SOCIAL CITIZENSHIP IN THE SHADOW OF COMPETITION

To my parents

Social Citizenship in the Shadow of Competition

The Bureaucratic Politics of Regulatory Justification

BRONWEN MORGAN
Oxford University

ASHGATE

Published by
Ashgate Publishing Limited
Gower House
Croft Road
Aldershot
Hants GU11 3HR
England

Ashgate Publishing Company
Suite 420
101 Cherry Street, VT 05401-4405
USA

Ashgate website: http://www.ashgate.com

British Library Cataloguing in Publication Data
Morgan, Bronwen
    Social citizenship in the shadow of competition : the
    bureaucratic politics of regulatory justification. - (Law,
    justice and power)
    1.Public law 2.Public law - Economic aspects
    I.Title
    342'.001

Library of Congress Cataloging-in-Publication Data
Morgan, Bronwen, 1966-
    Social citizenship in the shadow of competition : the bureaucratic politics of regulatory
    justification / Bronwen Morgan.
        p. cm. -- (Law, justice and power)
    Includes bibliographical references.
    ISBN 0-7546-2187-1 (alk. paper)
    1. Trade regulation. 2. Social values. I. Title. II. Series.

    HD3612 .M67 2003
    338.9--dc21
                                                                    2002032681

ISBN 0 7546 2187 1

Printed and bound in Great Britain by MPG Books Ltd, Bodmin, Cornwall

Contents

Acknowledgements

This book owes most of all to the intellectual stimulus and the institutional environment of the Centre for the Study of Law and Society at the University of California, Berkeley, and its doctoral programme in Jurisprudence and Social Policy. There I learnt to tread the myriad avenues that lead outwards from the judicial, doctrinal universe of law school, and began a project whose last days have taken me eastwards to another inspirational Centre, the Oxford University Centre for Socio-Legal Studies. The result is a book that is silent about courts, but still centrally about law. The path here has been made convivial and inspiring not only by these two institutions, but also by many individuals and other institutions along the way, whom I wish to thank and acknowledge. Thanks first to my dissertation committee, Martin Shapiro, Bob Kagan and Jonah Levy, for their invaluable feedback and shaping of the project while it was still a doctoral thesis. For invaluable support in funding my research and study, I thank the Fulbright Commission, the Australian and American Associations of University Women, the University of Sydney, Australia, the University of California at Berkeley, USA and the Faculty of Law at Oxford. My appreciation to Jim Jeffris of the Regulation Review Committee secretariat in the New South Wales Parliament, who kindly arranged for me to spend a month in the Committee's offices which was a vital entrée point to the remainder of my bureaucratic contacts. Finally my special thanks to some of the many whose company and conversation shaped my thinking and lifted my spirits: Roger Berkowitz, John Braithwaite, Javier Couso, David Engerman, Peter Fitzpatrick, Denis Galligan, Tom Ginsburg, Mark Harris, Breena Holland, Alex Huneeus, Josh Holmes, Chris Jewell, Liora Lazarus, Elizabeth Letcher, John Parks, Ed Rubin, Jeremy Waldron, Maggie Winslow and Karen Yeung.

Introduction

Consider three momentary snapshots in the wax and wane of ongoing struggles over globalisation. In 1999, waves of protestors in Seattle succeed in shutting down the talks convened for starting a new round of trade negotiations for the World Trade Organisation. In 2000 the activist organisations who mobilised the 'Battle of Seattle' begin to organise workshops for potential recruits on the architecture of international financial regulation, trade flows and the rules and processes governing the World Trade Organisation. In 2002, in Oaxaco, Mexico, Zapotec indigenous people stage a peaceful nine-day hunger strike to demand access to basic goods like electricity and water, filling the town square with thousands upon thousands of cardboard cutouts in the shape of hands of all colours, waving their entreaty from long wooden stems grounded by clear plastic bags filled with earth.

Only the first of these three is well-known, perhaps even iconic to the point of becoming threadbare. Only the first captures the colour and clash of 'high politics'. The last of the three, in lacking the element of clash, fails in this instance to capture the attention of the media, but shares the capacity with the first to capture the imagination and spirit of 'high politics'. The second, sandwiched obscurely between them, remains, at least in broad public debate in the shadows. But it is in the unpredictable elisions between the arcanae of technical bureaucratic minutiae and the fundamental questions about governance implied by such minutiae that my interest in regulatory politics resides. For it is there that the crucial nexus of politics in its deepest sense – the 'art of the possible' – lies.

This book explores questions about governing – both about how to govern, and why. More narrowly, it is a book about regulatory politics, by which I mean political conflict over state efforts to address social risk, market failure or equity concerns through rule-based direction of social and individual action. The question of '*how* to govern' raises issues of technocratic governance in the politics of regulatory design. The questions of '*why*' or 'to what ends' are governance choices directed raises an enduring tension between competing community values, often diffusely

1

captured by a loose distinction between 'economic' and 'social' goals. Bringing these two concerns together, the book focuses on an increasingly pervasive subset of institutions of technocratic governance I call meta-regulation, and explores how meta-regulation copes with tensions between the 'social' and 'economic' goals of regulatory politics.

Meta-regulation is in some ways an ugly word, a dry, impersonal term redolent of bureaucratic jargon. That is appropriate. For it is in the minutiae of technical bureaucratic politics, the thrust and parry of setting agendas, framing issues, and deciding priorities, that the real power to shape the ultimate ends of governance lies. The community politics of the ethical limits of global capitalism are passionate and highly wrought. They are fomenting broad-brush political change in many directions, from the emergence of new political parties or coalitions (One Nation in Australia, the Perot-Nader coalition on certain issues in the US) to the violent protests in Seattle and their progeny. The intensity of these politics is important to me, and core to the motivation of this project. But it is also the motivating *context*, and not the focus. This project is committed to the notion that it is the welter of technical decisions occurring day by day in the backstage committee rooms of political arenae that crucially shape the dramatic politics that eventually take centre stage, and that set the limits of possibilities for those politics. Since so many of these pages will trace the technicalities of meta-regulation, I aim to begin with a broader brush.

The notion of meta-regulation is simple at heart: it captures a desire to think reflexively about regulation, such that rather than regulating social and individual action directly, the process of regulation itself becomes regulated. The term has been used previously[1] to capture developments at the intersection of state regulation and self-regulation, where government monitors the self-monitoring of corporations. Meta-regulation in this book is equally reflexive, but focused more on reflexivity within the confines of the state, and defined rather more narrowly in order to capture the specific political conflict between 'social' and 'economic' goals in regulatory policy that interests me. It encompasses any set of institutions and processes that embed regulatory review mechanisms on a systematic basis into the every-day routines of governmental policymaking, such that a particular form of economic rationality becomes part of the taken-for-granted ways of policymaking. For example, under the reforms introduced by the Australian government that this book explores, governments require the application of a public benefit test to justify the maintenance of any public policy that prima facie restricts competition. Policies for which a public benefit cannot be demonstrated must be repealed or modified so that they do not reduce competition. This principle of regulatory reform is institutionalised as a *general mechanism of governance,* not confined to one-off efforts to reform particular policy sectors, but instantiating generally applicable, sector-neutral and continuously applied techniques of regulatory reform.

The core question is what extent (if at all) does meta-regulation attenuate social citizenship? The idea of social citizenship draws on T.H. Marshall's well known argument[2] that as industrial democracies became more wealthy and stable, they sought to extend the egalitarianism of political and civil equality to the social and economic realms. Once each individual citizen had equal *input* in the political realm (the opportunity to vote and participate in politics), as well as in the sphere of civil capacity (the opportunity to own property and participate in the market), social struggles shifted to secure entitlements to a minimum equal portion of the *output* in the economic sphere. There are two facets to social citizenship that are important themes in this enquiry. One is the more tangible facet of the social regulation and welfare policies that are the techniques of securing social citizenship. The other is somewhat more diffuse, but has to do with the sense of collective identity and social cohesion fostered by the overall pattern of regulatory policy choice in a particular political community. The principles and techniques of meta-regulation have at least the potential to attenuate both facets of social citizenship: whether and how they do is the heart of my enquiry.

In this introduction, I briefly state the two primary objectives of the book and the nub of the way in which I fill them out. I then contextualise the issues thus raised, introduce and justify the selection of Australia as the case study that forms the heart of the book, and provide an overview of the structure of the following chapters.

Objectives

The first important objective of the book is to assess the relative power of a narrow market-centred economic rationality to exclude or dominate competing ways of understanding regulatory policy choices. Briefly, what emerges is that meta-regulation does not destroy social citizenship, though it does alter its forms, instruments and discourses. Meta-regulation institutionalises a presumption in favour of market governance, and this causes bureaucrats to reframe or 'translate' aspects of social welfare that previously may have been expressed in the language of need, vulnerability or harm into the language of market failures or market distortion. For example, when justifying the regulation of professional qualifications of immigration advice agents, bureaucrats in the Department of Immigration initially framed the issue as one of protecting vulnerable clients from being given poor advice. At a later stage of review, the shaping influence of

National Competition Policy led to a reframing of the issue as one of correcting the market failure of information asymmetry between advisor and client. The welfare state's protective obligations of integrity towards vulnerable citizens were translated into the resolution of market failures in respect of information asymmetries that denied consumers the precondition of fully informed and autonomous choice necessary to participate in the market for migration advice.

Strategic translation, however, does not necessarily secure the retention of social citizenship. Even where social citizenship values *are* translated and taken into account, the culture of meta-regulation still resonates in salient ways. The framing effect subtly shifts the boundaries of what is taken for granted. Laws that were previously taken to reflect the expression of democratic will are reclassified as rents attained by self-interested special interest groups; laws that were previously assumed to protect the vulnerable are reclassified as distorting a fully competitive market for services. In the immigration advice example referred to above, for instance, when the overall structure was approached as a response to market failure, free advice to indigent clients provided by non-profit agencies became a "cross-subsidy which distorts the migration advice market". This had the result that it was counted as a cost rather than, as under the prior framework, a benefit. In this way certain critical modes of demanding justice, particularly those that rely on moral or distributive values, are silenced. Furthermore, the *institutional* solutions which bureaucrats advance to secure the 'translated' social citizenship values render them politically vulnerable. Again drawing on the example above, the solution offered to retain advice for the poor was to rely not on the income generated by registration fees but on direct budget subsidies, transparently costed. Given the political vulnerability of the class of people who need but cannot pay for immigration advice, this is a solution which preserves social citizenship analytically and conceptually, but threatens it practically and politically.

The second primary objective, which flows from the first, is to explore what the practice of meta-regulation means for our conceptions of collective identity. A mode of decision-making that gives priority to conceptual frameworks drawn from neo-classical economics will have not just instrumental implications, but also cultural or expressive meaning, in terms of the values it is socially understood to endorse or express.[3] What emerges here is that the culture of meta-regulation, centred in technical-bureaucratic arenae but increasingly 'leaking' over into broader community contexts, has important implications for the range of acceptable modes of justifying collective policy choices in regulatory politics. While in broad political debates about meta-regulation, attempts were made to articulate an alternative to economic rationality, one grounded on various conceptions of community morality, such alternatives had no power to 'bite' in the bureaucratic-technical politics that really mattered. The discourse of regulatory politics therefore was ultimately dominated by technocratic expertise articulated on behalf of highly differentiated sub-groups in society, in ways that sidestepped as far as possible the expression of collective values. The accompanying centrality of apolitical images of consumer sovereignty depoliticised social citizenship, masking the power relations encoded in policy conflicts. Even attempts to articulate discursive resistance to economic rationality (invoking, for example, shared vulnerability, ethical communities, multi-faceted need) tended to become, once applied in specific policy contexts, little more than demands for redistribution of material resources. Important though greater material equality is, the significance of the regulatory conversation mapped in this book seems rooted in something deeper; namely, a search for a way to conceive of what matters in political economy without reliance on the logic of utility or on any other instrumental rationality.

Broader Context

As the second objective of the book suggests, the issues explored through the lens of bureaucratic routines and techniques have a much broader social context. That context concerns the fate of social citizenship values in the wake of liberalising the post-war welfare state in industrialised democracies. Since the oil shocks of the 1970s, the welfare state, social democracy and the social citizenship aspirations that they fostered have come under continuous and rapidly increasing pressure from the pursuit of values and goals loosely associated with market competition. That there are tensions between the pursuit of competitive efficiency and that of social citizenship is part of what I mean to convey by speaking of competition as casting a *shadow* over social citizenship. The shape and texture of that shadow can be captured at two levels – the relatively concrete one of policies and institutions, and the more intangible one of discourse and ideology.

At a concrete level, much of the shadow concerns pressures on the redistributive policies of the welfare state, and the pervasiveness of economic liberalisation.[4] Across the industrialised democracies of the Organisation for Economic Co-operation and Development (OECD), inequality between rich and poor has risen relentlessly and economic liberalisation has become a standard policy prescription, whether it be at the international level in the spread of free trade regimes, or the domestic level in the privatisation of major infrastructure services previously provided by the state. A host of associated techniques that 'reinvent the state' by contracting out service provision or imposing market disciplines on previously insulated professional or public sectors are also familiar instances of the shadow of competition.[5]

This is not to suggest that the shadow of competition is monolithic. Some writers argue that welfare state policies have not always been substantially retrenched under the pressure of international competition or initiatives that hollow out the national state,[6] while others suggest that forms of 'social liberalism' that temper market forces within a nation can actually *improve* international competitiveness.[7] But if the effects of competition's shadow at a material level are somewhat ambiguous, at a discursive level, they are pervasive. At the most diffuse level, the shadow merely imports considerations of instrumental rationality conceived of in narrow cost-effectiveness terms: 'getting more for less'. Somewhat more pointedly, policy decision-making is increasingly guided by full-blown cost-benefit analysis, and the influence of a neoclassical mode of economics that has a normative preference for market incentive-based governance lies behind many of the concrete policy and institutional choices that collectively constitute the 'shadow of competition'.

In this shadow, political dialogue increasingly consists of arguments about which means will most effectively achieve a shared goal of increasing economic growth and productivity. Within this scope of politics, there has been, in parallel with the growing influence of economic rationality, a persistent resistance to the parameters set by the terms of this discourse, particularly its narrow conception of the public good. Perhaps the two most significant axes of the expanded conception of public good that is conveyed by the notion of social citizenship have focused on redistribution or equity more generally, and on ecological sustainability. Resistance has in some cases been populist, such as where social movements focused on welfare, poverty and environmental issues highlight the importance of values that diverge from the structures of profit and capital accumulation so central to economic rationality. Other strands of resistance have been more technical, such as efforts to widen what is *measured* by standard economic indicators: the Human Development Index or the 'greening' of Gross Domestic Product.

Until recently, much of the resistance referred to above did not challenge general assumptions about governance structures, but rather raised governance issues when a specific reform in a particular sector was at stake. General resistance to economic rationality was aimed at highlighting alternative values or working on measurement criteria. Since the development of the 'anti-globalisation movement', however, the conflict between economic and social rationality has moved to challenge assumptions about governance at a markedly more general level, particularly in terms of the degree of democratic inclusiveness in international policy decision-making.

While the growth of such a movement is not my focus in this book, its emergence provides an apt entrée into the concerns of the project, because it indicates that what was once technocratic and specialised is increasingly a matter of wider concern. Technocratic governance, or the trend towards substituting relatively transparent, participatory forms of politics with economistic technocracy, has for some time now been a feature of sector-specific regulatory reform in industrialised democracies. But its *general* application has only become more marked in recent times (though it has been prevalent in the developing world through the avenues of the International Monetary Fund (IMF) and the World Bank for much longer). The growing remit of the World Trade Organisation (WTO) and the spread of independent central banks are examples of the growth of generalised technocratic governance in the OECD world, as are the regulatory management regimes at the heart of this book. While further descriptive detail will be given in the first chapter, let me confine myself for the moment to emphasising that like central banks and WTO dispute resolution, meta-regulation is a deployment of economic technical expertise in an institutional setting that both possesses 'clout' and is insulated from representative participatory politics.

It is important that despite this insulation, there is, as the emergence of the anti-globalisation movement indicates, an increasing intersection of technical regulatory politics and more diffuse 'everyday' politics where broader conceptions of collective values are debated. The importance of this broader valency is the other part of what I mean by the 'shadow of competition'. It is not simply that securing competitive efficiency is often in tension with, and is given priority over, the pursuit of social citizenship values. By itself, this aspect of the shadow captures political conflict over the allocation of resources, which insofar as a clash between the 'economic' and the 'social' is concerned is as old as capitalism itself. What is newer, this book argues, is that the mechanisms of technocratic governance that embed the values of economic rationality, and increasingly of competitive efficiency more specifically, into everyday routines of regulatory politics are becoming more deeply institutionalised. There is potential for meta-regulation to become a social institution in the deep sense of an array of norms that in an increasingly taken-for-granted way, shapes the agenda of regulatory politics.

An apt analogy here would be the way that the rule of law, a complex, multi-faceted institution of the kind I am alluding to here, has itself cast a shadow. Socio-legal literature has long spoken of the 'shadow of the law'[8] as a reference to the ways in which legal institutions and legal rules can shape social interactions in areas ostensibly unconnected to the law. In the shadow of the law, social relations often take on milder characteristics of the nature of legal interactions – formal, arms-length, depoliticised, often adversarial. The shadow of competition gives social relations a texture imparted by the influence of not legal, but *economic* rationality. Part of my interest in delineating meta-regulation as an emerging institution of governance is to capture its systematic effects on the quality of social relations insofar as they emerge in participation in regulatory politics. This includes, up to a point, paying attention to winners and losers in substantive sectors of regulatory policy. But like the rule of law, which has long garnered fierce disputes as to its political merits,[9] meta-regulation can be ambiguous in terms of its substantive political implications.

Thus while some attention will be given to the instrumental impact of meta-regulation, the weight of the argument is directed towards exploring its more expressive implications. Economic rationality, in meta-regulation, is understood in this book as a complex mixture of expertise and ideology utilised by bureaucrats and interests as a powerful strategic resource.[10] It is a key resource in struggles over the authority to determine the criteria for 'correct solutions' in regulatory policymaking. It is not only capable of being deployed by powerful central agency bureaucrats who favour the maximisation of the forces of market competition, but also of deployment by dissenting groups who nonetheless employ creative strategies of 'translation' in order to harness the discursive power of economic rationality. Translation strategies show the Janus faces of deploying knowledge as power. On the one hand they facilitate leverage for otherwise politically weak groups, making it possible for them to harness the organisational resources of much more powerful institutions in the service of interests opposed to, or ignored by those very groups.[11] On the other hand, the very ubiquity of this deployment of expertise, while it might limit the scope of its concrete impact on vulnerable groups in the short term, gives it a more diffuse power as a shared discourse, one that comes to define and colour the perception of meaning, in particular by shaping the nature of unstated assumptions. Thus the culture of meta-regulation, the way it shapes how actors understand the scope, goals and appropriate techniques of regulatory policy, is a mixed heritage, one that both is and is not monolithic. In terms of its instrumental impact, economic expertise is sufficiently politically malleable that a range of substantive outcomes seem possible under its sway. But in terms of its expressive effects, its hegemonic presence is more difficult to dislodge.

Outline

The trajectory of this book reflects the ambiguity of the mixed heritage alluded to above. In its account of whether and how, if at all, social citizenship has been attenuated by the shadow of competition represented by meta-regulation, it charts a constant dialectic between interpretive fluidity and institutional solidity. As an interpretive study of political legitimation strategies, both discursive and institutional, the project is an example of an endeavour that Paul Kahn has recently urged upon scholars in relation to the rule of law: a "study of the culture of [meta-regulation]... *as a distinct way of understanding and perceiving meaning* in the events of our political and social life".[12]

Chapter One sets forth the conceptual conditions of the practice of meta-regulation by developing an extended analogy with the rule of law. I discuss two features of the rule of law that crucially shape our understanding and perception of meaning under its sway: institutional autonomy and the 'taming of politics'. I then suggest that meta-regulation also exhibits these features in ways strikingly analogous to the rule of law. Seen from this perspective, meta-regulation is part of a culture of rulemaking that reiterates Weberian rationalisation. Just as law once rationalised political power in the service of market capitalism, now meta-regulation seeks to rationalise the production of law, once more in the service of market capitalism. Just as in a state committed to institutionalising the rule of law, government lawyers may come to play salient roles in political judgments about the proportionality of regulatory action,[13] so under meta-regulation economic experts shape those same limits. Meta-regulation thus becomes a mode of incipient *non-judicial legality*.

In addition to laying the conceptual ground, Chapter One also descriptively fleshes out several different modes of meta-regulation in support of the general relevance of the phenomenon. Chapter Two provides more detailed historical context for the *particular* instance of meta-regulation at the heart of the empirical research of the book: the Australian initiative adverted to in the opening pages. Known in its entirety as the National Competition Policy (NCP), it has a meta-regulatory regime as one of its principal features. The Australian initiative is an ideal case study of otherwise widely applicable and spreading trends. This is so because on the one hand, it is broadly representative of Anglo-American OECD industrialised welfare states,[14] and has come under similar pressure, in the shadow of competition, to scale back government and implement wide-scale economic reforms. At the same time, the Australian context, and in particular the initiative itself, are distinctive enough to sharpen the *salience* of the case study as an instance of a spreading technique of governance.

There are five main aspects of this 'representativeness-distinctness'. First, the shadow of competition has typically exercised its strongest influence in the context of small, open economies. It is no accident that some smaller peripheral countries such as New Zealand[15] and Chile[16] drew attention in recent decades for their particularly rapid and extreme modes of reinventing the state. While Australia's economy is closer to medium-sized, it is still significantly exposed to international trends, and like New Zealand and Chile, it is considered to be at the forefront of general approaches to reinventing the state.[17]

Secondly, the sheer scale, scope and comprehensiveness of the meta-regulatory regime in the Australian initiative is unprecedented. Over a five year period (later extended to seven years), the reforms required every state government and the federal government to scrutinise every piece of legislation on their books to determine whether it was subject to review. More than 1,700 pieces of legislation were actually listed for review. All new legislation is subject to the regime. Some AUS\$4.2 billion have been made available thus far as targeted incentives for compliance with the reforms, and brand new institutions have been designed, staffed and funded to oversee the process. The breadth and depth of the programme's ambitions to change the status quo could not be more comprehensive.

Thirdly, the economic rationality embodied in the Australian meta-regulatory regime possesses a novel structural feature which gives it particular 'bite'. It goes further than 'mere' cost-benefit assessment of regulatory policy choices. Cost-benefit analysis requirements and consideration of alternative regulatory strategies are measured in relation to a yardstick that is more substantive than simple 'net benefit': that of maximising market competition, a requirement written into the intergovernmental agreement that lays the framework. This substantive yardstick means that regulatory impact analysis in Australia is more like environmental impact analysis than generalised cost-benefit analysis. Just as environmental impact assessment seeks to attain the maximum feasible extent of environmental protection rather than simply achieve aggregate net benefit, so the National Competition Policy regime seeks to achieve maximum feasible extent of market competition. The substantive yardstick sharpens the focus of the cost-benefit analysis considerably, and also has a stronger 'framing' effect on the issues targeted.

Fourthly, the federal structure of Australia, especially the role in meta-regulation played by different states governed by different political parties, provides an internal comparative benchmark for assessing just how much politics matters. In particular, Australia has historically prided itself on an egalitarian tradition of social citizenship, yet National Competition Policy was initiated by a Labour government. The tension between social citizenship and the shadow of competition is therefore especially acute in the case of Australia.

Fifth, and finally, the Australian initiative is likely to be influential in the possible future spread of meta-regulatory regimes internationally. Australian approaches to managing economic regulatory policy have a history of international influence. For example, the Trade Policy Review Process in the WTO was modelled on procedures developed by an Australian body now known as the Productivity Commission, and the Trade Policy Review Body was initially staffed by some key former members of that Commission.[18] In the case of the National Competition Policy, countries as diverse as Canada, Germany and Mexico as well as industrialising countries in the Pacific Rim have already shown considerable interest in the structure of the reforms, the former trio all sending officials on investigatory visits to Australia in this regard.[19] Moreover, the OECD, whose prominent support for meta-regulation has been driven primarily by a small but influential key network of some five or six advocates that includes two Australians,[20] is an important player in setting international agendas.[21] As what one commentator has called "the single most important builder of business regulatory epistemic communities",[22] the OECD may well become a motor for spreading the salience of the Australian regime to other nations or to international processes.[23]

The middle three chapters of the book explore, at increasingly specific levels, what happened when bureaucrats, interest groups and the wider political community engaged with the day-to-day practice of meta-regulation. While the first two chapters present a relatively systematised, ordered picture of what meta-regulation entails, these chapters introduce complexity and malleability into the picture. As Kahn suggests, once the details of actual practices are explored (as opposed to their conceptual conditions), the focus turns to the "layered character of multiple, juxtaposed meanings".[24] Chapter Three explores the layers as they emerge in broader debates in the political community, drawing primarily on a wide-ranging parliamentary inquiry into National Competition Policy. Chapters Four and Five explore the way in which more bureaucratic-technical practices also generate multiple, juxtaposed meanings by virtue of the political malleability of meta-regulation, although here the incipient legality of meta-regulation imposes greater constraints on this malleability. Chapter Four focuses on the general level of setting the agenda for meta-regulation, and explores the practices of a network of central agency officials, as well as the intellectual underpinnings of those practices in a public choice perspective on regulation. Chapter Five, comprised of five sub-parts, continues the focus on the technicalities of bureaucratic practice, this time in four specific policy sectors. The four case studies cover the regulation of social policy aspects of utility services, of rice production, of immigration advice and information, and of public sector auditing. The final sub-section of this chapter looks at some of the practices of the national independent agency that monitors compliance with meta-regulation.

Read together, these three chapters illustrate three possible fates of social citizenship under meta-regulation: silence, translation and attempts to voice alternatives to economic rationality. These chapters do at times emphasise the strategic political games played around meta-regulation, and the selection of case studies is chosen to highlight the disparate effect of different political administrations in power. But this 'causal' political dimension is included not so as to ultimately propose 'better regulation strategies': that is the policy objective of meta-regulation, but not the intellectual objective of this account of meta-regulation. That intellectual objective is, rather, to stand back from the raw policy outcomes and understand the totality of practices, routines and institutions that comprise meta-regulation as a mode of incipient non-judicial legality. This claim is given particular prominence in the closing section of Chapter Five, but is also grounded in the gradual accumulation of empirical detail that builds across the trajectory of Chapters Three, Four and Five.

That trajectory, however, is one which is at the same time persistently destabilised by the constant dialectic between institutional solidity and fluid interpretive conflict that emerges in the details of implementation. The malleability that characterises meta-regulation's incipient legality is a crucial aspect of the passionate conflicts over the tension between social and economic goals that dominate the 'everyday politics' of meta-regulation. That malleability, along with the passionate conflicts generated as a result, was perfectly illustrated in the course of a key moment of the Australian story that unfolds later in this book. In June 1995, as eight Australian state and federal parliaments went about the business of passing 'mirror legislation' enacting national regulatory reform, two very different, but both highly dramatic, visions of what was occurring emerged. The first, from the leader of Australia's 'third' party, the centre-left Democrats, lamented:

> The intentions [of the bill] are laudable but nonetheless dangerous and their corrosive effect on our culture and our social life is everywhere to be seen by those with eyes not blinded by the religious ecstasy of economic rationalist ideology...One cannot legislate for goodness. A government can, over time however, pass a series of laws which so undermine the fabric of society that anti-social behaviour flourishes and the moral and

cultural cement that binds citizens together in a society is inexorably dissolved. The bill before us today marks one of the stages of that dissolution.[25]

In stark contrast, a view from the right of politics mocked the very opposition (the Labour party) that had sponsored the legislation at federal level:

[The bill] spells an end to the opposition's socialist dreams, the managed economy and public ownership. It spells the end of what opposition members talk about now and what they have talked about in past years. The bill signals the inevitable victory of economic rationalism in Australia.[26]

It is to these high-colour politics that the final brief chapter returns, mining the backlash against National Competition Policy for intimations of just how its mode of incipient – and possibly insidious – legality shapes our conceptions of collective identity. But the route to such considerations, alluring as they are, takes us necessarily through the grey thickets of the 'everyday politics' of bureaucratic regulation. Such is the nature of the art of the possible.

Notes

[1] Gunningham, N., Grabosky, P. and Sinclair, D. (1998), *Smart Regulation: Designing Environmental Policy*, Clarendon Press, Oxford; Parker, C. (2002), *The Open Corporation: Effective Self-Regulation and Democracy.* Cambridge University Press, Cambridge.

[2] Marshall, T.H. (1950), *Citizenship and Social Class and Other Essays*, Cambridge University Press, Cambridge.

[3] Pildes, R. and Sunstein, C. (1995), 'Reinventing the Regulatory State', *University of Chicago Law Review*, Vol. 62, pp.1-129, p.70.

[4] Cerny, Philip (1995), 'Globalisation and the Changing Logic of Collective Action', *International Organisation* Vol. 49, pp.595-625; Sassen, S. (1996), *Losing Control? Sovereignty in an Age of Globalization*, Columbia University Press, New York.

[5] Considine, Mark (1988), 'The Corporate Management Framework as Administrative Science: A Critique', *Australian Journal of Public Administration* Vol. 47, No. 1, pp.1-18; Williams, W. (1988), *Washington, Westminster and Whitehall*, Cambridge University Press, New York; Pollitt, C. (1990), *Managerialism and the Public Services: the Anglo-American Experience*, Basil Blackwell, Cambridge, Mass; Massey, Andrew (1993), *Managing the Public Sector: A Comparative Analysis of the United Kingdom and the United States*, Edward Elgar, Aldershot, UK; Brookfield, Vermont; Painter, Christopher (1994), 'Public Service Reform: Reinventing or Abandoning Government?', *Political Quarterly*, Vol. 65, pp.242-262; Vogel, Steven (1998), *Freer Markets, More Rules: Regulatory Reform in Advanced Industrial Countries*, Cornell University Press, Ithaca.

[6] Pierson, P. (1994), *Dismantling the Welfare State?*, Cambridge University Press, Cambridge.

[7] Porter, M. (1998), *The Competitive Advantage of Nations*, MacMillan Press, Basingstoke.

[8] Galanter, Marc (1974), 'Why the 'Haves' Come out Ahead: Speculations on the Limits of Legal Change', *Law and Society Review*, Vol. 9, pp.95-160; Mnookin, R. and Kornhauser, L. (1979), 'Bargaining in the Shadow of the Law: the Case of Divorce', *Yale Law Journal* Vol. 88, pp. 950-97; Jacob, Herbert (1992), 'The Elusive Shadow of the Law', *Law and Society Review*, Vol. 26, pp.565-590.

[9] Thompson, E.P. *Whigs and Hunters: the Origins of the Black Act*, Penguin, London; Galanter, M. (1974), 'Why the 'Haves' Come out Ahead: Speculations on the Limits of Legal Change' *Law and Society Review* 9 95-160.

[10] Dezalay, Yves (1995), 'Introduction' in Dezalay, Y. and Sugarman D. (eds), *Professional Competition and Professional Power*, Routledge, London; Dezalay, Yves and Garth, Bryant (1996), *Dealing in Virtue*, University of Chicago Press, Chicago.

[11] Latour, Bruno (1986), 'The Powers of Association', in Law, J. (ed), *Power, Action and Belief: A New Sociology of Knowledge?*, Routledge and Kegan Paul, London; Watts, Michael (1993), 'Development: Power, Knowledge, Discursive Practice', *Progress in Human Geography*, Vol. 17, pp.257 ff.

[12] Kahn, P.W. (1999), *The Cultural Study of Law: Reconstructing Legal Scholarship*, University of Chicago Press, Chicago., emphasis and brackets added.

[13] Daintith, T. and Page, A. (1999), *The Executive in the Constitution*, Oxford University Press, Oxford, p.342.

[14] Wilensky, H. (1974), *The Welfare State and Equality: Structural and IdeologicalRoots of Public Expenditures*, University of California Press, Berkley; Esping-Anderson, G. (1990), *The Three Worlds of Welfare Capitalism*, Polity Press, Cambridge.

[15] Kesley, J. (1995), *Economic Fundamentalism*, Pluto Press, Sydney.

[16] Couso, Javier (n.d.), 'The Economic Constitution of Chile: The Lochner Era Reborn?', unpublished paper on file with author.

[17] New Zealand and Chile do not have formal meta-regulatory regimes of the kind that Australia has introduced.

[18] Braithwaite, Interview (2001), *Interview*, B. Morgan, December 2001.

[19] Ranald, Interview (1996), *Interview*, B. Morgan; Hilmer, (2001), *Interview*, B. Morgan.

[20] Perton, V., Member of Parliament of Victoria, Chairman of Scrutiny of Acts and Regulation Committee (1997), *Interview*, B. Morgan, January 29 1997. ; Downing, T., Senior Policy Officer, NSW Cabinet Office (1998), *Interview*, B. Morgan, February 7 1997. The two in question are Roger Wilkins and Sue Holmes. Canada's Scott Jacobs is the other significant national influence on the OECD initiatives. Both are Anglo-American federations and as indicated (and to be discussed further in Chapter Two), the politics of federalism are highly salient to the particular regime that developed in Australia.

[21] Salzman, James (2000), 'Labour Rights, Globalisation and Institutions: The Role and Influence of the Organisation for Economic Cooperation and Development' *Michigan Journal of International Law*, Vol. 21, pp.769 ff.

[22] Braithwaite, J. and P. Drahos, P. (2000), *Global Business Regulation*, Cambridge University Press, Cambridge. p.29.

[23] For example, the OECD has already used detailed guidelines developed in 1999 by one of the Australian states in connection with National Competition Policy in developing its own conception of 'best practice' standards for regulatory quality: Braithwaite, Interview (2001), *Interview*, B. Morgan, December 2001.

[24] Kahn, P.W. (1999), *The Cultural Study of Law: Reconstructing Legal Scholarship*, University of Chicago Press, Chicago, p.36.

[25] Senator Coulter (then leader of the Democratic Party), Commonwealth Hansard, Senate, 22 June 1995: 1772-1775.

[26] Victorian Hansard, October 11 1995:360.

1 Economic Adjudication and the Rule of Law

My primary aim in this chapter is to make an argument that certain complexes of *non-judicial* institutions, procedures and techniques bear important analogies with the role of legal institutions in fostering global capitalism. I want to suggest that these sites of 'economic adjudication' are key to the dynamics of contemporary regulatory politics, and in particular to the trajectory of the increasingly fractious tensions between the 'social' and 'economic' faces of an increasingly interdependent global economy. At the same time, I want to explore these bureaucratic regulatory institutions specifically as incipient modes of legality, so that the exploration is essentially one concerning the role of law in political economy.[1]

The chapter has three main parts. In the first, I cast in abstract form the analogies between judicial and non-judicial legality that I wish to develop. Meta-regulation is the primary form of non-judicial legality in which I am interested: that is, institutions and processes that embed regulatory review mechanisms into the everyday routines of governmental policymaking. In the second part, I sketch empirical examples of meta-regulation, focusing on efforts at both national and international levels to systematise the regulation of regulators, and in particular those who produce legislation. I include a brief layout of the nascent regime of economic adjudication in Australia that forms the basis of the empirical research elaborated in future chapters, though Chapter Two will contextualise that in much more depth. In the third part, I develop the analogy between meta-regulation and the rule of law, concluding on a note that emphasises the malleability of both modes of legality. That malleability is critical to the politics of implementation that the bulk of the book explores. But the construction of meta-regulation as a mode of incipient legality is a crucial context for those fluid, fragmented politics, and it shapes my final interpretation in the last chapter of the cultural meaning of those regulatory politics.

Some of the material in this chapter, particularly in the first and third parts, is fairly schematically presented. This is because I hope this chapter will function as a hinge between social theory and interpretive empirical inquiry, always a difficult transition to make. The empirical case studies explored in future chapters will move increasingly further from any monolithic assumptions, highlighting both the conceptual malleability and the political contestability of meta-regulatory politics. Indeed, if the resonance of my analogy between meta-regulation and the rule of law is to be at all persuasive, it should only be expected that this emergent institution is as complex and contradictory as it is capable of reification.

Judicial and Non-judicial Legality in Political Economy

Consider three situations, mundane enough and possibly familiar. Each is in substance about economic exchange. In each, law plays a crucial role.

Situation one: a business woman has multiple contracts with large numbers of individuals living in different parts of one nation, to sell them the same product. Market conditions vary substantially across the country. Nonetheless, should things go awry, she can turn to the judicial system to enforce her contracts in roughly the same way no matter where the breaching party is based. Moreover, a second business woman thinking of setting up business in the same product arena can also rely on uniform and predictable enforcement of the same kind of contract, should she set up business, and can thereby calculate the likelihood of her success or failure.

Situation two: two companies in different states in a federal regime both sell cigarettes. However, one province has banned the sale of cigarettes. The federal constitution provides a guarantee that interstate trade will be free. The company from the banning state can turn to the judicial system and seek a declaration that the provincial law banning cigarettes burdens interstate trade and is therefore invalid.

Situation three: two multinational companies both net tuna. One company sells the tuna to a country that has banned the import of non-dolphin-friendly tuna. The other company lobbies its national government to turn to a panel of the World Trade Organisation to plead their case that the national law ban contravenes the rules of international trade law.

The three situations share some key features. All involve individual businesses seeking to conduct an exchange of goods for economic gain. All three involve a legal (judicial) pronouncement that an identified action is unjustifiable when evaluated in light of previously agreed-upon rules. This is one legal facet of the scenarios. However, it is not the *only* legal facet.

For in the second and third situations, the action requiring justification *is itself* law – i.e. a legislative act is the target of the judicial assessment. That legislative act is regulation: an effort by the state to address social (smoking) or environmental (dolphin-culling) risk.

I want to argue that while all three situations tell us something remarkably similar about the instrumental role of (judicial) law in political economy, the difference between the first on the one hand, and the second and third on the other, is that the instrumental role of (legislative) law in political economy is equally important. The general notion of the rule of law tends to blur within its broad frame of reference two aspects of 'law': law as dispute resolution and law as rulemaking. In the context of the modern regulatory state, a focus on the role of law as rulemaking is by no means new, as the vast literature on independent regulatory agencies and judicial review attests. There is an equally large literature on the *politics* of regulatory reform, telling stories which blend elements of dispute resolution, rulemaking, political lobbying, value conflicts and the role of expert knowledge. Much of the first literature, however, is judicially focused; and much of the second literature is sector-specific. By contrast, by focusing on meta-regulation, this story is about the dynamics of regulatory reform as a *general mechanism of governance,* not confined to one-off efforts to reform particular policy sectors, but instantiating generally applicable and continuously applied techniques of regulatory reform. It is also a story about the *non-judicial* institutionalisation of meta-regulation, a development whereby the values of economic thinking are being systematised and embedded in routines that increasingly subject law itself to the rule-of-economics. Before I give a concrete descriptive account of just what sorts of institutions, routines and procedures are typical of the rule-of-economics, let me say a little more about what kind of perspective I am taking on the concept of law here.

Weber's vision of law as a crucial means of rationalising social behaviour in ways that facilitate the ends of a capitalist economy provides the background for my categorisation of the three situations outlined above.[2] The three situations show that law is, from the perspective of political economy, instrumental in facilitating capitalism. The important facet of law's instrumental role in this context is its capacity to rationalise the uncoordinated behaviour and decisions of unconnected individuals, to render their effects calculable, predictable and systematic. In the first situation, the decisions of judges enforcing the common law norms of contract provide a systematic way of making relatively predictable the outcome of multiple disperse interactions between individuals from a variety of social backgrounds. In the second and third situations, law is still important in this way. Judicial (or quasi-judicial) decisions in both situations (those of a constitutional court and those of an international panel of experts) rationalise social exchange. But in these two latter situations, law – as *legislation* rather than judicial decisions – is *also the target* of the rationalising process, as well as its means. That is, 'law' is both the means of the rationalising process (via the decisions of constitutional courts or WTO Panels) and the target of its decisions (the offending legislation passed by democratically elected subnational or national governments).

I want to highlight this increasing importance of law as a target of rationalisation. In the first story the decisions of judges (law) rationalise socially mediated exchange between individuals by coding their actions as justified or unjustified according to common law. In the second, the decisions of judges rationalise legally mediated exchange by coding certain provincial legislation (law) as an unjustifiable barrier to free trade. In the third situation, national rather than provincial legislation is coded as an unjustifiable restriction on free trade, and not by judges but by quasi-judicial panels. That is, one way of viewing this kind of supervision of the content of national laws imposed by the WTO at international level is that the laws that helped nation-state capitalism flourish are now hindering global capitalism, and that techniques are emerging which seek to 'rationalise' such laws. The ways in which the European Court of Justice manages the internal EU market[3] might be seen as a further illustration of the kind of economically instrumental role I am assigning to law.

At this point I am still emphasising the importance of law (legislation) as the *target* of rationalisation, in contradistinction to the first story where law (judicial decisions) is the tool of rationalisation. In fact, though law (in the form of rules) is being reflexively rationalised in the second and third situations, I constructed those situations to reflect the fact that one means of such 'reflexive rationalisation' can be law itself (judicial or quasi-judicial power to decide disputes). At least where there is a context such as a constitutional guarantee, or international agreements to adhere to the certain principles, there is no reason why law (legislation) cannot be rationalised by more law (judicial interpretation). But now I want to stress the significance of *non-judicial institutions* as a means of rationalising law. This in itself is not new: Weber himself wrote extensively about the role of accounting methods in this respect. But I want, in the contemporary world of regulatory politics we currently inhabit, to focus not on accounting, but on neo-classical economics.

Even in the quasi-judicial institutional context of the WTO itself, economics is clearly a powerful animating conceptual framework for how to envision the role of the panels. Recent writing argues, for instance, that the WTO represents a new "world trade constitution" in which domestic majorities have committed to institutions that restrain the ability of interest groups to obtain protectionist legislation at the public expense.[4] This characterisation strongly echoes the conceptual framework of public choice analysis of regulation, which draws strongly on neo-classical economics, albeit giving a particular role to political institutions. Such a framework is not typically elaborated by courts, however much it has caught the imagination of at least some sectors of legal academia. Imagine, for example, a Committee of Wise Economists with the power to decide the boundaries of justifiable national regulation. Like a national supreme court deciding on whether commerce between its constituent states is justifiably impeded (or like the European Court of Justice deciding whether Article 95 of the Amsterdam Treaty justifies a Member State departing from an agreed Community standard), a Committee of Wise Economists would be requiring and enforcing a process of rational public justification.

But would the character, standards and outcomes of such a justificatory discourse differ in important ways from the justifications accepted by judges and lawyers? An instrumentalist Weberian vision might suggest that similar ends may well be pursued by both lawyers and economists: the rationalisation of social behaviour in general, and increasingly of legislative activity in particular, so as to facilitate the smooth development of capitalism.[5] Meta-regulation as an integral aspect of rationalisation is perhaps analogous, in its zeal for the dream of comprehensiveness, clarity and completeness, to codification of the common law in the nineteenth century: a need to impose rational order, this time on positive law. Furthermore, where judicial law may have combined rationalisation and continuing flexibility through the incrementalism of the common law, meta-regulation tries to achieve flexibility by being reflexive – that is, providing a systematic process for constant revision and self-analysis by government of its own means of governance.

Thus the overall trend of legal and (at least neo-classical) economic rationality can be viewed as parallel techniques towards a common end. Rationalisation is not, however, just about enhancing the calculability and predictability of social coordination. It is also about legitimation – providing a relatively coherent justification for the patterns of conduct that result. From this perspective, legal and neo-classical economic rationality draw on rather different logics of justification, though both may be seen as self-referential. But the self-referential nature of legal justification is more oriented to the past and to tradition, drawing on analogical reasoning from precedent even while incorporating the possibility of forward-looking change. Justification in the context of neo-classical economics, on the other hand, is almost wholly forward-looking, seeking always to maximise the overall efficiency, or net social welfare, of particular political choices. The relevance of this difference will be discussed at the end of this chapter.

In the second part of this chapter, I explore three instances where the rationalisation of law through predominantly neo-classical economic lenses is proceeding apace. In all these contexts, we can observe routines, procedures, criteria and institutions evolving which aim to systematically rationalise the production of new and existing legislation in ways that maximise the smooth operation of competitively structured economic exchange.[6]   As I have indicated, I call this general development meta-regulation. Within that broad term, different degrees of meta-regulation can be observed. First and most loosely, nations can implement regulatory management systems, a capacious term for a set of somewhat diffuse routines, procedures and evaluative criteria that might ensure 'regulatory quality'. Secondly, and more developed, I describe a specific regulatory management system in Australia that arguably approximates the building of institutions of 'economic adjudication'. Finally, I allude to recent developments that presage an *intersection* of meta-regulation and the development of international trade rules. This intersection of trade concerns and national-level regulatory reform potentially gives national legislation the presumptive character of "behind-the-border impediments to international trade", which can be challenged as unjustifiable in a dispute resolution context. It could possibly even lead to the situation where a country would be expected to institutionalise meta-regulation as a condition of membership of international trade regimes. If such directions were to materialise, it would forge practical links between meta-regulation and the rationalising effects of the rule of law, as well as the conceptual analogies that I sketch in the third part of this chapter. But first, to empirical description.

Meta-regulation

OECD Efforts

The OECD, a non-governmental organisation based in Paris, has for almost two decades now given quiet but persistent attention to systematic collection of information about domestic regulatory reform processes. The Public Management section of the OECD publishes a series of country reports which track progress on regulatory reform in a sector-by-sector manner across countries and over time. In the last 5 years or so, the notion that regulatory reform can be analysed as an *economy-wide* phenomenon has been increasingly emphasised by the OECD.[7] In 1995, the OECD promulgated a Recommendation it calls an "international quality standard" on the production of government regulation.[8] Since 1995, it has explicitly developed a range of 'best practice' criteria by which it identifies the sorts of institutions and processes that will guarantee a high standard of 'regulatory quality' in different countries. In other words, the approach is rather like treating the legislative output of a particular nation-state as a product or good of that nation-state, which should meet certain quality standards in order to be acceptable to the citizens of that country.[9]

The content of the 'quality standards' for regulation suggested by OECD basically mirrors the concerns of regulatory politics in recent decades, namely the trends towards, variously, deregulation, a maximisation of market competition, incentive-based methods of shaping economic activity and so on. The OECD has long lists of criteria which 'best quality regulation' should achieve, but the most important are counter-posed to qualities which the OECD claims have traditionally characterised regulation in the past. Thus 'new-style regulation' should be cost-effective and efficient rather than purely 'effective', bottom-up rather than top-down, empirically based rather than produced in response to the demands of interest groups, and should make strategic use of markets rather than replace them.

The general trend of such recommendations is by now an all too familiar refrain in regulatory politics. And one of the techniques for achieving 'best-quality' regulation, the requirement that new or existing regulatory regimes be justified by reference to cost-benefit analysis, is not new. It began with military policy and dams in the US in the 1930s, but has been a general feature of executive activity in the US since the late 1970s, and has since the mid-1980s onwards has become increasingly pervasive at least as a formal requirement in a number of OECD countries – cost compliance assessment in the UK, regulatory impact analysis in Australia etcetera. However the OECD has been increasingly emphasising the necessity of a 'regulatory management system', that is a set of routines and procedures with institutional support within a country to embed the 'new thinking' about regulation into the internal procedures of government policymaking. By 1999, four years after the OECD's Recommendation on the content of best practices in this regard, twenty-four OECD countries were using regulatory impact analysis to guide their regulatory policy decision-making process, compared to only three in 1980.[10] Moreover, fourteen of these countries had established specific units and personnel in central bureaucracies to monitor and support the new routines.[11] A particularly highly developed example of such a 'regulatory management' system is that which was established in Australia in 1995 under the auspices of a policy initiative known as 'National Competition Policy'. The connection between the Australian initiative and the OECD is not coincidental, for the small but influential key network of some five or six advocates within the OECD for this systematisation of regulatory reform principles include two Australians.[12] This also has implications for the possible future spread of the kind of regime that is explored in this book, for the OECD, as what one commentator has called "the single most important builder of business regulatory epistemic communities",[13] is an important player in setting international agendas.[14] The use, for example, by the OECD of detailed guidelines developed by one of the Australian states in applying the reforms discussed below, demonstrates the salience of this regime for broader international developments.[15]

Australian Regime

In April 1995, to vociferous political credit-claiming and media fanfare, the nine governments that jointly and concurrently govern Australia signed a triad of intergovernmental agreements known as National Competition Policy (the NCP reforms).[16] Although the reforms fall under the rubric of 'competition policy', their import ranges far wider than the arena of anti-trust rules. NCP in Australia is essentially about a redefinition of the state's regulatory and public provision functions, at all levels of governments in the federation. The very fact that the reforms were framed in terms of *competition* policy rather than regulatory reform is part of that redefinition: it puts the effect of regulatory reform on competition at the very centre of the regime, thus relatively marginalising other facets of the public interest that may be served by regulation.

The NCP reforms apply to rule-making procedures in the Australian polity at both the legislative and the formal administrative level.[17] Although limited aspects of NCP are embodied in 'mirror legislation' (i.e. statutes passed in identical terms by the six states, two territories and federal government) the main outlines of the reforms are recorded in *intergovernmental compacts*, the legal status of which is not entirely clear. In form, they resemble most closely international treaties, but the parties are sub-units of one domestic state, rather than distinct national states.

The Competition Principles Agreement (CPA) is the intergovernmental compact that instantiates a wide-ranging regulatory management regime. It applies to rules that are made either formally through legislative processes, or by an accretion of policy decisions that treat government entities differently from private entities. The CPA aims to eliminate all rules that restrict the operation of competitive market forces unless a publicly reasoned case demonstrates the public interest that necessitates their existence. It does so by imposing a set of largely procedural requirements on all levels of government rule-making, requirements that must be complied with before any rule becomes law. I use the qualification *largely* procedural because there is an important substantive facet to the test that all rules must satisfy: the rule must represent the option least restrictive of competition, unless a more restrictive option would be demonstrably more beneficial to the public interest. The agreement applies not only on a continuing basis to new rules and programmes coming into force after April 1995, but also, on a rolling basis over five years, to the totality of *existing* rules and programmes across all levels of government. Its scope is ambitious in the extreme.

Compliance with the CPA is secured by a mix of layers of executive oversight and fiscal incentives. Each state and the Commonwealth creates an executive unit to oversee and coordinate the review and reform of legislation department by department. Although these state-level units have no substantive penal powers to punish lack of compliance, an incentive 'carrot' method of securing compliance exists instead. As a quid pro quo for effective implementation of the regulatory reform required by the CPA, the agreement provides for the payment of some AUS\$4.2 billion to state and territory governments by the federal government, known as "competition payments". Receipt of the competition payments is conditional on satisfying a newly created national independent agency – the National Competition Council[18] – on an annual basis that "effective implementation" of the NCP reforms is taking place. The creation of new institutions, the reorganisation of existing networks of officials to give a central place to National Competition Policy, and the fiscal incentives provided to enforce it, all make the Australian reform package a particularly significant instance of meta-regulation.

A particularly blunt description of the overall package occurred during the parliamentary debate on the implementing legislation in the state of Victoria. The description characterises the reforms almost as if they were a new and excitingly simple recipe – and indeed, they were marketed to the public very much in these terms, as a fail-safe way to increase the size of the economic pie to the benefit of all. The speaker was a member of the ruling Coalition (conservative) government. The second paragraph encapsulates the CPA reforms which are the main focus of this research:

> Firstly, you unleash [anti-trust legislation] across the board to affect all state operations. Secondly you take away the unfair advantages government enterprises have ... You then distil from government enterprises the natural monopolies – the railway lines, the transmission lines, the ports and so forth – and put them to one side. You then take the competitive elements and put them in the marketplace. That very simple process was set out and agreed to by the Council of Australian Governments (COAG).

> You then look at all the legislation you have and you take out any unnecessary protection that may exist, whether it is for professions or whether it is for other areas, and you say 'That is out' unless of course there are certain reasons why particular parts of that legislation should be left in. Effectively COAG has agreed that if you are going to do that, that is fine but it is a reverse onus of proof: you have to prove that it is necessary that you leave it in, so the onus is on you to show that. There are many areas both in the professions and in other areas where that is easily shown.

> Then there is the access to natural monopolies, which effectively ensures that all those natural monopolies that you took out are equally accessed by the new competitive bodies. This is the way the world is going and it is the way this state must head.[19]

In this 'structural adjustment' plan, there are two guiding assumptions. First, governmental operations should be guided by the same system of constraints and incentives that shape competitive markets in the private sector. Secondly, government rules should promote and support a market-based system of constraints and incentives, unless a positive case is made for the net public benefit served by any anti-competitive effects that might result from the introduction or continuation of regulation. The presumptive view that regulation all too often secures rents for special interest groups is implicit in the characterisation of legislation as "unnecessary protection".

It is worth emphasising the element of *inbuilt presumption* against a particular subset of government regulation in the way the regime is structured. Recall the primary aim of the CPA: to eliminate unjustifiable restrictions on competitive forces, "unnecessary protection" in the words of the politician above. In order to achieve this, the principal visible outputs of government – formal rules – are treated as a product that is subject to a regime of quality control. The core quality standard of the CPA regime – the standards that define what is 'necessary' and what is 'unnecessary' protection – is that laws and regulations are demonstrably the *least restrictive alternative to competition*.

That there should be an explicit presumption *against* any legislation impacting on competition was clear from the beginning. The Committee of Inquiry whose report formed the basis of the NCP reforms argued that in order "to overcome the resistance of protected groups" when dismantling "unjustifiably restrictive regulations", governments should accept "the principle that there is a presumption that competition is desirable, placing the onus on those proposing continuation of a restriction to demonstrate why it is justified in the public interest".[20] This presumption creates a design bias against what the OECD calls 'traditional regulation' legislation as a means of achieving collective objectives, whether social or economic. It institutionalises a preference in favour of market mechanisms or incentive-based frameworks over command-and-control frameworks of regulation. It is a preference built in as a requirement to examine ways of securing the public benefit sought, without using prescriptive rules encoded in law. That is to say, competitive market frameworks allowing the interaction of unrestricted individual preferences are the preferred mechanism for pursuing all ranges of public interest goals in policymaking. Second-best alternatives include 'soft law' (e.g. codes of conduct) or informal ways of shaping otherwise unrestricted individual preferences (e.g. self-regulation, government-backed accreditation). And only as a last resort can formal legislative intervention, under the CPA regime, be justified.

Thus overall, the structure of the CPA meta-regulatory regime prescribes an explicit substantive aim, which is to maximise the degree to which competitive market structures provide a framework for service delivery or addressing social risk or equity concerns. Complementing this substantive aim are extra procedural hurdles to discourage political intervention as a way of achieving these goals, particularly if encoded in formal command-and-control regulation. Just as constitutions place extra-political constraints on the lawmaking process, so too the CPA regime places a different kind of extra-political constraint on lawmaking. The constraint institutionalises scepticism about assumptions the welfare state tended not to question – the efficacy of command-and-control regulation and the positive social benefits flowing from such regulation. It is a constraint around which institutions have been built and to which significant resources have been committed. It is a constraint embedded in a regulatory management system, the substance of which reflects a perspective on political economy which emphasises law's instrumental role in facilitating market capitalism. Because of the degree of institutionalisation of the system, especially its enforcement structure and the development of a new agency, it is arguably a nascent instance of institutions of 'economic adjudication'.

The Intersection of Meta-regulation and International Trade Regimes

A regulatory management regime such as that described above in Australia's National Competition Policy requires sub-national units to justify at a national level their legislative and regulatory activity in terms the 'least restrictive alternative to competition'. Whether amounting to 'economic adjudication' or not, if the compliance requirements of international trade regimes were to intersect with this kind of regulatory management regime, the rule-of-economics would apply not just within national boundaries but across nation-states. Furthermore, if such a linkage were buttressed by a dispute settlement mechanism such as the one the WTO possesses, the shadow of 'economic adjudication' would correspondingly lengthen.

These thoughts are not purely speculative. Recent initiatives within the OECD have begun thinking through just such a systematic intersection between international trade regimes and national regulatory management systems. The opening paragraph of a recent OECD paper encapsulates the idea:

> As trade barriers at the border fall through successive trade negotiations, it is increasingly evident that domestic regulation may represent a significant source of residual trade barriers. Current national regulatory systems were developed when the nation-state was seen as the primary economic unit; with the increased importance of the global economy today, regulatory reform may be necessary to ensure that the expected benefits of globalisation are realised and that the different national systems do not become barriers to international trade and investment.[21]

The idea of linking regulatory reform into trade regimes is already more than just a series of OECD papers. In February 2001, a meeting in Singapore occurred entitled the APEC-OECD Cooperative Initiative on Regulatory Reform.[22] It discussed the idea of integrating what it called 'market strengthening' or 'competition advocacy' into the conditions of trade between APEC countries. 'Competition advocacy' is defined as "the promotion of competitive market principles in governmental policy and regulatory processes" and distinguished from competition law and competition policy. It is much broader than either of those two, and Australia's procedures as described above constitute a good example of competition advocacy.

When domestic regulatory reform is something about which a trade partner could complain in a forum like the WTO, it has the effect that the nation in question justify its domestic regulatory regime in terms acceptable to that particular dispute resolution forum. This is already happening to an extent under the Trade Policy Review Process in the WTO, where an extensive pre-prepared report on a particular country's level of compliance with trade obligations is produced at regular intervals by WTO-employed economists, and subsequently discussed in an open forum with the aid of independent commentators.[23] While this process does not at present have any particular formal sanctions attached to it in and of itself, the 'public shaming' effect it has may function as a hook for the imposition of regulatory management systems within national borders. What is important is the potential for trade regimes to act as an *enforcement* tool for domestic meta-regulatory regimes, both for their initial introduction and for their ongoing compliance.

Without specific reference to the WTO, the OECD reports are focusing upon "six efficient principles of regulation to ensure an environment that takes account of the trade effects of regulation and can underpin further trade liberalisation".[24] These principles would presumably function as the benchmark assessment of sufficiently high 'regulatory quality' to comply with trade conditions. The six are: transparency; non-discrimination; avoidance of unnecessary trade restrictiveness; use of internationally harmonised measures; recognition of equivalence of foreign regulatory measures; and competition principles.

What is particularly interesting about these criteria is that they are a mixture of rules familiar from trade (non-discrimination), meta-regulation (avoidance of unnecessary trade restrictiveness equivalent to the 'least restrictive alternative to competition' in the Australian context), and from a more political-constitutional culture of legal accountability (transparency). The debate about constitutionalisation of trade is in part a debate about legitimate process (focusing on transparency) and in part one about the legitimate threshold of substantive criteria – what will count as a 'necessary' restriction on trade in the global market? The way in which the criteria operate is a kind of blend of rule-of-law concerns and rule-of-economics concerns. This intersection of trade/competition issues and regulatory reform would, if institutionalised, produce a constantly repeating question: is a particular piece of national regulatory legislation protectionism or legitimate protection? disguised protectionism or a legitimate policy choice? covert protectionism or a considered societal choice? In all these forms, this dichotomy appears repeatedly in the OECD material, in a context that always requires a choice on one side or the other of the dichotomy to be *justified*.

The discipline of justification is at the core of this development, and this suggests an analogy with the rule of law. The rule of law allows individuals to demand justification of *decisions* (and sometimes rules) in terms of formal legal authority. Meta-regulation allows central government agencies and (depending on how transparency is institutionalised) civil society and business to demand justification of *policy choices* in terms of legitimate government objectives, defined in relation to market competition and competitive efficiency objectives. While the types of statements that constitute acceptable justifications under the rule of law on the one hand and the rule-of-economics on the other will differ, there are nonetheless important similarities in the structural logic of these two social institutions, which the next section develops.

Meta-regulation and the Rule of Law: 'Not Will but Reason'

The rule of law is clearly not a monolithic concept, and some of its internal varieties and ambiguities will be discussed in the next section. The aim of the argument here is however to isolate two relatively simple but important features that characterise any notion of the rule of law, that are in a sense constitutive of the social and normative functions served by the general notion of the rule of law.[25] I then want to argue that these two features also characterise the development of regulatory management systems, or meta-regulation.

Two features typically characterise any discussion of the rule of law. What these two features together convey is, in a nutshell, that the binding decisions taken in the collective political arena should (up to a point)[26] reflect 'not will but reason'. There is an institutional dimension to this imperative, and a cognitive dimension.

The institutional dimension of the rule of law requires that the limits of binding decisions taken in the collective political arena should be decided by actors and institutions who are independent from, and operate autonomously in relation to, 'pure' political actors and decision-makers. This is in fact a limit to pure democracy, a constraint on 'the will of the people' – the rule of law, by requiring the consent and approval of an institutionally autonomous group of actors, imposes the limits of legality on the expression of democratic will in the political arena. Though literature on law and politics endlessly debates the precise extent of law's autonomy, the general observation of that autonomy has been clearly stated, both analytically[27] and sociologically.[28] The specific development of a separation between judicial and political institutions, with the former developing a distinctive logic governed by its own battery of internal meta-rules, is one facet of this autonomy.

The cognitive dimension of the rule of law supplements this institutional constraint on 'will' by supplementing will with reason. Democratic majoritarianism justifies political action by virtue of the expression of majority will, and not by reference to the rational, logical, moral or ethical content of the binding decisions taken by political collectives. The rule of law, however, imposes a supplementary rationality, that of legal reason, onto politics. It is in a sense a mode of 'taming' politics, of ensuring that decisions taken thereby conform to the calming dictates of legal reason. The notion that legal reason can legitimate politics is linked historically to a moral conception of law's function as being to suppress the passions (the original 'police power').[29] But in modern liberal democracies, where broad social consensus on morality is difficult to attain, 'legal reason' is much more a matter of procedural regularity than of substantive limits.

These two dimensions of the rule of law are closely related. The 'taming of politics' is facilitated by the institutional separation of legal actors from political actors. The autonomous application of law, even when it is only *procedurally* autonomous, has the effect of taming politics because it 'triangulates' the relationship between governor and governed by inserting a third party with decision-making power over both.[30] The third party's power is exercised ostensibly neutrally, and even if not neutrally, at least in response to very different incentives from those holding purely political power. In a way, the partial insulation of different branches of the state from each other (and in particular the judicial branch) is at the heart of the basic notion of separation of powers, a historically classic device for 'taming politics'.

The development of regulatory management regimes can be viewed as an analogous device for applying to collective political decision-making the discipline of 'not will but reason'. Indeed, meta-regulation can be viewed as a variation on the basic idea of separation of powers. First, consider the dimension of institutional autonomy, the extent to which regulatory management regimes depend on at least partial independence from democratic politics. Over time, the institutionalisation of Australia's meta-regulatory regime has led to a separation of competencies *within* the arena of the executive. In other words, separate executive units and independent agencies have sprung up within government to monitor and enforce the application of meta-regulatory criteria. A situation of semi-autonomous institutional structures characterises the sphere of meta-regulation.

Second, consider the cognitive dimension of meta-regulation. Majoritarian democratic procedures, under the influence of perspectives drawing on public choice theory, have increasingly lost legitimacy by being seen as too vulnerable to 'special interests' who secure 'rent' by self-interested pursuit of laws that do not benefit the general public. This is where meta-regulation steps in to add an additional constraint upon 'pure politics'.

Meta-regulation is a strategy for managing the production of formal legal rules (primary and secondary legislation). Just as constitutions 'tame politics' with legal reason, meta-regulation seeks to supplement legal reason with a more explicitly economic rationality. In so doing, meta-regulation questions the assumption that adherence to legal procedural mandates will necessarily produce 'rational' laws, and imposes an additional hurdle which must be cleared by all proposals for rule-based intervention into the economy.

Like legal reason, the economic rationality of cost-benefit analysis which dominates meta-regulatory regimes lays claim to an objectivity and neutrality that will temper the arbitrary exercise of political power. Thus there is an analogy between the way in which law claims to 'tame politics' and the aspirations of meta-regulation: meta-regulation imposes economic reason on politics. The logic of taming politics by the application of neutral, objective expertise is structurally similar. Both the rule of law and the rule-of-economics institutionalise a discipline of 'not will, but reason' upon binding decisions taken in the collective political arena.

Multiple Versions of the Rule of Law

My purpose in emphasising these analogies between the rule of law and the kinds of institutions and procedures that make up regulatory management regimes, has been to convey a particular vision of the social function of such regimes: an instrumental role in facilitating capitalism, in essence. Of course, this is highly political, a facet illustrated by the fact that the introduction of such regimes is on the one hand, typically presented by their adherents as a technocratic apolitical endeavour, and on the other hand, resisted by key groups in society as a mask for neo-liberal politics.

In fact of course, complex and diffuse institutional phenomena such as the rule of law or the rule-of-economics, are never reified 'things' that 'represent' particular constellations of substantive values and political decisions. Rather they are malleable ideals, capable of interpretation in multiple ways, a locus for argument about the legitimate thresholds of allocating power to different groups and interests within a society. The presentation of certain versions of the rule of law as the 'correct' version, or the 'universal value' reflects the ideological role such a notion plays in collective politics; it does not contradict the malleability of the ideal itself. That malleability has been reflected in the academic literature, where the 'rule of law' has been given shifting meanings.[31] Two primary meanings can be discerned, which could be termed 'thin' and 'thick' versions – 'thick' versions adding a variety of substantive ends to the 'thin' version which is more proceduralist, means-focused.

The 'thin' version of the rule of law is a formalist conception, referring to the relatively modest claim that state power is exercised according to law, no matter what the content – i.e. that political authorities respect existing laws, whatever these are. Hayek's succinct formulation is (leaving aside the implications he draws from this): "stripped of all technicalities this means that government in all its actions is bound by rules fixed and announced beforehand".[32] Even this minimalist conception of the rule of law requires that the meaning of existing laws is declared by institutionally autonomous personnel applying 'not will but reason'.

A 'thicker' conception of the rule of law requires more than that the current political regime respect its own legality; it refers to the existence of a particular set of substantive guarantees that accrue to citizens by virtue of legal mechanisms. As soon as we speak of a 'thicker' conception of the rule of law, we are in the realm of regulatory politics. Since a requirement that rules be fixed and announced beforehand is commonly linked with a requirement that the rules be *general*, discussion of the rule of law can easily slide into an assertion that the substantive guarantees secured by law include prohibitions on regulatory intervention into the economy. Hayek for example argues that the need to govern only by prospective general rules excludes by necessity "measures designed to control access to different trades and occupations, the terms of sale, and the amounts to be produced or sold".

The slide from a formalist emphasis on the importance of general, pre-announced rules to an assertion that specific modes of intervention into political economy are precluded by the rule of law occurs because of anxiety about discretion. Many aspects of regulatory intervention into the economy provide selective benefits or impose selective controls on sub-sections of society: this kind of selectivity is certainly discretionary and some argue it is arbitrarily so. It is *arbitrary* political discretion that is seen as incompatible with the rule of law. Yet governance without any discretion is inconceivable, and the content of what is designated as 'arbitrary' is typically filled by substantive political visions. Albeit somewhat schematic, it is useful to delineate three different substantive political visions which animate commonly relied-upon visions of the rule of law.

I will do no more than mention the first vision, which would 'thicken' the formalist conception of the rule of law by emphasising political liberties, or human rights, as the content of the guarantee.[33] While this is a vitally important facet of the rule of law, it is not the primary focus of this book, in part because the institutions involved are typically courts and my interest here is in non-judicial bureaucratic institutions. Furthermore, courts in the Australian context play a less direct role in shaping social and economic regulatory policies than they do in human rights issues.[34]

A second substantive vision is that anchored in broadly neo-liberal substantive politics, embedded in a vision of the rule of law as part of *market liberalism*. A market liberalism perspective emphasises the kinds of substantive guarantees considered to be essential preconditions for the smooth functioning of a market economy: for example, rules that specify property rights, rules that facilitate voluntary contracting, rules that ensure the stability of banks and currencies, anti-trust rules. This conception of the rule of law is frequently implicit in international development reform packages advocated by institutions like the World Bank for countries transitioning from military or communist rule into a market democracy.

A third perspective, which could be termed *tempered market liberalism*, would extend the substantive guarantees secured by law to include not only political and civil liberties, but also "the establishment of the social, economic, educational and cultural conditions which are essential to the full development of [human] personality".[35] Tempered market liberalism of this kind connotes a set of substantive guarantees frequently associated with the various facets of the welfare state, guarantees that aspire to promote social citizenship, in addition to civil and political citizenship. Social citizenship here aims to ameliorate key deficiencies of market liberalism, such as social risks arising from market failures and uncontrolled externalities, as well as the fact that markets are insensitive to distributive issues.

The promotion of such guarantees *as a facet of the rule of law* (as opposed to a concern of social justice more generally) is controversial. This is because provision of social citizenship frequently involves a degree of positive governmental action, necessarily discretion-saturated, which potentially conflicts with the notion that even a purely formalist notion of the rule of law will constrain arbitrariness by reining in discretion. Certainly there is tension between the substantive goals of market liberalism and tempered market liberalism, explicit in the labels since the latter seeks to respond to key limitations of market liberalism. But tempered market liberalism still envisages securing social citizenship goals through legal means, albeit rule-based bureaucracies more than judicial interpretation. For example, environmental regulation, nursing home regulation, new drug testing, motor vehicle safety regulation, rule-based state programmes for redistributing income to disadvantaged citizens, rules that required health insurance or medical services to be provided to citizens in need, rule-based programmes for subsidising the cost of higher education for selected citizens, are all examples of this perspective on the rule of law. And in international development, the importance of establishing these kinds of social guarantees has been stressed as a necessary aspect of technical assistance in establishing the rule of law.[36]

At some point, 'thick' versions of the rule of law risk blurring into arguments about a complete social philosophy for guiding collective decision-making. This malleability, though, is just what makes the notion of the rule of law a rich and complex resource for argument in the collective political arena about the limits of binding decisions. And all three versions of the rule of law, however malleable, impose a discipline of rationalisation upon the process of political decision-making. That rationalisation occurs by virtue of the role that legal institutions, insulated from politics and applying a form of impartial reason, play in securing the guarantees. In the 'thin' formalist version and the market liberalism version of the rule of law common law courts are crucial providers of these dimensions of decision-making. In the case of a human rights-focused version of the rule of law, constitutional courts may become important players. And in the case of the vision of social citizenship under tempered market liberalism, despite the *tension* with the rule of law noted above, there is still a strongly rationalising ethos involved, insofar as rule-based bureaucracies (operating at least partially autonomously from 'pure politics' and also subject to the discipline of judicial review) are crucial providers of the substantive guarantees at stake.

The Rule of Law and Meta-regulation Juxtaposed

The ethos of rationalisation is a function not only of the institutions involved but also of their method of reasoning. In essence, the discipline of justification, closely tied to a sense of proportionality, is key here. The rule of law allows individuals to demand justification of *decisions* (and sometimes rules) in terms of formal legal authority, and possibly a varying range of substantive guarantees in addition to such formal authority. The limit this places on political decision-making is at its core a requirement that decisions be justified in a transparent, evidence-based manner. This is really the heart of much constitutional balancing and judicial review of regulatory laws. Seen like this – a structured careful, evidence-based way of making means-end assessments with institutions insulated from political pressures – the analogy with the institutions of meta-regulation is easier to observe. Just as constitutions place extra-political constraints on the lawmaking process, so too meta-regulation places a different kind of extra-political constraint on lawmaking.

The analogy between meta-regulation and the rule of law here begins to deepen. The combination of institutional autonomy and expert manipulation of discourses grounded in claims to neutral rationality gives those who flesh out the meaning of the rule of law considerable interpretive power. That interpretive power is particularly strong from the point of view of how an issue is discursively framed. The rights and duties recognised by the legal system constitute the terms and boundaries of the justificatory debate – whether to the benefit or detriment of broader political values is hotly contested, as a long-running debate over 'rights talk' evidences.[37]

Meta-regulation, like the rule of law, also catalyses a process of justification in a context where the resulting interpretive power discursively frames the debate. The extra-political constraint imposed by meta-regulation institutionalises scepticism about assumptions the welfare state tended not to question – the efficacy of command-and-control regulation and the positive social benefits flowing from such regulation. Applying and interpreting such constraints is an interpretive enterprise, a quest for an 'interpretive fit' between the range of possible regulatory solutions and the criteria laid down by the meta-regulatory regime. This quest for an 'interpretive fit' has deliberate Dworkinian echoes,[38] illuminating the structural similarities between a society's commitment to the rule of law, and its commitment to a regime of meta-regulation. In other words, the enterprise of seeking interpretive fit within meta-regulation is at least in part a principled enterprise, and not simply a question of the most powerful interests winning out. It is an enterprise which seeks to elicit the boundaries of 'justifiable regulation', and to decide how far those boundaries should incorporate ideals of social citizenship.

Its primary interpretive community is very different, however, from that which imposes legal reason on politics. Meta-regulation is located in a community which is dominated by the expertise, values and intellectual orientations of professional economists, particularly in final decision-making roles. As a result, even if outcomes are not rigidly dictated by neoclassical economic perspectives, increasingly the debate as a whole is conducted *in terms of* efficiency criteria and the language of externalities and market.

Despite the analogy with a Dworkinian search for integrity in regulatory reform, however, the meta-regulatory setting for this search is very far from the austere, protected stratosphere of Dworkin's Herculean judge. The competition for interpretive persuasiveness that flows from the conversation of meta-regulation is more explicitly political, more pragmatic and open-textured than judicially-located battles over the limits of justification. It takes place in bureaucratic agencies and legislatures rather than in courts. In addition to economists, its participants are bureaucrats, interest groups and, on occasion, parliamentary committees. Of course, such participants supplement the interpretive stances of judges and lawyers in the judicial arena too. But it is part of the argument of this book that meta-regulation is an *incipient* mode of legality, not necessarily a fully fledged one. The institutions and personnel that comprise a meta-regulatory regime do not have the degree nor longevity of insulation from politics that judicial institutions have enjoyed. Debates about how to institutionalise the rule of law in developing and post-communist countries are increasingly conscious of the limits imposed by the absence of a well-entrenched separation between law and politics.[39] I would suggest that meta-regulatory regimes are at a similar stage of evolution in industrialised democracies – edging slowly towards the kind of discursive and institutional autonomy enjoyed by judicial institutions, but at present still closely tied to administrative contexts where pragmatic justifications dominate.

Nonetheless, the self-referentiality of neo-classical economic reasoning increasingly wards off this open-textured pragmatism. But because of the contested nature of the field of regulation, the dominance of economic discourse is not hegemonic. The substantive political implications of meta-regulation are, like the rule of law, potentially malleable. In closing this chapter, I turn to a brief overview of the possible dimensions of meta-regulation's contested malleability. The purpose of sketching alternatives here is really just to complete the analogy built with the rule of law. The detail of what is involved in different interpretations of meta-regulation will be filled out much more substantially as the book proceeds, primarily in Chapters Three, Four and Five.

Malleable Meta-regulation

Just as there are multiple visions of the rule of law, there are multiple visions of meta-regulation. The core logic of meta-regulation, like that of the rule of law, is, as I have argued, one of justification. The rule-of-economics demands a justification by governments of policy choices, and the parameters of justifiable regulation, or of legitimate government objectives are defined in relation to either a 'benchmark' standard of maximum market competition, or at least a net benefit to the community assessed in a economistic cost-benefit framework. Within this broad shared logic, however, several types of justification exist, and they could broadly be categorised in analogy with the discussion regarding the rule of law above, 'thin' versions, and 'thick' versions.

First, then, 'thin' meta-regulation. The analogy to a purely formalistic version of the rule of law is what I call 'check-list rationality'. In essence here, governments are free to intervene in whatever manner they choose provided they fulfil specified procedures of thinking through a range of alternatives, comparing the costs and benefits of each one, and ensuring that there is sufficient empirical evidence to buttress the claimed cost-benefit structure. As long as justification is offered, policy choice is not constrained. The hurdles are purely procedural and purely formal. They impose a burden on how decisions are made, but not on what decisions are made.

By contrast, 'thicker' versions of meta-regulation do impose some substantive constraints on policy choice. The contrast here is principally between market liberalism and tempered market liberalism. Both visions have a prima facie commitment to market governance, consistent with the implicit assumption of a conceptual framework drawn from neo-classical economics. But depending on the ideological fervour with which that framework is interpreted, meta-regulation might be malleable enough to incorporate a variety of techniques or policy solutions that would temper the worst externalities of markets or their most extreme distributive impacts.[40]

A neo-liberal vision of meta-regulation as a technique for imposing or facilitating market governance is implicit in much of what is written by proponents of meta-regulation. These proponents are often situated in central government agencies and frequently speak in economistic terms of the aim of meta-regulation as being to provide a bulwark against inefficient rent-seeking by special interest groups.[41] Increasingly, popular understandings of the potential impact of international trade regimes at a domestic level link the principles that typify meta-regulatory regimes with neo-liberal political agendas Perhaps because of the fierceness of the political opposition which this association has engendered, evident in the anti-globalisation movement, it appears that as meta-regulatory regimes mature, a second perspective on their justificatory logic is emerging. This may well be a change of emphasis rather than an alternative, and it may even be 'window-dressing'. Nonetheless it does expand the malleability of what meta-regulation means for regulatory politics. This perspective advocates that markets be tempered, though it sometimes frames this not so much as 'tempering' as correcting for externalities, market failures or distributive insensitivity in order to strengthen the long-term viability of the market framework.

The rhetoric of the OECD-APEC forum mentioned earlier in this chapter is an interesting instance of ambiguity in this context, where it is not entirely clear whether more importance is being given to the ultimate primacy of market governance, or to the inevitable limitations of that mode of governance. However the presence of countries with very different levels of development in trade negotiations appears to be a factor that encourages greater recognition of the need to temper market governance. For example, negotiations for free trade arrangements between the countries of the Americas indicate that the notion of 'market strengthening' is being widened to *officially* include 'social goals'.[42] And the development of Australia's meta-regulatory programme is another example: in recent times it has acquired a new focus on 'adjustment packages' for those most vulnerable to distributive effects of the reforms generated under meta-regulation. This second perspective may amount to little more than 'paying off the losers' but it does import a stronger focus on tempering market liberalism in ways that emphasise the political malleability of meta-regulation.

The rest of the book will of course develop the variability of meta-regulation in more detail, but at this point it is appropriate to summarise what has been established. Meta-regulation involves the commitment of resources, institutions and personnel to the instrumental use of economic reason in law-like ways that has considerable implications for the ongoing development of global capitalism. It is a 'cutting edge' of capitalism's rationalising techniques, a form of non-judicial legality that is increasingly pervasive across western industrialised countries, and likely to be incorporated into multilateral trade regimes that will spread its influence even further. The bureaucratic regulatory institutions built around meta-regulation, like judicial institutions, contribute to rationalisation because they are partially insulated from politics, exercise partial veto power and are seen as neutral rational actors. As a technique of rationalisation, meta-regulation involves the development of institutions that systematically and purposively render calculable and predictable patterns of regulatory policy choice, in addition to providing a relatively coherent justification for them.

But the predictability and coherence of this process should not be over-emphasised. Rationalisation is always incomplete, always destabilised by the malleability of politics and the political nature of so-called neutral expertise. Some actors see meta-regulation as a legitimating technique for perpetuating a neo-liberal version of globalisation and deregulation, one that will attenuate social citizenship. Others cast it in more pragmatic terms as a rational constraint on the distortion of regulatory politics by 'vested interests', but a constraint that leaves open a range of market tempering possibilities. Any evaluation of meta-regulation at this level can only be made in a specific local context. Of the range of meta-regulatory developments surveyed in this chapter, that of Australia, as argued in the Introduction, is the most ripe and apt for exploration. The next chapter duly gives some flesh and blood to the actors and institutions populating the trajectory of meta-regulatory developments in Australia, as well as some historical and political context to the specific regime of meta-regulation at the heart of the project.

Notes

[1]   I use the phrase 'political economy' here to emphasise my perspective that *all* accounts of the role of law in structuring, facilitating and shaping economic exchange are accounts of political relations. Though the law, and the economy, may variously be portrayed as neutral, technical and apolitical, I assume that such a portrayal is in itself a political move. This does not mean it is a purely cynical exercise, for important ends can be achieved by attempts to separate law, or the market, from 'pure politics'. But the attempts will always be incomplete and will always have a political resonance. Hence I do not wish to separate 'politics' at a conceptual level from 'law' and 'economics'. The differences that matter exist at the level of institutions, routines and procedures, and the allocation of final decision-making power.

2   This is not to sideline Marx. Both Weber and Marx could be viewed as casting law as a means of rationalising socially mediated exchange in a manner that facilitated the growth of nation-state capitalism. Of course Marx's critical stance cast this rationalisation as a veneer for the exercise of raw power in contrast to Weber's more Whiggish sense of cumulative progress, but they share a sense of law's instrumental role in political economy. Where they part company sharply is on the role of law in legitimation of social relations, an angle I return to later in the book.

3   Weatherill, Steve, (2000), 'New Strategies for Managing the EC's Internal Market', *Current Legal Problems*, Vol. 53, pp. 595-619.

4   McGinnis, J. and Movsesian, M. (2000), 'The World Trade Constitution: Reinforcing Democracy Through Trade', *Harvard Law Review*, Vol. 114, pp.511-605.

5   Of course, just as the modes of justification sanctioned by law are not monolithically pro-capitalist, nor will the modes of justification facilitated by economic rationality necessarily exclude the tempering of market capitalism. That both the rule of law and meta-regulation have malleable political implications is a point taken up in more detail later in the chapter.

6   The regulatory management systems advocated by the OECD in fact emphasise the production of efficient regulation – in the sense of regulation that avoids the imposition of excessive compliance costs and produces a net social benefit. By contrast, the Australian model prioritises *competitively structured* exchange, and the potential linkages between trade regimes and regulatory management systems would focus more on barriers to trade. For the present purposes, these are all criteria that facilitate a free-market version of capitalistic social relations.

7   OECD (1995), *Recommendation of the Council of the OECD on Improving the Quality of Government Regulation*, PUMA, 9 March 1995, Paris; OECD (1996), *Regulatory Reform: A Country Study of Australia*, Public Management Service; OECD (1997), *The OECD Report on Regulatory Reform: Synthesis*, Paris; OECD (1998), *Regulatory Reform*, Paris.

8   OECD (1995), *Recommendation of the Council of the OECD on Improving the Quality of Government Regulation*, PUMA, 9 March 1995, Paris.

9   As we shall see later in this part, by linking trade and regulation, the OECD is beginning to suggest that regulatory quality should be acceptable not just to citizens of the country in question but to those outside its borders who wish to trade with its citizens or invest within its borders.

10   Jacobs, Scott (1999), *The Second Generation of Regulatory Reforms*, IMF Conference on Second Generation Reforms, p.17, available at http://www1.oecd.org/subject/regreform/speeches/.

11   Deighton-Smith, Rex (1997), 'The Machinery of Regulatory Reform' *The OECD Observer* Vol. 206, June/July 1997, p.33.

12   Perton, Victor, Member of Parliament of Victoria, Chairman of Scrutiny of Acts and Regulation Committee (1997), *Interview*, Morgan. January 29 1997; Downing, Terry, Senior Policy Officer, NSW Cabinet Office (1998), *Interview*, Morgan. February 7 1997. Canada is the other significant national influence on the OECD initiatives. Both are Anglo-American federations and as we shall see in Chapter Two, the politics of federalism were highly salient to the particular regime that developed in Australia.

13   Braithwaite, J. and Drahos, P. (2000), *Global Business Regulation*, Cambridge University Press, Cambridge, p.29.

14   Salzman, James (2000), 'Labour Rights, Globalisation and Institutions: The Role and Influence of the Organisation for Economic Cooperation and Development' *Michigan Journal of International Law*, Vol. 21, pp.769 ff.

15   Braithwaite, Interview (2001), *Interview*, Morgan. December 2001. The guidelines in question are Centre for International Economics (1999), *Guidelines for National Competition Policy Legislation Reviews*, Centre for International Economics, available at www.intecon.com.au and on file with author, Melbourne.

16   The three agreements are the Conduct Code Agreement, the Competition Principles Agreement and the Agreement to Implement the National Competition Policy and Related Reforms. See Appendices.

17   They also apply, by virtue of the first intergovernmental agreement, beyond rule-making procedures to the actual conduct of businesses in the public and private sectors, although this is of less direct concern to this research. This agreement, the Conduct Code Agreement (CCA) extends federal anti-trust rules to all public sector businesses as well as to unincorporated businesses. This ensures that the norms of market competition govern all business decisions and conduct, regardless of their location in the public or private sector.

18   One of two new bodies set up under the legislative amendments to the Trade Practices Act 1974 (Cth) as part of the NCP reforms. The other body is an independent agency, the Australian Competition and Consumer Council (ACCC) which is an expanded amalgam of the formerly existing Trade Practices Tribunal and the Prices Surveillance Authority. ACCC's role lies mainly in monitoring conduct rather than policymaking.

19   Victorian Legislative Assembly (1995), *Hansard*, 11 October 1995, p.612.

20   Hilmer, Rayner, et al. (1993), *National Competition Policy*, Independent Committee of Inquiry into National Competition Policy, p.205.

21   OECD, (2000), 'Trade and Regulatory Reform: Insights from the OECD Country Reviews and Other Analyses', Working Party of the Trade Committee, December 2000, available at http://www.oecd.org/ech.

22   OECD (2000), The APEC-OECD Co-Operative Initiative on Regulatory Reform, November 2000, available at http://ww.oecd.org. It is interesting to note the groups hosting the APEC-OECD initiative: the government of Peru, the OECD and the APEC secretariat – an intriguing mixture of national government, non-legal international organisations, and the bureaucracy of a international legal treaty regime. The connection with Peru can be explained thus: the conference chair was Margarita Trillo, Convenor of the APEC Competition Policy and Deregulation Group and Head of International Relations and Technical Cooperation at INDECOPI (National Institute for the Defense of Competition and Protection of Intellectual Property), Peru. Trillo is a good example of an official whose place in a policy network gives her as much or even more affinity with a transnational agenda as with national interests. In Chapter Four, economically qualified central agency officials at state level in Australia form a network which is a key factor in developing meta-regulation's capacity to trump, on occasion, state-level responses to regulatory reform.

23   Braithwaite, J. and Drahos, P. (2000), *Global Business Regulation*, Cambridge University Press, Cambridge, p.209. In another interesting instance of cross-fertilisation between Australia and international meta-regulatory processes, the Trade Policy Review Process was modelled on procedures developed by an Australian body now known as the Productivity Commission, and the Trade Policy Review Body was staffed by some key former members of that Commission

(Braithwaite, Professor of Law, Research School of Social Sciences and Member of Business Council of Australia (2001), *Personal Communication*, Morgan).

24   OECD, (2000), 'Trade and Regulatory Reform: Insights from the OECD Country Reviews and Other Analyses', Working Party of the Trade Committee, December 2000, available at http://www.oecd.org/ech, para.2.

25   While it cannot but be acknowledged that there are multiple versions of the *meaning* of the rule of law (a point I discuss in detail in the next section), here I am simply aiming to identify at the most general level possible features that are common to the 'logic' of competing accounts of the meaning of the rule of law. Paul Kahn's first chapter in *The Cultural Study of Law* helped me clarify my nascent sense of the interplay between will and reason. Judith Shklar's useful article 'Political Theory and the Rule of Law' (Shklar, J. (1987), 'Political Theory and the Rule of Law', *The Rule of Law: Ideal or Ideology?*, Hutchison and Monahan, Toronto University Press, Toronto) discusses a bifurcation between ancient and modern conceptions of the rule of law (the 'rule of reason' versus an institutional conception) that reflects the two limbs I have identified.

24   Varying accounts of where this threshold should be drawn underpin the multiple conceptions of the rule of law referred to in the next section.

27   Hart, H.L.A. (1961), *The Concept of Law*, Clarendon Press, Oxford.

28   Nonet, P. and Selznick, P. (1978), *Law and Society in Transition: Toward Responsive Law*, Harper and Row, New York; Teubner, Gunther (1993), *Law as an Autopoietic System*, Blackwell, Oxford.

29   Hirschmann, Albert (1977), *The Passions and the Interests: Political Arguments for Capitalism Before its Triumph*, Princeton University Press, Princeton.

30   Shapiro, Martin (1981), *Courts: A Comparative and Political Analysis*, University of Chicago Press, Chicago.

31   Couso, Javier (no date), *The Economic Constitution of Chile: The Lochner Era Reborn?*, Unpublished paper on file with author; Raz, Joseph (1977), 'The Rule of Law and its Virtue' *Law Quarterly Review*, Vol. 93, pp. 195ff; Nonet, P. and Selznick, P. (1978), *Law and Society in Transition: Toward Responsive Law*, Harper and Row, New York; Hayek, F. (1979), *Law, Legislation and Liberty*, Routledge, London; Hendley, K. (1996), *Trying to Make Law Matter*, University of Michigan Press, Ann Arbor; Krygier, M. (2002), 'Selznick's Subjects', in Kagan, R., Krygier M. and Winston K. (eds), *Legality and Community: On the Intellectual Legacy of Philip Selznick*, Berkeley, Berkeley Public Policy Press.

32   Hayek, Friedrich (1962), *The Road to Serfdom*, Routledge, London, p.54.

33   Dyzenhaus, David (ed) (1999), *Recrafting the Rule of Law: The Limits of Legal Order*, Hart Publishing, Oxford; Mendez, J., O'Donnell, G. and Pinheiro, P.S. (eds) (1999), *The (Un)Rule of Law and the Underprivileged in Latin America*, University of Notre Dame Press, Notre Dame.

34   The *intersection between* human rights and regulatory policymaking is of increasing interest and importance, particularly at the international level where resistance to the pervasiveness of market liberalism is increasingly cast in terms of human rights. That is beyond the scope of this book however.

35   International Congress of Jurists (1959), *The Rule of Law in a Free Society: A Report on the International Congress of Jurists in Delhi*, Norman Marsh (ed), International Congress of Jurists, New Delhi, India, pp 4-14.

36   Kendall and Stiles (1998), 'Civil Society Eempowerment and Multilateral Donors: International Institutions and New International Norms', *Global Governance*, Vol. 4, pp. 199-216.

37 Scheingold, Stuart (1974), *The Politics of Rights: Lawyers, Public Policy and Political Change*, Yale University Press, New Haven; Minow, Martha (1990), *Making All The Difference: Inclusion, Exclusion and American Law*, Cornell University Press, Ithaca; Silverstein, Helena (1996), *Unleashing Rights: Law, Meaning and the Animal Rights Movement*, Michigan University Press, Ann Arbor; Schlag, Pierre (1998), *The Enchantment of Reason*, Duke University Press, Durham.

38 Dworkin, Ronald (1986), *Law's Empire*, Belknap Press, Cambridge, Massachusetts.

39 Mendez, J., O'Donnell, G. and Pinherio, P.S. (eds) (1999), *The (Un)Rule of Law and the Underprivileged in Latin America*, University of Notre Dame Press, Notre Dame; Couso, Javier (n.d.), 'The Economic Constitution of Chile: The Lochner Era Reborn?', unpublished paper on file with author.

40 Yet another dimension of malleability might involve, as with the rule of law, a connection with human rights: for example, the connection between human rights and access to markets made in debates over China's accession to the WTO. However, I will not pursue this dimension here, for the fieldwork in the national context was unsuitable for grounding such a dimension, which appears to be pursued with much more vigour at the international level.

41 Senior Official F, National Competition Council (2001), *Interview*, Morgan, 3 April 2001.

42 Summit of the Americas (2001), *Declaration of Quebec City*, Summit of the Americas, http://www.nuevamayoria.com/english/library/idocumentos.htm, esp. p.4.

2 Public Law and Political Economy in the Australian Administrative State

This chapter uses a narrative of political history to flesh out more concretely the ongoing analogy between judicial and non-judicial rationalising institutions that underpins my argument linking meta-regulation and the rule of law. The inevitably selective historical narrative presented in this chapter highlights functional analogies between developments in public law on the one hand and in political economy on the other. To reiterate what I mean by rationalisation, I am referring to the development of institutions that systematically and purposively render calculable and predictable the uncoordinated behaviour and decisions of unconnected individuals, in addition to providing a relatively coherent justification for the patterns of conduct that result. Rationalisation is an instrumental phenomenon, serving the interests of both the *efficiency* and the *legitimation* of the relevant system.

By portraying specific political and institutional reform initiatives in the history of the Australian administrative state as instances of rationalisation, I do not wish to suggest that they are not also at the same time products of strategic and contingent political choices and actions. Indeed I hope to blend a sense of both facets into the telling of the narrative, in such a way as to give increasing prominence to the contingencies of politics as we move closer to the reforms with which the remainder of the book is concerned. The tension between characterising a set of institutions and procedures as a technique of rationalisation on the one hand, and a provisional outcome of contingent politics on the other hand, is both productive and apt. It is apt because the presentation of reform as a neutral, technical and apolitical inevitability is increasingly a mode of politics, in and of itself. And it is also productive because the notion that law, or the market, can be somehow separated from 'pure politics' is at one and the same time, a cultural resource with important resonance – both expressive and instrumental – and also perpetually incomplete.

The incomplete nature of that separation is what makes the bureaucratic politics of regulatory justification politically interesting because it introduces malleability into the phenomena observed. Building on the end of the first chapter, this chapter will show how the political implications of reforms that rationalise regulatory policy choice have frequently been capable of representation from more than one angle. The two relevant poles are a more neo-liberal vision of market governance and a more tempered pragmatic version. These two visions reflect the thematic conflict underpinning the normative issues in this book: a conflict between social citizenship and competition.

But perhaps of more central importance at this stage than political malleability is the task of fleshing out rationalisation through a description of *institutions* that are important to the relationship between law and political economy. This will be done at two levels: in relation to policy application and in relation to policymaking. The first level concerns citizen-state relations, the second inter-institutional relations. At the first level, rationalising institutions and techniques both justify, and render calculable, predictable and systematic, the individuated decisions of state officials in relation to particular citizens. At the second level, rationalising institutions and techniques render calculable, predictable and systematic the otherwise uncoordinated effects of either different departments within the state, or of the variations between sub-national rulemaking on the Australian polity as a whole. Regulatory management systems, including institutions of economic adjudication, are a subset of such techniques that also provide an arena for justifying the constraints they thereby place on regulatory choices. In respect of these I go into deeper detail, and the aim is to convey a sense of the types and strength of institutions built around meta-regulation, the analytical criteria built into them, and the (sometimes malleable) politics of inception that produced them.

Obviously policymaking and policy application (or decision-making and rulemaking in the traditional terms of public law) are rarely distinct in practice. Nonetheless they are conceptually distinct enough that typically different institutions develop to address the specific tasks they pose. Schematically we might say that, at least in Australia,[1] in any particular administrative department Weberian hierarchical bureaucratic oversight and judicial institutions together typically rationalise policy *application* affecting citizen-state relations, with judicial institutions playing a particularly significant role in the legitimation limb. Policy*making* on the other hand is rationalised by a more overtly political process occurring primarily within central government agencies, as departments of finance, treasury and cabinet coordinate, plan and prioritise a range of competing demands on government. The justification of such policies has also traditionally occurred in the party political realm and the media, such that legitimation involves more of a community-political dialogue than the technical reason typically applied by rationalising institutions.

However, nascent institutions of economic adjudication are, as the argument of this book has it, increasingly important actors both in rendering regulatory policymaking across sectors systematic and predictable, *and in justifying the resulting patterns.*

We see therefore in this chapter instances of judicial institutions being key to some rationalising processes and non-judicial institutions to others. There is also some degree of typical 'fit' in terms of techniques of rationalisation such as due process techniques and cost-benefit analysis and other economic analysis techniques. But while due process fits judicial institutions better and economic analysis fits non-judicial institutions, this is not a rigid association. Judicial institutions can and sometimes do apply economic rationality; non-judicial institutions can display strong commitments to due process. What matters is the extent to which such techniques are insulated from democratic politics and open-textured pragmatic arguments – the more they are, the more we can observe the features of neutral rationality and institutional autonomy that mark out a mode of legality. And the more that non-judicial modes of legality are animated by a highly self-referential rationality such as neo-classical economics, the more this will tend to occur. The narrative trajectory in this chapter emphasises an overall move towards intensifying the degree of economic rationality shaping regulatory policy choice.

Egalitarianism in a Context of Market Liberalism

In amplification of the way I am approaching the underlying dynamic of regulatory politics (as a tussle between social citizenship and the forces of competition), this brief and highly selective historical overview of the Australian welfare and regulatory state emphasises tensions between egalitarianism and the relative size and degree of government intervention into the economy. The political bargain underpinning the Australian regulatory and welfare state has sometimes been referred to as the 'Australian settlement', to indicate its relatively idiosyncratic nature in the context of comparative political economy. Most OECD countries with a strongly egalitarian ethos to their political economy demonstrate relatively high levels of government shaping of the economy, whether through corporatist or statist strategies. Concomitantly, most OECD countries with a governance strategy of market liberalism typically pursue egalitarian outcomes to a lesser degree than corporatist or statist political economies.[2] In Australia, however, egalitarianism was, due to the nature of the historical bargain underpinning the basic patterns of Australian political economy, *consistent* with low levels of micro-level state intervention.

This 'Australian settlement' made possible an unusual combination of egalitarian goals with a version of market liberalism. The political bargain primarily focused on supporting generous levels of wage security by means of a nation-building strategy of political and legal intervention in three crucial areas: restrictive immigration policies, protectionist tariffs and quotas in the manufacturing sector, and a highly centralized and legalistic wage bargaining system[3] which used courts to set wage levels nationwide. The particular brand of state-economy relations that resulted from this political bargain between labour and capital has been described as a kind of "statist laissez-faire".[4] 'Statist laissez-faire' combined relatively strong state intervention at the macro-economic level with a laissez-faire attitude to the micro-economy operating at firm and transaction level, as well as low levels (in comparative perspective) of direct government spending on welfare.[5]

Through the 1950s and 1960s, the 'welfare state' operated primarily through this indirect means of macro-economic regulation. The combination of protective tariffs (still at an average rate of 40% as late as 1970)[6] and restrictive immigration made it possible for the centralised wage bargaining system to secure high living standards more through full employment and high minimum wages rather than through social security transfers and income support systems. Although both the latter existed from the mid-1940s, they were minimalist and highly selective[7] and Australia's level of social security spending was one of the lowest in the OECD until the 1970s.[8] Nonetheless, up until the 1970s, before immigration policies became less restrictive and women moved in large numbers into the workforce, Australia's political economy bargain was consistent with a general ethos of egalitarianism even while the administrative state remained small.

The socio-economic context changed sharply in the 1970s as the oil crisis and the slump in commodity prices led to spiralling balance of payments problems and an increasing lack of competitiveness in primary industry. This undercut the economic prosperity that subsidised the protection of secondary manufacturing industry. It also meant that the post-war wave of immigration was no longer soaked up by expanding employment. These pressures led to two main changes in the regulatory policy mix, which might be crudely characterised as a rollback of economic regulation and an expansion of social regulation and welfare state provision.

On the one hand, sectors exposed to these international pressures began to be subjected to deregulation from the macro-economic state constraints hitherto protecting them. The Labour government of 1972-75 deregulated protective tariffs. The conservative Coalition (Liberal-National) government (1975-83) left these roll-backs in place and the new Labour government elected in 1983-1996 intensified the restructuring, beginning with deregulation of the financial sector. This government also introduced an independent agency initially called the Industry Commission and a decade later renamed the Productivity Commission, to foster independent input into economic regulatory policy. Although its role is purely recommendatory, it was nonetheless unusual at the time (and remains so) to give any significant influence over such sensitive policy issues to an institution at a remove from political control.

On the other hand government regulation in order to foster social policy goals increased significantly from the 1970s onwards. The Labour government of 1972-75 introduced extensive regulatory initiatives in environmental policy, health and safety and equal opportunity measures. There was an expansion of public provision on a monopoly basis of goods and services that supplemented the market economy in health, education and aged care. Direct provision of welfare expanded with the introduction of single mothers' pensions, maternity and child care benefits and a family allowance.[9] Indirect provision of welfare through community services at the state and local level grew over the 1970s by 25% (measured on employment level in community services).[10]

The 1970s expansion of direct social welfare measures was not retrenched by the conservative Coalition (Liberal-National) government (1975-83), nor did they succeed (despite efforts) in dismantling the centralised wage negotiation system. Both immigration and tariff barriers had by now been lowered, which meant that centralised wage regulation was the last of the three key planks which had made it possible for Australia to pursue relatively egalitarian policies. In 1983, the Labour government added a national health system to this mix.

Thus the 1970s and early 1980s saw two primary developments in tension with each other: the expansion of social regulatory policy and direct welfare provision on the one hand, and the fiscal squeeze created by the changing international economic context on the other hand. At the same time, the institutional and policy balance that had made possible the 'Australian settlement' – egalitarianism secured by market liberalism – was increasingly tenuous. Centralised regulation of the labour market was the only significant aspect of this settlement left in place. A modest amount of tempered market liberalism had shored up the stability of the settlement, but created in the process new tensions. In response to these new tensions, three sets of institutional reform that developed between the 1970s and the 1990s are particularly important.

The three sets of reforms relate more directly to processes of rationalisation. The first set, the 'new administrative law' was introduced in the mid-1970s in the wake of the growth of the administrative state described above. These reforms centred on due process values and judicial and quasi-judicial institutions, and were sponsored and promoted largely by legal professionals. The second, the 'new managerialism' of the 1980s, sought to rationalise the state itself as the tension between fiscal squeeze and the expansion of social regulatory policy cut in. These reforms were primarily about internal administrative reorganisation, inspired by attempts to give cost-efficiency and flexibility a higher priority than the values of equity and universal treatment historically prioritised by the state. These reforms did not build new institutions as such and were sponsored and promoted primarily by professional bureaucrats, especially in central agencies such as Finance, Treasury and Cabinet.

The third set of reforms comprise those I have called meta-regulation. Sponsored and promoted by a coalition of business interests and technocratic officials, these reforms intensified the application of economic rationality introduced by the new managerialism. In contrast to the new managerialism, however, which applied internally within the arena of the state, meta-regulation imposed constraints on the interface between state and society, at the agenda-setting policy stage of introducing or continuing regulatory policies underpinned by law. Early attempts to introduce meta-regulation built on existing institutions and merely introduced new procedures and techniques of oversight with limited scope that amounted to what I have called a 'regulatory management regime'. However, the regime at the centre of the book, encoded in the National Competition Policy, was considerably more comprehensive and built new independent bureaucratic institutions that arguably amount to institutions of economic adjudication. While this characterisation is slightly tendentious, it is deliberately so, in an effort to draw out the analogy between the rule of law and meta-regulation discussed in the first chapter.

The 'New Administrative Law': Judicial Rationalisation of Policy Application in the Administrative State

In the 1970s and 1980s, the federal government in Australia introduced a range of institutional innovations which were known for some time as the 'new administrative law' but have more recently been referred to as the Commonwealth Administrative Law Package.[11] These reforms were primarily aimed at fostering due process values in decision-making made by government officials. The goal was to ensure that individual decisions were correctly and fairly made without endangering the systemic efficiency of the administrative decision-making agencies. Although the efficiency of the administrative state itself (rather than the broader political economy) was a background concern in introducing these reforms, the advocates of reform were more focused on the positive benefits of imposing legal reason on administrative decision-making. They argued that the 'new administrative law' would constrain the arbitrary exercise of discretion and enhance the rule of law. Insofar as this would in part render more predictable and systematic the effects of bureaucratic decisions, and in part justify the impact of such decisions on particular individuals, the new administrative law can be viewed as an effort to rationalise the growth of the administrative state that had was taking place up to and at the time.

The reforms were championed and shepherded through the political process mainly by lawyers. It was lawyers who headed the 1971 Kerr Committee, and 1973 Bland and Ellicott Committees of Inquiry, and the reports from these committees strongly shaped the ultimate reforms.[12] The initial package consisted of three main planks: the codification of the grounds of judicial review in the *Administrative Decisions (Judicial Review) Act* 1977, the institution of the Ombudsman, and the introduction of a generalist merit review tribunal known as the Administrative Appeals Tribunal (AAT). In 1982, the package was expanded by the passing of the *Freedom of Information Act* and in 1988, a Privacy Commissioner was created in response to a Law Reform Commission recommendation. Finally, championed by various coalitions of social movements and lawyers, a Human Rights Commission was set up to review government decisions in accordance with commitments derived from various international treaties. This leant more than just a procedural hue to the notion of 'correct, fair, non-arbitrary' treatment.

It is notable that all these reforms apply to the making of executive *decisions* or to the post-hoc effect of discriminatory practices upon particular individuals. As such, they rationalise the *application* of regulatory policies rather their formation. The process of lawmaking itself remained a predominantly political one, subject to checks by independent legal bodies mainly at the margins, for constitutional reasons or at the level of delegated legislation. This was consistent with a deferential judicial approach based on the tenet that legislative or quasi-legislative processes were unsuitable for consideration in adjudicative fora, and were adequately held in check through the political accountability secured by the parliamentary system of responsible government. Such an approach fitted comfortably within the Australian political culture's emphasis on parliamentary sovereignty, which it inherited from Britain. Despite the existence of a written constitution, the courts in Australia do not as a whole play a large role in the making of regulatory policy,[13] nor in setting the agenda for welfare state policies: rather they primarily rationalise particular applications of those policies.[14]

This limited effect on the policymaking process disappointed many who had larger structural hopes for the impact of the new administrative law. Particularly legal academic writing that explicitly or implicitly advocated a tempered version of market liberalism in political terms, harboured hopes that the application of legal reason to individual decision-making might have spill-over effects onto the broader policymaking process. But the new administrative law package was to disappoint them in this respect: the due process values it fostered had a decidedly individualistic focus.[15] The Committee reports on which the changes were based stressed a concern for the protection of 'individual citizen rights' against the arbitrary exercise of executive discretion that motivated the reforms, rather than any desire to design a mechanism to alter or contribute to government policy. Each of the reforms, whether judicial review, ombudsman or merits review by tribunal, shared the characteristics of assessing the impact of governmental *decisions* in terms of their fidelity to due process values. The policy-making processes of government were only indirectly affected.

To the extent that policymaking *was* affected, the 'new administrative law' package tended to have a formalising impact on the implementation of rule-based programmes and regulatory measures, decreasing the amount of discretion and resulting in increasingly more detailed prescriptive rules.[16] Particularly in its early stages it was often criticised as being overly adversarial and legalistic.[17] These criticisms reflected dissatisfactions both from the left, who had hoped for a more radical democratisation of broader policymaking processes,[18] and the right, who feared a negative impact on administrative efficiency.[19] By the early 1990s, moves were in place that concentrated on increasing flexibility and informality in the administrative law package, primarily through increased use of mediation in the AAT. The direction of these moves echoed the general tenor of the second set of reforms: the new managerialism.

The New Managerialism: Non-judicial Rationalisation of Policymaking Processes within the State

The new managerialism[20] was a shorthand reference to the composite of reforms which the Hawke Labour government of 1983 initiated in an effort to rationalise the costs and increase the efficiency of public administration, but which have been expanded by the right-wing Coalition since 1996. In contrast to the due process focus of the 'new administrative law', these reforms emphasised economic rationality, in particular cost-effectiveness and decentralised decision-making power. The linkage between the two was achieved by internal restructuring and new rules which devolved operational decision-making, but retained central control over spending limits and policy direction.

According to Stewart and Kimber,[21] the federal public service departments of the early 1980s were clearly traditional rational-legal bureaucracies, pyramidal in shape and characterised by procedure-based formalisation, specialised tasks and roles, and multiple layers of hierarchical management. In 1984, the introduction of the Financial Management Improvement Programme (FMIP) to the Commonwealth Public Service decentralised decision-making power with respect to budgetary allocations within the department. In the opposite direction, however, the formation of the Senior Executive Service (SES) along American lines intensified the hierarchical link of accountability between minister and head of department. These were enforced by outcome-based performance appraisal agreements introduced in 1986.

In 1987, the entire departmental structure was substantially reorganised, with a resulting decrease in both the number of departments and, within each department, the number of hierarchical layers and internal differentiation. Day-to-day departmental operations became significantly less hierarchical, using flat management structures, lateral co-ordination and semi-autonomous 'project teams' to increasing extents. But the simplified structure facilitated an increase in central control from the senior echelons of the public service, who were more easily able to set policy agendas and overall budgetary limits. Economic incentives in the form of performance pay in 1993 were introduced. Overall then, the new managerialism mixed more intense hierarchical control over budgetary levels and overall policy direction, with decentralisation and lateral networks being introduced at operational levels.[22]

Since no reforms ever encounter a blank administrative slate, tensions developed between the effects of the new administrative law and the aims of the new managerialism. Budgetary formalisation decreased under the FMIP, as did the grounds of recruiting personnel – procedures became looser and more discretionary. But the 'new administrative law' reforms led to increased formalisation, in the sense of increasingly detailed rules governing the actions of civil servants.[23] This formalising impulse was supplemented by direct government regulation in the equal opportunity and health and safety policy areas applying to the public sector. Thus the decreased formalisation occurring in the internal environment of departments was offset to some extent by the increased formalisation arising from pressures elsewhere within the state sector.

To an extent, these tensions can be cast in terms of a tension between social citizenship and an economic rationality which prioritises efficiency. The due process emphasis of the type of formalisation induced by the new administrative law often sat uneasily with the operational flexibility sought by the new managerial reforms. But it is a little misleading to cast this as a simple contest between economic and social objectives, as suggested by the very label for the philosophy inspiring the reforms – economic rationalism.[24] In the context of this particular set of reforms, it was not so much a question of monolithic pursuit of a limited set of values, as a desire to reorganise the structure of governance. Under Labour's version of new managerialism, there was a significant 'social justice' component, reflected primarily in human resource policies focusing on diversity, and in Access and Equity programmes established across a wide range of departments and agencies.[25]

While the effectiveness of this was probably limited,[26] what was important about the new managerialism was its focus on administrative restructuring. In particular, it was significant that rationalisation across departmental structures involved a combination of operational decentralisation and increased budgetary/policy control. It indicates a move towards a new model of rationalisation that departs from the classic Weberian bureaucratic model, moving more towards a fluid decentralised structure more analogous to a market. Lacking the decentralised coordinating mechanism of the price function, however, central direction over budgetary limits and policy direction still characterised the governance structure under managerialism (not only by necessity but no doubt also by political attractiveness).

This emphasis on the governance structures that frame policymaking intensified in the third set of reforms. Given the political context of the 1980s, which included considerable pressure to cut public spending, changes in governance structures tended also to be accompanied by an emphasis on containing or cutting costs. This is consistent with market liberalism, inasmuch as it is a strategy which aims to keep the size of government small. But the notion of cost efficiency (producing the most for the least input of resources) is *also* consistent with Weberian bureaucratic rationalisation, and is thus not necessarily a reform strategy that reconfigures state-economy relations, but rather promotes reform *inside* the state. Social welfare programmes of the 'tax-and-spend' type could be controlled and shaped by the new managerialism, but building decentralised governance structures within the state did not necessarily impact on governance issues as *vis-à-vis* government-business relations. These issues came to be systematically addressed through what I have called meta-regulation.

Meta-regulation: Non-judicial Rationalisation of Regulatory Policymaking

Meta-regulation encompasses any set of institutions and processes that embeds regulatory review mechanisms into the every-day routines of governmental policymaking. Like the new managerialism, meta-regulation affects policymaking more directly than policy application. Unlike the new managerialism, however, the reforms relate more directly to *lawmaking*, as opposed to bureaucratic policymaking or budgetary decisions. In what follows, I explore in more detail than with the first two phases of rationalising reform, details of the political coalitions that built an impetus for meta-regulation in Australia. I do this because the particular subset of meta-regulation, the National Competition Policy, grew out of those politics and an important facet of this story is the uneasy and complex relationship between the framing power of ideas as cultural expression of collective ideas, and the naked material interests served by the promulgation of such ideas.

The pressure flowing from the interaction of the domestic and international economies had continued to increase during the 1980s, and politicians had responded in the regulatory field mostly by slowly (and painfully) dismantling tariff barriers in different manufacturing sectors.[27] The effective rate of assistance for manufacturing was reduced from 22% in 1983-84 to 15% in 1990-91.[28] But the political cost and time involved in implementing sector-by-sector reforms was high, and the pace of reform comparatively slow. The non-tradable sector, especially public infrastructure and the building industry, became increasingly significant to any potential improvement in the competitiveness of the overall Australian economy, because as inputs for all other goods and services production, they had such a high effect on flow-on costs.

Governing parties in the late 1980s and early 1990s thus came under pressure from business interests to expand the scope of political economy reforms to encompass a much broader spectrum of the domestic economy. Business groups sought a solution that would permanently implant in government bureaucracies an *ongoing mechanism* for automatically reviewing political strategy in all areas of regulatory policy. Meta-regulation was the response which was developed.

A weaker form of meta-regulation might be labelled a 'regulatory management system', where existing forms of 'best practice' in the making of regulations are brought together and generalised as systematically desirable. However, a stronger version of meta-regulation would actually *build new institutions* and *design effective enforcement mechanisms* to embed the meta-regulatory logic into everyday routines of policymaking. I argue that aspects of the package of reforms Australia introduced as the National Competition Policy come closest to implementing this strong form of meta-regulation, by building institutions of economic adjudication. The emergence of those institutions did have precedents, however, in weaker regulatory management systems that had been painstakingly built over the course of the 1980s, at both state and federal level.

Regulatory Management Systems

This section briefly outlines the politics of two forms of regulatory management systems introduced at state and federal level in Australia during the 1980s. These systems demonstrate typical features of the kind of meta-regulation that I have argued is analogous in structural logic to the rule of law. They all share institutions, routines and procedures which can be characterised as an attempt to rationalise the making of policy on a systematic basis such that a particular form of economic rationality becomes part of the taken-for-granted ways of policymaking. At the same time, these regulatory management systems can be *distinguished* from the more powerful regime built under the auspices of National Competition Policy described in the following section, when the shared features are compared in terms of degree. For this reason, I emphasise the fact that these early forms of meta-regulation all share the following three features: weak institutions, especially in the enforcement context; diffuse analytical criteria; and low visibility politics of inception.

This last feature does not imply low political salience *per se*. The politics of the inception of these regimes is, like those of National Competition Policy in the next section, potentially malleable, but it is noteworthy that these early regimes began their lives in contexts more closely tied to neo-liberal visions of market governance.

State-based regulatory impact analysis of secondary legislation   Meta-regulation in Australia began at the state level where it applied only to regulations made by government departments and the executive, and not to full-scale legislative programmes. The regimes aimed to stem the proliferation of inflexible, badly targeted or unnecessary rules with an inadequate empirical base. The major tool for achieving this goal was the imposition of a requirement that Regulatory Impact Analysis (RIA) become part of routine policymaking procedures.

A major imperative for the first state RIA regime, which was in the state of Victoria, was a report released in 1980 by the Confederation of Australian Industry and the Victorian Chamber of Manufacturers on the impact of government regulation in Australia ('the CAI/VCM report').[29] The report reviewed empirical research on the net impact of government regulation in Australia and conducted a detailed case study of the foundry industry to assess the costs and benefits of regulation affecting that industry. Overall, although the study emphasised the burden placed on the business community by regulatory initiatives, it avoided any strongly ideological agenda of deregulation. Rather, it argued for the introduction of new processes and analytical approaches that would clarify the objectives and justifications for introducing or renewing regulatory programmes. The sample procedures suggested by the report drew on Canadian and American attempts to try and implement regulatory reform.[30] Although it stated that the Canadian example was of most direct relevance to Australia, the specifics of the scheme in fact closely reflected United States President Reagan's Executive Order 12,291. Echoes of 'Reaganomics' notwithstanding, the report was pitched as an initiative to enhance the technical basis of regulation, rather than as a political attack on government intervention *per se*.[31]

The CAI/VCM report was sponsored by, and reflected the interests and goals of, peak business associations. However, the political logic of Victoria's RIA regime was not that of a straightforward rightwing ideology. The regime came into existence under the auspices of the Cain *Labour* government, with the passing of the Subordinate Legislation (Review and Revocation) Act (Vic) in 1984. Shortly after the release of the CAI/VCM report in 1980, a Regulation Review Unit was created in 1981, housed in the central Department of Premier and Cabinet.[32] The Unit had five civil servant members from various departments, including not only central finance departments more committed to free-market approaches but also planning and labour departments more loyal to industry assistance approaches. It also had one union and one business representative. Its brief was broader than specific regulatory relief and extended to economic development policy more generally. By April 1984, the Unit had produced a blueprint entitled *Victoria: The Next Step – Economic Initiatives and Opportunities for the 1980s*. The report had an entire chapter devoted to regulatory relief, and as an adjunct to publishing the chapter, the Unit submitted a draft bill for the consideration of the Legal and Constitutional

Committee, a bipartisan House Committee with a reputation for a fairly apolitical and legal approach to matters under their jurisdiction.

The draft bill laid out the basic components of an RIA regime more or less in accordance with the suggestions made in the CAI/VCM 1980 report on the impact of regulation. It focused on delegated legislation[33] made under authorising provisions of statutes, and applied to both new regulations and (as a consequence of a systematic sunsetting programme) to old regulations as they periodically expire. The basic structure (subsequently adopted by other states)[34] has two principal mechanisms: an economic rationality component, centred on a written cost-benefit analysis of proposed rules and their feasible alternatives, and a due process component, centred on public participation in the rule-making process. Both consultation and analysis must occur before regulations and rules are passed into law.

The bill's working title was the Subordinate Legislation (Deregulation) Bill. Once the bill was referred to the Legal and Constitutional Committee, however, it became the object of interest and support by quite different key players, notably the Victorian Council of Social Services, a peak association of community and welfare interest groups, and the Department of Community Welfare.[35] These groups were concerned about the extent to which analytical requirements might give short shrift to non-economic concerns. They were however supportive of the component of increased and newly mandatory consultation in the RIA regime, though they expressed caution about how equitable access to the new regime was likely to be. Overall, the bill's passage through the Legal and Constitutional Committee resulted in a greater emphasis on due process than on economic rationality. The tension between deregulatory and democratic potential in the bill was masked by casting it as a technical solution for 'better, not less, regulation', and relatedly, changing the name of the bill to the more neutrally worded Subordinate Legislation (Review and Revocation) Bill. In this form, it passed, though not without dissent.

As the Legal and Constitutional Committee pointed out in its 1984 report,[36] there was a significant amount of internal governmental dissent over the proposed reforms. When the Committee canvassed departments for submissions on the bill, the Premier's department developed a 'government policy line' on regulatory reform and suppressed independent submissions by particular departments and agencies, instructing them to direct their contributions through the central department. Upon objection by the Committee, they conceded only in providing summaries of departmental submissions to the Committee, thus giving the appearance of consensus which one suspects was illusory.[37] The stark variation in departmental response indicates that 'programme' departments viewed meta-regulation as a threat to their mission and as a thinly concealed attempt to 'hollow out' the state. That the bill passed is probably linked to its 'umbrella' nature – it was a *system* of regulatory management, not a particularised policy initiative affecting only targeted departments or interest groups, and thus central political agencies had sufficient political muscle to pass it over such departmental objections. As an 'umbrella bill', the regulatory management system thus put into place had 'something for everyone', and rested on a mix of uneasily co-existing aspirations.

Three primary sets of ideas can be isolated as motivating the enactment of the Victorian RIA regime. The first was economic development, and was often expressed in rhetoric about business needing room to breathe and the fettering and suffocating effect that regulation had on business activity. The second was democratic participation, which was valued both for its capacity to prevent capture and unequal access to the regulatory making process,[38] as well as in the sense of fostering a critical dialogue regarding the goals and means of regulation. An analogy was made to the values enhanced by Freedom of Information legislation.[39] Finally, the RIA regime hoped to secure more intelligent decision-making in regulatory politics, in the sense of rules which are based on empirical, objective data and systematic scientific analysis of their probable effects. Systematic objectivity, embodied in techniques of cost-benefit analysis, would – it was hoped – function as an antidote to the uncertainty and manipulation characteristic of politics.

These three sets of ideas, particularly in combination, are comparatively diffuse, though they do dovetail with the notion that meta-regulation is a rationalisation of policymaking both in terms of efficiency and of legitimacy. Ideally, the need to tender objective expertise renders regulatory policy decisions more calculable in a manner that facilitates economic development and greater efficiency, and aspires to do so in an even-handed manner by securing the opportunity for full public participation. This however is fairly abstract and arguably aspirational. In terms of more immediate particularistic political interests, the regulatory management systems outlined here were highly politically ambiguous and contained significant internal tensions.

Take for example, the due process component of the system. This entails public notice of the proposed rule followed by a defined period during which public comment is solicited and inclusion of public comments in material submitted to oversight committees. A record of those consulted must also be included in the final regulatory impact statement submitted to a parliamentary oversight committee. From one perspective, even-handed processes primarily help prevent rent-seeking behaviour by powerful interest groups, an aspiration which fits well with the impulse to base regulation on objective data. From another perspective, though, democratic participation can correct imbalances in economic power (including the power to manipulate 'objective data') between well-resourced and more vulnerable members of society. This second perspective casts democratic participation and due process as a more overtly political value, one that is more expressive of social citizenship than it is useful for improving the technical efficacy of the regulatory process.

The same can be said for the economic rationality component of these systems. The Regulatory Impact Statement (RIS) required under this branch of the system must do four things:

a)   state the objectives of the proposed rule;
b)   identify different means of achieving those objectives including means which do not involve the state (e.g. self-regulation, voluntary codes of compliance etc);
c)   assess the financial and social costs and benefits of each alternative including resource allocation, administration and compliance costs and where quantification is not possible, an outline of the social costs and benefits;
d)   explain and justify why the rejected alternatives are not appropriate.

This is a relatively diffuse analytical framework. It effectively prescribes an aggregate social welfare balancing act. Although it is also intended to encourage policymakers to consider less interventionist modes of reaching policy goals, at its base the guiding criterion is merely that some kind of 'net benefit' be demonstrated in order to render secondary legislation enacted by these governments justifiable. This is 'economic rationality' in two senses: not only in the more general sense of instrumental rationality measured at aggregate levels, but also as a matter of contingent practice, given that the technical capacity to produce a cost-benefit analysis is typically (though not necessarily) delegated to those with economic expertise. In terms of familiar political tensions between market liberalism and tempered market liberalism however, there is in the design of the state RIA regimes no obvious ideological preference: all would depend on the measurement and articulation of particular costs and benefits.

The conceptually diffuse nature of these regulatory management systems is one aspect that might limit their potential impact on regulatory policymaking. Even more important however, are the institutional scope and design of the system. In terms of scope, their ambit was defined in formal rather than substantive terms and they encompassed only secondary and delegated legislation. This meant that they targeted neither primary legislation nor the significant bulk of 'soft law' which governed many regulatory arenas. State RIA regimes were therefore both under-inclusive and over-inclusive. Their formally defined ambit meant they applied to many rules which were not actually of much concern to the pro-reform constituencies. And their restriction to secondary rules meant that they did not 'bite' on deep substantive policy issues very often – especially in a parliamentary system where lawmaking is controlled by the party in power and *primary* legislation usually (though by no means always) deals with major policy issues in detail, thus foreclosing major change at the level of secondary rules.

Enforcement mechanisms, while varying slightly across states, were also weak. For the most part, states co-opted existing institutions, and in particular, parliamentary oversight committees to whose list of tasks RIA oversight was simply added. For example, New South Wales relies solely on supervision by a parliamentary committee (the Regulation Review Committee) which has historically had little power or prestige. In Victoria, parliamentary committee oversight is supplemented by a specialist independent executive body known as the Office of Regulation Review, which retains sole power over certifying regulations as being in compliance with the RIA regime. Without certification, Cabinet approval cannot be obtained. Despite Victoria's stronger institutional support, for both states, the main sanction backing the enforcement of the system's requirements is the power to force a disallowance of an impugned regulation. Amendments cannot be suggested, and the power is in many ways too blunt to be used effectively, particularly given that the type of committees assigned oversight are weak, bipartisan technical committees who usually perform more of a 'check-list' review function than a robust questioning of regulatory policy choices.

Overall then we can see that even if the early politics of inception of meta-regulation at state level sprung from a more neo-liberal political orientation, some tempering of that was necessary to secure passage of the reforms. This was followed by a cautious approach to implementation that emphasised the 'thin' nature of meta-regulation's requirements.

Federal regulatory impact analysis Like the states, the Commonwealth (federal) government also has a history, prior to National Competition Policy, of attempting to impose broad general requirements of both due process in rulemaking and cost-benefit analysis of pending regulatory schemes. The history is distinctive from that of state schemes primarily in the way that the two strands of meta-regulation – due process and economic rationality – were pursued through separate political avenues. Arguably, this led an absence of the amorphous bipartisan appeal discussed above in relation to states and doomed the reforms to political fragility or ineffectiveness. What follows is a brief overview of first the early attempts to impose economic rationality requirements at federal level and secondly, a failed due process initiative.

At the federal level, a very weak RIA-type regime focused only on requiring broad cost-benefit analysis (and not on consultation) was set up around about the same time as state regimes: the mid-1980s. Analogous pressures to those discussed at state level led the business community to press for regulatory relief at all levels of the federation. In May 1985, in the immediate wake both of Victoria's innovation in meta-regulation and the first re-election of the Hawke Labour government, the Business Regulation Review Unit (BRRU) was established in the Department of Industry, Technology and Commerce (DITAC) during the period of 'new managerialist' reforms.[40] The conditions for effective regulatory review by the BRRU were not auspicious. First, it was located in a department that did not support its mandate. DITAC had a general 'industry assistance' approach to regulatory policy. By contrast, BRRU was responsible to the powerful Structural Adjustment Committee, a Cabinet Committee deeply committed to pro-competitive micro-economic reform. The ill fit between the strong neo-liberal orientation of BRRU to its tasks, and the much more tempered vision held by its hosting department undercut the impact of BRRU's routines and powers.

Secondly, unlike the committees and agencies of the state regimes, the BRRU had no formal powers to block regulation and was established by executive order only. Given the lack of trust and cooperation arising from its placement noted above, the fact that it was in practice unthreatening to recalcitrant departments made its unwelcome message ineffective. Finally, it also suffered from continual resource shortages during its existence.

In the early 1990s, a separate initiative focusing mainly on expanded consultation and participation in rulemaking wound its way tortuously through the federal legislative calendar, but ultimately was never passed. The legislation, entitled the Legislative Instruments Bill, mainly addressed due process issues, with some marginal attention given to the utility of broad cost-benefit analysis of new regulations *as an aid to effective consultation*.[41] Unlike the mandate of the BRRU, it would only have applied to subordinate legislation and thus did not bite directly at the policy level. Overall it had a legalistic procedural cast, most likely the result of it having been sponsored by the Administrative Review Council, an independent advisory body staffed almost wholly by lawyers. Its eventual derailment was partly a casualty of the 1996 change of government from left to right. This indicates how a due process initiative, when decoupled from the cost-benefit analysis dimension, took on a political hue much more reminiscent of social citizenship, a shift which the incoming conservative government resisted.

Together with the ineffectual institutional context supporting the economic analysis requirements of the RIA-type regime, these two federal initiatives therefore show how important both institutional design and broad-based (if ambiguous) political appeal are to the successful introduction of meta-regulatory regimes. As we shall see in the next section, the institutional design of the Competition Principles Agreement overcame these institutional weaknesses and even improved on the state versions of meta-regulation. The corollary of this was a much higher and more visibly contested political salience.

National Competition Policy and the Competition Principles Agreement

The principal design features of the meta-regulatory regime embedded within the National Competition Policy have already been described in the previous chapter. This section elaborates on the political context which brought into being National Competition Policy as a whole. It then briefly recapitulates some of the key features of the Competition Principles Agreement in such a way as to draw a contrast with the earlier versions of meta-regulation that preceded it – a contrast that can be accounted for partly by virtue of the rather different political history.

As stated earlier, one very important feature of the political landscape that produced National Competition Policy was the pressure from an increasingly integrated international economy for large-scale reforms that might enhance national productivity and competitiveness. By the mid-1990s, the bulk of federal legislative business for the parliamentary year derived from implementing the Uruguay Round of the General Agreement on Trades and Tariffs,[42] indicating the extent to which international economic policy dominated the domestic political agenda. Business groups pressing for regulatory reform were now urgently focusing on restrictions within the domestic economy that resulted in higher infrastructure costs (transport, gas, electricity, water) and those sheltered from the direct effects of trade. The spectre of the need for international competitiveness haunts the turn to the national arena as the next forum for regulatory reform. In its second annual report on Regulation and its Review, the Commonwealth Office of Regulation Review (ORR) said:

> ... global developments make it all the more important that Australia strive
> for effective regulatory regimes. Increasingly, a country's regulatory
> environment is regarded as a crucial factor in overall assessments of
> international productivity, and it can affect Australia's success in keeping

and attracting industries that are able to locate in the country most advantageous to them.[43]

Thus there were strong economic pressures in the early 1990s to intensify regulatory reform. Indeed, these pressures were such that the right faction of the Labour government dominated the policy-setting agenda, and early on in their term of office began implementing deregulatory reform in the financial sector which opened up Australia's economy significantly to the international economy. But the political cost and time involved in implementing sector-by-sector reforms was high, and the pace of reform by that method comparatively slow. Further, even a right faction-dominated Labour government had to take into account continued broad public support for the social regulation and public provision that had been put in place since the 1970s. Since their 1983 gain to power, they had essentially pursued a strategy of 'no regulatory growth'. The only major new social programme that was put in place in the early 1990s was in the environmental arena (the setting up of the National Environmental Protection Council). Systematic restructuring in health, education and community services also took place, which was billed as reorganisation rather than cutback.

Some of these tensions in the fit between interest group pressures and political opportunities could be addressed by approaching further regulatory reform as an *economy-wide* strategy which did not target any particular policy sector. Existing state and federal meta-regulatory regimes provided one obvious model. Meta-regulation was described as a search for "more selective, appropriate and better designed regulation" rather than a pitch for deregulation *per se*.[44] It allowed the government to continue to rely on packaging further reforms as technical restructuring rather than changes in policy, thus balancing the pressures to achieve international competitiveness with continued broad public support for social regulation and public provision. This approach represented a shift from the more aggressively neo-liberal approach of the BRRU regime to a much more pragmatic, tempered packaging of meta-regulation.

But the politics of the reform package that ultimately emerged as National Competition Policy went beyond the relatively low-visibility politics typical of those that produced earlier versions of meta-regulation in Australia. In comparison to those earlier versions, National Competition Policy had far greater political salience and a much greater commitment of high-level political will behind it. This was largely because it emerged in the context of, and was designed to address, not only the business-sensitive governance issue of the degree of regulatory intervention into the economy, but also the federal issue of distribution of the power of regulatory political choice across the federal components of the Australian political landscape.

The non-tradable sectors of the domestic economy (especially the utilities sectors), the provision of professional services, and key agricultural support schemes, were all state-controlled arenas over which the federal government had no direct power, yet which had important implications for national productivity. The politics of federalism thus provide an important source of explanation for why a federal Labour government would reach consensus with six conservative-led state governments and one state Labour government on a policy which constrained the freedom to make regulatory policy choices of all the constituents to the agreements. The answer to that question is both organisational (focusing on the growth of an executive-centred bargaining network which facilitated an avenue for national policymaking) and substantive (focusing on a reorganisation of policy responsibility in combination with fiscal incentives that was attractive to both state and federal governments).

The organisational locus for the political bargaining that led to the NCP reforms was the national forum of the Council of Australian Governments (COAG). COAG is an institutional outgrowth of the 'new federalism' that former Labour Primer Minister Bob Hawke had espoused after his fourth election to office in 1990. The new federalism was designed to counter policy coordination made historically difficult by the fiscal peculiarities of Australian federalism. Since mid-century, the federal government's de facto monopoly on income tax receipts, combined with a constitutional prohibition on states raising excise taxes, had established an entrenched 'vertical fiscal imbalance' in the Australian federal system. The federal government currently raises about 75% of tax revenue but spends only 54% of it, while the States raise only 25% and spend 46% of it.[45] The disparity between raising and spending money arises because much of state income comes from federal grants, often accompanied by stringent conditions, skewing the power balance in fiscal affairs towards the centre.

In 1990, Hawke initiated an annual Special Premiers' conference of all the state and territory leaders, but under the leadership of the less consensus-oriented Keating, the vertical fiscal imbalance once again took priority over policy coordination. The conferences became embittered slanging matches, with the states and territories competing fiercely for federal money.[46] When, in 1991, political leaders agreed to examine a national approach to competition policy, the states realised their opportunity to gain more leverage than was usual, for their cooperation in areas within their residual constitutional powers (health, education, the professions, essential services infrastructure) was essential to the design of a feasible reform package. The Special Premiers' Conferences, with some institutional restructuring, became COAG, a forum of genuine bargaining and negotiation marked by a significantly more cooperative spirit than previously. COAG meets irregularly, but in practice it is every four or five months, provided none of the nine parliaments have been prorogued for an election.[47]

The NCP reforms took four years from that initial agreement to come into being. Those four years were dominated by narrowly bounded debates within the microeconomic reform 'policy community', a political space situated largely 'inside the state' with a one-way flow of information out towards the policy community. The critical state actors were politicians and bureaucrats from Treasury, Finance, the Structural Adjustment and Expenditure Review committees of federal cabinet, the Industry Commission (now the Productivity Commission) and the Trade Practices Commission (now the Competition and Consumer Commission). The relevant policy community consisted of peak business groups,[48] journalists, trade union officials, and some academics.[49] These groups had been monitoring developments in competition policy reforms on an ongoing basis, but beyond this, there was initially little or no wider public interest, as is common with many regulatory reform efforts, including the state RIA regimes already discussed.

In late 1992, an independent inquiry headed by the Dean of the New South Wales Graduate School of Management, Professor Fred Hilmer, was commissioned. Its initial terms of reference were narrow, and related mainly to extending the scope of the anti-trust or competition law regime so that activities such as the provision of urban infrastructure and professional services might be evaluated against a background of competition law. Due to constitutional limitations,[50] such an extension could not be done simply by passing legislation, but had to be done through intergovernmental agreements made between the federal and state governments

As the inquiry evolved, its remit broadened, moving from relatively technical and narrow aspects of competition *law* to competition *policy* viewed as a wholesale way of viewing institutional design and political choice across the spectrum of regulatory politics. This broad conception of 'competition policy' sought to take into account the role of both the market and the state in economic exchange. Thus competition policy involved the private sphere (anti-competitive behaviour by firms or citizens in the economic sphere), the public sphere (the effects of legislative restrictions on competition) and the intersection of the two (parity between public and private enterprises competing for the same market).

These three aspects of 'competition policy' translated into the key planks of National Competition Policy. The first aspect underlay expansion of the remit of traditional competition law as well as mandated structural reform of public utilities and mandatory public access to infrastructure which remained under monopoly control. The second aspect catalysed the legislation review component of NCP: i.e. the meta-regulation regime. The third aspect gave rise to requirements that states institute 'competitive neutrality' as between public and private businesses. These different facets added up to a comprehensive framework of justifiability for the design of regulatory policymaking from first principles. It was a framework intended to embed into the everyday routines of regulatory policymaking the question of "the nature and extent of competition in society or the way and amount in which you want to use competitive forces in society".[51]

While the reforms did not of themselves require more competition *per se*, they did mandate a process of rational justification which, as noted in Chapter One, gave presumptive force to the priority of competition. The 'last word' on whether such a presumption would actually prevail was ultimately political, but the institutions designed to implement it passed the decision-making procedure through an analytics derived from an essentially public choice economics analysis of the production of regulatory frameworks. While the intellectual underpinnings of the reforms will be discussed in more detail in Chapter Three, it is sufficient here to highlight an important difference in the CPA meta-regulation from that used to date in the general regulatory management systems discussed above. Indeed, the inquiry consciously sought to create this difference, explicitly in order to ensure that the regime thereby introduced would have a thicker, more powerful rationalising impact than one of mere 'checklist rationality'. It was intended to catalyse an analytical process that would force consideration of policy options at a strategic level, and to do so with a substantive though defeasible end in mind – the question of whether social arrangements could be infused with more competition than they currently possessed.

In contrast to prior regulatory management systems, therefore, meta-regulation under NCP required not only that the benefits outweigh costs in enacting or renewing regulatory policy, but also that the objectives of the legislation *can only be achieved by restricting competition*. In other words, the economic rationality at the core of the arrangements is not simply a utilitarian social welfare calculus, but more specifically a market-oriented standard that requires all legislation to be vetted for whether or not it unjustifiably restricts competition. Competition, and not just aggregate social welfare, becomes the presumptive political good. Market governance is designated presumptive institutional preference. As emphasised in Chapter One, that presumption can of course be reversed, or become demonstratively inapplicable provided a burden of proof is discharged by the regulating government. But the rationality imposed by the regime is more substantive than procedural, and this gave the reforms a much greater potential policy salience – and consequently, greater political controversiality.

In August 1993, the Hilmer report was made public.[52] At the February 1994 Hobart COAG meeting, heads of government accepted the principles of the Hilmer report. They commissioned an examination of its practical implications (for current anti-trust law) and requested drafts of the legislation and intergovernmental agreements that would be needed to implement the Hilmer recommendations. The Legislation Drafting Group that prepared these drafts was coordinated by the Structural Policy Division of Commonwealth Treasury and supervised by the COAG Microeconomic Reform Group. Participating Commonwealth officials tended to be highly specialised, primarily in anti-trust policy issues, and all were either familiar with legal issues or had immediate support from legal advisers. In addition there were many of them: a veritable "phalanx".[53] State officials tended to be either generally qualified lawyers with no specialist knowledge of anti-trust or competition law, or policy officers experienced in areas other than microeconomic policy; furthermore one or at most two representatives from each state typically came to meetings of the group. The result of this imbalance meant both that Commonwealth preferences and policies dominated and that the conceptual framework reflected the assumptions of professional economists and competition lawyers.[54]

Once the NCP package of reforms entered a broader arena of debate than the narrow microeconomic policy community, two main developments occurred. The first continued to press for moves that would temper the analytical orientation of the conceptual framework, which was heavily influenced by neo-classical economics. Some significant gains were made here, especially a 'public interest amendment' to the intergovernmental agreements. Later developments returned the debate to the intergovernmental arena and here it was given an institutional 'bite', particularly in terms of the framework for enforcement, that would distinguish it from its weaker ancestors at state and federal level.

Early criticism of the NCP package focused predominantly on its conceptual framework. Fears that the dominance of economic modes of analysis would constrain or dilute the pursuit of social justice values gave rise to the formation of what I shall refer to as a 'dissenting coalition'. In the interim between the drafting of the agreements and their final signing and legislative implementation, a number of key unions, consumer, environmental and social welfare groups formed a coalition to present a united front of opposition to the reforms. Sensing that the political momentum of the reforms was too great to succeed in blocking them, they fought for the addition of a crucial 'interpretation clause' to the CPA. This clause mitigated, at least in theory, the strength of the rebuttable presumption in favour of 'marketisation' and maximum competition in regulatory policy choice. Concerned that this would erode hard-won social benefits and programmes, the dissenting coalition sought to flesh out more specifically the factors that would 'balance out' the desirability of maximising competition and market structures. They succeeded in inserting into the CPA compact an interpretation clause that became known as the 'public interest' clause. The clause required that whenever the merits or appropriateness of any legislative programme was being assessed under NCP reforms, the following factors should be taken into account: government legislation and policies relating to ecologically sustainable development; social welfare and equity considerations, including community service obligations; government legislation and policies in regard to occupational health and safety, industrial relations and access and equity; economic and regional development, including employment and investment growth; the interests of consumers generally or of a class of consumers; the competitiveness of Australian businesses; and finally, the efficient allocation of resources.

The 'public interest' clause is a compendium of the principal kinds of interests at stake in the NCP reforms. It was regarded by the dissenting coalition as a possible bulwark against the potential for the reforms being used to justify the promotion of economic competitiveness at the cost of all other social goals.[55] It was politically important in part because like the earlier regulatory management systems, there was a potentially strong due process component to the CPA requirements as well as the economic rationality schema just discussed. The justification process catalysed by the NCP reforms, as well as the oversight function performed by the National Competition Council, all had to take place transparently and with public access. Broadening the range of concerns that had to be explicitly addressed would therefore make proportionately more difficult any final political decision to ignore 'social' concerns in favour of 'economic' ones.[56]

The incorporation of the public interest clause into the intergovernmental agreements was crucially important to the political acceptability of the final outcome.[57] It created an ambiguity about the full implications of the reform package that made it possible for significantly different visions of those implications to be painted in the legislative sessions that later implemented the intergovernmental agreements. The federal Labour government referred repeatedly to the public interest clause when the bill passed parliamentary muster,[58] in order to defend itself against attacks that it was imposing a narrowly ideological vision of economic fundamentalism on the country. It also insisted that the reforms were not intended to apply to the 'core activities' of departments and programmes for delivering social policy services such as education and health.[59] By contrast, the Victorian Liberal-National Coalition government stated bluntly:

> [The bill] spells an end to the opposition's socialist dreams, the managed economy and public ownership. It spells the end of what opposition members talk about now and what they have talked about in past years. The bill signals the inevitable victory of economic rationalism in Australia.[60]

The amorphous nature of the political implications, however, while important to the public face of the reform package, was not the real driving force of its adoption, and within the 'inner circle' of policymakers, there still remained significant political obstacles before a final outcome could be announced. The August 1994 Darwin COAG meeting brought these to light. One axis of significant disagreement was the distribution of fiscal benefits flowing from the reforms. By agreeing to the NCP reforms, the state governments would forego the certainty of the revenue they had raised to date from government monopoly business in urban infrastructure provision. There had been a hope that that increased economic growth would raise state taxes enough to compensate, but the Darwin COAG meeting revealed the extent of the imbalance between the net gain of the Commonwealth and that of the States.[61]

The states, realising that Commonwealth access to any of these fiscal benefits necessitated cooperative action by all elements of the federation, regrouped and presented a united front to the Commonwealth, with the principal cleavage issue being shares in the financial 'spoils'. Last-minute negotiations between New South Wales, Victoria, Queensland and the Commonwealth produced an agreement on revenue-sharing. The states secured guaranteed extension and indexation of the general Commonwealth Financial Assistance Grants on a rolling three-year basis, as well as a greater share of the specific competition payments than the Commonwealth had originally offered. In total some AUS$16 billion dollars were promised to the states over the course of the next decade.

There was, however, a sting in the tail to this success for the states. The money was contingent on adequate state fulfilment of the intergovernmental agreements, and in particular the meta-regulatory regime as embodied in the legislation review programme. The institution with decision-making power to substantially enforce that condition was the National Competition Council,[62] which as described in Chapter One was a new independent agency built on the principles of technical (mainly economic) expertise rather than that of political representation. The existence of this supervisory power in a separately resourced, independent oversight agency, together with a conceptual framework of economic rationality for the application of that oversight considerably more substantively pointed than general cost-benefit analysis, in combination produces a meta-regulatory system of much greater political salience than the earlier weaker versions at state and federal level.

At the April 1995 COAG meeting, the triad of intergovernmental agreements was signed by all Australian heads of government. In the end, federal-state politics were key to securing the passage of the reforms. The design of the NCP package was a power-sharing arrangement which shifted a significant amount of power from the state to the federal arena, particularly power over public infrastructure, an area critical to international economic competitiveness. In return, the states were not only given significant financial incentives in the form of the competition payments, but the breadth of the NCP package allowed the state governments (in every case but New South Wales, governed by the right) to apply broadly neo-liberal reforms to social policy areas such as the delivery of community services. The federal Labour government not only acquired more power to share in decision-making over regulatory reform in sectors not core to its electoral prospects (the financial sector, agriculture, the professions), but also retained sufficient political control over the agenda of meta-regulatory review in the Commonwealth to be able to make credible promises that sectors such as the labour unions, postal and shipping services would not be subjected to the full rigour of the reforms. And beyond the concatenation of specific political interests, for *all* the governments signing up to the reforms the strengthening of COAG – a web of intergovernmental executive committees that effectively bypassed state Parliaments – as a powerful policymaking forum, provided the advantage of a future locus which would enhance executive power no matter who held office.

In summary, the political narrative of the inception of National Competition Policy thus presented has two facets – one is the contingency of the political fractures and coalitions that had to be built and sustained in order to pass the reforms. The contingency is reflected by the extent to which meta-regulation has been presented at times as a neo-liberal deregulatory initiatives, at other times as a pragmatic discipline with room for tempering market governance with social citizenship initiatives.

Co-existent with political malleability and contingency, however, is a very real set of institutional innovations which I have characterised as the culmination of a three-pronged wave of reforms (some judicial, some non-judicial) that sought to rationalise state power over the last twenty-five years in Australia. The non-judicial institutional innovations embodied in meta-regulation have gradually taken on a more solid, embedded cast over time. The type of economic rationality embodied in the earlier, institutionally weaker regimes took the form of a template of general cost-benefit analysis and a requirement that rules meet a standard of 'net benefit' in the context of an overall goal of maximising general social welfare. Though the aggregate nature of cost-benefit analysis tends to be insensitive to distributive goals, and cost-benefit analysis in effect mandates 'neutral economic expertise' as the appropriate technique for regulatory justification, this version of economic rationality nonetheless remains relatively diffuse. It amounts to a restatement, but in the language of economics, of the familiar injunction to a legislature to make laws for the "peace, welfare and good government" of the community it rules. The CPA meta-regulatory regime by contrast had a sharper focus, organised around a general presumptive (but rebuttable) goal of maximising market competition and requiring rules to meet the standard of being the least (market)-restrictive alternative for securing the desired goal. This regime also created a new independent agency for oversight purposes, one with important leverage from the significant financial penalties it was capable of imposing on recalcitrant states.

Both facets at play in this chapter – institutional solidity and political malleability – are important. Political malleability is at the root of the ensuing tale of the early interpretive conflicts playing out as meta-regulation moved from political rhetoric to administrative routine. Yet institutional solidity is equally important, for the enduring legacy of the reforms may well bite deep enough to merit drawing an analogy with the way that the rule of law seeks to entrench a culture of legality into modern administrative states – one where institutions insulated from democratic politics wield rationalised, routine interpretive power and in so doing exercise a partial veto on such politics that is typically cast as a constraint of neutral rationality.

The chapters that follow explore in more depth this intersection of fluid interpretive conflict and enduring institutional and policy change, showing how social citizenship is threatened by the institutional solidity of meta-regulation, but, due to its political malleability, not extinguished. Chapter Three explores the discursive terrain mapped out by debates about the political and cultural meaning of National Competition Policy between the micro-economic policy community and the broader Australian community. Chapter Four explores the agenda-setting stage of implementing the reforms, focusing on alterations in everyday policymaking routines and the bureaucratic institutional change secured by the reforms. Chapter Five explores several case studies in more detail in order to show not only the policy outcomes, but also the ways in the politics of meta-regulation simultaneously establishes and undermines discursive categories that speak to distinctive conceptions of collective membership and thus to notions of citizenship.

Notes

1   It is unwise to generalise about the link between rationalisation and institutional choice outside of a specific political arena. In the USA, for example, judicial rationalisation (through judicial review of the rulemaking process) of policy*making* is arguably stronger than in most other industrial democracies where public law plays a more individualised dispute resolution role. The potential for judicial institutions to contribute both to the rationalisation of policy application and of policymaking is always there, as captured most famously in Abram Chayes' article on the distinction between the structural effects of public law litigation and the dispute resolution effects. Though the legal culture, political institutional context and procedural tools that exist in the USA are arguably an exceptional combination in this regard, the European Union also provides an example (Chayes (1976), 'The Role of the Judge in Public Law Litigation' *Harvard Law Review* Vol. 89, pp.1281-1316).

2   Esping-Anderson, Gospa (1990), *The Three Worlds of Welfare Capitalism*, Polity Press, Cambridge.

3   Castles, Stephen (1988), Australian Public Policy and Economic Vulnerability: a Comparative and Historical Perspective, Allen and Unwin, Sydney; Castles, Stephen (ed) (1991), Australia Compared: People, Policies and Politics, Allen and Unwin, Sydney.

4   Bell, S. and Head, B. (1994), 'Australia's Political Economy: Critical Themes and Issues', in Head, B. (ed) *State, Economy and Public Policy in Australia*, Oxford University Press, Melbourne.

5   Esping-Anderson, Gospa (1990), *The Three Worlds of Welfare Capitalism*, Polity Press, Cambridge.

6   Schwartz and Rhodes, R. (n.d.), 'Internationalisation and the Liberal Welfare States: The UK, Australia and New Zealand', unpublished paper on file with author, p.27.

7   Yeatman, Anna (1990), *Bureaucrats, Technocrats, Femocracts: Essays on the Contemporary Australian State*, Allen and Unwin, Sydney, p.155.

8   Castles, F. (ed) (1991), *Australia Compared: People, Policies and Politics*, Allen and Unwin, Sydney.

9   Roe, Jill (1976), *Social Policy in Australia: Some Perspectives 1901-1975*, Cassell Australia.

10   Schwartz and Rhodes, R. (n.d.), 'Internationalization and the Liberal Welfare States: The UK, Australia and New Zealand'', unpublished paper on file with author, p.31.

11   Administrative Review Council (1995), *Better Decisions: Review of Commonwealth Merits Review Tribunals*, AGPS, Canberra, Appendix B, p.184.

12   Commonwealth Parliament of Australia (1971), *Administrative Review (Kerr) Committee Report*, AGPS, Canberra; Commonwealth Parliament of Australia (1973), *(Bland) Committee on Administrative Discretions: Final Report*; Commonwealth Parliament of Australia (1973), AGPS, Canberra; *(Ellicott) Committee on Review of Prerogative Procedure*, AGPS, Canberra.

13   An important exception to this is the role of the constitutional guarantee of freedom of interstate trade (s.92 of the Australian Constitution), analogous to the US commerce clause. While the history of the interpretation of this clause's contribution to the rationalisation of regulatory policy within Australia as a federation is not the

subject of this book, it is briefly mentioned at the start of the next chapter in the context of drawing analogies with trade law (see footnote 8, Chapter 3).

[14] Indeed in the case of much regulatory policy such rationalisation is occasional rather than systematic as a matter of practice. Australian regulatory policy historically has evidenced a largely conciliatory mode of enforcing governmental rules, and a heavy reliance on state discretion in the provision of government benefits and welfare (Braithwaite, J. and Grabowsky, P. (1986), *Of Manners Gentle: Enforcement Strategies of Australian Business Regulatory Agencies*, Oxford University Press, Melbourne.) Rulemaking has largely been an informal process of interest group negotiation with relevant government departments. An important exception was the highly legalistic and centralised tripartite bargaining for wage levels that took place in the Arbitration Court; however during the 1990s this has been diluted or sidestepped, particularly since the conservative Coalition government won power in 1996.

[15] De Maria, William (1992), 'The Administrative Appeal Tribunal in Review: On Remaining Seated During the Standing Ovation', in McMillan, J. (ed), *Administrative Law: Does the Public Benefit?*, Australian Institute of Administrative Law, Canberra.

[16] Stewart, J. and Kimber, M. (1996), 'The Transformation of Bureaucracy? Structural Change in the Commonwealth Public Service 1983-93', *Australian Journal of Public Administration*, Vol. 55, No. 3, pp.37-48.

[17] Administrative Review Council (1995), *Better Decisions: Review of Commonwealth Merits Review Tribunals*, AGPS, Canberra, Chapter 3.

[18] De Maria, William (1992), 'The Administrative Appeal Tribunal in Review: On Remaining Seated During the Standing Ovation', in McMillan, J. (ed), *Administrative Law: Does the Public Benefit?*, Australian Institute of Administrative Law, Canberra.

[19] O'Connor, Deidre (1991), 'Future Directions for Australian Administrative Law' *Canberra Bulletin of Public Administration* Vol. 66, pp.135-137.

[20] Considine, Mark (1988), 'The Corporate Management Framework as Administrative Science: a Critique' *Australian Journal of Public Administration*, Vol. 47, No. 1, pp. 1-18; Yeatman, Anna (1990), *Bureaucrats, Technocrats, Femocrats: Essays on the Contemporary Australian State*, Allen and Unwin, Sydney; Zifcak, Spencer (1994), 'New Managerialism: Administrative Reform in Whitehall and Canberra', in Rhodes, R.A.W. (ed), *Public Policy and Management*, Open University Press, Buckingham; Stewart, J. and Kimber, M. (1996), 'The Transformation of Bureaucracy? Structural Change in the Commonwealth Public Service 1983-93', *Australian Journal of Public Administration*, Vol. 55 No.3, pp.37-48.

[21] Stewart, J. and Kimber, M. (1996), 'The Transformation of Bureaucracy? Structural Change in the Commonwealth Public Service 1983-93', *Australian Journal of Public Administration* Vol. 55 No.3, pp.37-48.

[22] Stewart, J. and Kimber, M. (1996), 'The Transformation of Bureaucracy? Structural Change in the Commonwealth Public Service 1983-93', *Australian Journal of Public Administration*, Vol. 55 No.3, pp.37-48.

[23] Allars, Margaret (1991), 'Managerialism and Administrative Law', *Canberra Bulletin of Public Administration*, Vol. 66, pp.50-62.

[24] John Quiggin, 'Rationalism and Rationality in Economics' (1999) *Queensland Economic Review* Vol. 3, pp.4 ff.

[25] Zifcak, Spencer (1994), 'New Managerialism: Administrative Reform in Whitehall and Canberra', in Rhodes, R.A.W. (ed), *Public Policy and Management*, Open

University Press, Buckingham; Administrative Review Council (1995), *Better Decisions: Review of Commonwealth Merits Review Tribunals*, AGPS, Canberra.

[26] Yeatman (1990), *Bureaucrats, Technocrats, Femocracts: Essays on the Contemporary Australian State*, Allen and Unwin, Sydney.

[27] Capling, Ann and Galligan, Brian (1992), *Beyond the Protective State: The Political Economy of Australia's Manufacturing Industry Policy*, Cambridge University Press, New York.

[28] Hilmer, Rayner, et al. (1993), *National Competition Policy*, Independent Committee of Inquiry into National Competition Policy.

[29] Confederation of Australian Industry and Victorian Chamber of Manufacturers (1980), *Government Regulation in Australia.*

[30] Victoria Legal and Constitutional Committee (1984), *Report on the Subordinate Legislation (Deregulation) Bill*, Parliament of Victoria, pp.132-138.

[31] Although Reagan espoused a fairly militantly anti-regulatory ideology, the EO 12,225 was actually an extension of earlier versions of regulatory impact analysis instituted by President Ford in 1974 (Ford, Executive Order 11,821 (1974), *Executive Order*, 27 November 1974) and President Carter in 1978 (Carter, Executive Order 12,044 (1978), *Executive Order*, 24 March 1978). Although the Carter version was aimed more at inflation than at deregulation, there is therefore still a bipartisan cast to the technique, even in the US (McGarity (1991), *Reinventing Rationality: the Role of Regulatory Analysis in the Federal Bureaucracy*, Cambridge University Press, Cambridge).

[32] Victoria Legal and Constitutional Committee (1984), *Report on the Subordinate Legislation (Deregulation) Bill*, Parliament of Victoria.

[33] In fact not all forms of delegated legislation were caught by the scope of the bill, since it applied mainly the most formal kind that needs approval by the Governor-in-Council before it becomes valid.

[34] See for example the Subordinate Legislation Act 1994 (Vic) and the Subordinate Legislation Act 1989 (NSW).

[35] Perton, Victor, Member of Parliament of Victoria, Chairman of Scrutiny of Acts and Regulation Committee (1997), *Interview*, Morgan. January 29 1997.

[36] Victoria Legal and Constitutional Committee (1984), *Report on the Subordinate Legislation (Deregulation) Bill*, Parliament of Victoria, pp.4-6.

[37] Perton, Victor, Member of Parliament of Victoria, Chairman of Scrutiny of Acts and Regulation Committee (1997), *Interview*, Morgan. January 29 1997.

[38] Victoria Legal and Constitutional Committee (1984), *Report on the Subordinate Legislation (Deregulation) Bill*, Parliament of Victoria, p.148.

[39] Victoria Legal and Constitutional Committee (1984), *Report on the Subordinate Legislation (Deregulation) Bill*, Parliament of Victoria, p. 190, 195.

[40] I rely upon Forster, Head, and Wanna (1991), 'The Effectiveness of the Business Regulation Review Unit', in McCoy, H.A. (ed), *Deregulation or Better Regulation*, Centre for Australian Public Sector Management, Brisbane for the account of the Business Regulation Review Unit given in the text).

[41] Administrative Review Council (1992), *Rule Making by Commonwealth Agencies*, AGPS, Canberra.

[42] Office of Regulation Review (1995), *Regulation and its Review: Second Annual Report*, Productivity Commission of the Commonwealth Government, Canberra.

[43] Office of Regulation Review (1995), *Regulation and its Review: Second Annual Report*, Productivity Commission of the Commonwealth Government, Canberra, p.2.

44   Office of Regulation Review (1995), *Regulation and its Review: Second Annual Report*, Productivity Commission of the Commonwealth Government, Canberra, p.9.

45   Campbell, Colin and Halligan, John (1992), *Political Leadership in an Age of Constraint: the Australian Experience*, University of Pittsburgh Press, Pittsburgh, p.146.

46   Churchman, Susan (1996), 'National Competition Policy – Its Evolution and Implementation: A Study in Intergovernmental Relations', *Australian Journal of Public Administration*, Vol. 55, No. 2.

47   In practice, this can occur with frustrating frequency: the November 1996 COAG meeting was cancelled for this reason and the April 1997 COAG almost met the same fate. In the first two years of office of the federal Liberal-National (Conservative) government, elected in 1995, there was only one COAG meeting.

48   Primarily the Business Council of Australia, but also the Metal Trades Industry Association, Primary and Allied Industry Council, Confederation of Australian Industry and the Australian Chamber of Commerce and Industry.

49   Gerritsen (1994), 'Microeconomic Reform', *State, Economy and Public Policy in Australia*, Head, Oxford University Press, Melbourne; Carroll and Painter (1995), 'The Federal Politics of Microeconomic Reform: An Overview and Introduction', *Microeconomics Reform and Federalism*, Painter, Federalism Research Centre, ANU, Canberra.

50   Federal competition law in Australia rests on the power to make laws with respect to corporations (s.51(xx) of the Constitution), but the commercial activities most prominent in the non-traded sector are typically not carried out by corporations, but by partnerships or non-corporate government entities.

51   Hilmer, (2001), *Interview*, Morgan, p.2.

52   Hilmer, Rayner, et al. (1993), *National Competition Policy*, Independent Committee of Inquiry into National Competition Policy.

53   Churchman, Susan (1996), 'National Competition Policy – Its Evolution and Implementation: A Study in Intergovernmental Relations', *Australian Journal of Public Administration*, Vol. 55, No. 2.

54   Churchman, Susan (1996), 'National Competition Policy – Its Evolution and Implementation: A Study in Intergovernmental Relations', *Australian Journal of Public Administration*, Vol. 55, No. 2.

55   Moore, Gary, Director of New South Wales Council on Social Services (NCOSS) (1997), *Interview*, Morgan. February 20 1997.

56   The original inquiry did not support the need for a public interest interpretation clause, seeing it as weakening the onus of proof in favour of pro-competitive arrangements by, in effect, legitimating just the kind of rent-seeking politics which the reforms sought to counter. Otherwise put, the inquiry considered that the due process and democratic transparency facets of the reforms, coupled with the continuing role of politicians in the final decision-making phase, would automatically import such 'public interest' considerations and thus explicit specification was redundant: Hilmer, (2001), *Interview*, Morgan.

57   Moore, Gary, Director of New South Wales Council on Social Services (NCOSS) (1997), *Interview*, Morgan. February 20 1997; Hilmer, (2001), *Interview*, Morgan.

58   Australian Legislative Assembly (1995), *Hansard*, 30 June 1995, pp.2795, 2796, 2819.

59   Australian Legislative Assembly (1995), *Hansard*, 30 June 1995, p.2796.

60   Victorian Legislative Assembly (1995), *Hansard*, 11 October 1995, p.360.

61   Churchman, Susan (1996), 'National Competition Policy – Its Evolution and Implementation: A Study in Intergovernmental Relations', *Australian Journal of Public Administration*, Vol. 55, No. 2, p.98.

62   See (in Appendices) the third intergovernmental agreement of the NCP reforms: Agreement to Implement the National Competition Policy and Related Reforms. The NCC cannot itself actually authorise the payments: this must be done by the Commonwealth Treasurer, but in practice the recommendations of the NCC as to whether payments are made to states or not are effectively final.

3 The Contested Terrain of Regulatory Conversation

National Competition Policy was initially forged in the enclosed domain of a micro-economic policy community whose shared norms and mode of discourse were relatively technocratic. While the prescriptions of expert discourse crucially shape the interstitial bureaucratic politics of meta-regulation in ways that are central to its incipient legality, this chapter aims to establish a broader context before delving into those technical bureaucratic politics in Chapters Four and Five. It is in this chapter that the broader cultural absorption of the possible meanings of this new legality is explored. Here, in legislative debates and parliamentary inquiries, is where individuals and groups who do not share the closed circuits of expert discourse attempt to make sense of its prescriptions in the 'everyday' terms of pragmatic political discourse. These sites provide a window onto the expressive dimensions of meta-regulation.

As a technique of rationalisation, meta-regulation seeks not only to enhance the efficiency of regulatory policy decision-making, but also to legitimate the resulting patterns. It does so by establishing a culture of rational justification, and here meta-regulation is best viewed from the perspective of its communicative[1] or expressive[2] role. The expressive dimension of meta-regulation directs attention to the values it is socially understood to endorse at a level where what is at stake are broader cultural consequences rather than the specifics of winners and losers. Regulatory reform in a particular sector, while it obviously does implicate broader social values, often generates a narrower kind of conversation about specific policy goals and techniques of governance, one tailored to the local peculiarities of, say, the deregulation of agricultural support schemes, as we shall see in Chapter Five. Such conversations tend toward the technical and particularistic, and though four examples will be traced carefully in Chapter Four, the cultural consequences of those discussions are better illuminated if we first put them in the context of responses to meta-regulation as a systemic, economy-wide reform initiative.

At that systemic, economy-wide level, meta-regulation sparked a dialogue about the extent to which markets should or should not dominate diverse areas of social and political life in general. National Competition Policy instituted a comprehensive framework of justifiability for the design of regulatory policymaking from first principles. It was a framework intended to embed into the everyday routines of regulatory policymaking the question of "the nature and extent of competition in society or the way and amount in which you want to use competitive forces in society".[3] The intellectual underpinnings of this aspiration derive from expert technocratic discourse: that of a public choice perspective on regulatory politics, whose prescriptions are visible in the structure of the reform package. These will be explored first, as they are the catalyst for the ensuing regulatory conversation. The essence of the vision communicated by this perspective will be stated briefly here and elaborated on as the chapter develops.

A public choice perspective on regulation assumes a particular version of the 'public interest' that advocates that the imposition of public rules on private actors should be restricted to the improvement of market efficiency, while 'non-market' goals are addressed by explicitly political responses. This 'two-step' approach implies a distinction between market infrastructural values and social citizenship values regulation. The facilitation of competitive or efficient markets justifies regulatory intervention as a *technical* corrective. But pursuit of what could be broadly described as 'social justice' values is viewed as distorting efficiency objectives if pursued through regulation, and thus best pursued explicitly (and independently) as a *political* corrective.

Once the reforms entered the public domain, competing stories were marshalled by the participants in the debate, stories which spoke to the perceived fate of social citizenship under a meta-regulatory regime with market competition at its conceptual centre. The variety of these stories speaks to the malleability of meta-regulation's cultural meanings. The range of interpretive fluidity that developed seemed constrained by the fact that the assumptions of a public choice perspective on regulatory politics dovetailed comfortably with a neo-liberal vision of market liberalism. While we have already seen in Chapter Two that a more pragmatic, 'tempered market liberalism' was considered feasible by some architects of the reform package, early legislative debates over the package tended to represent it as expressive of a neo-liberal attack on the social citizenship values of the post-war welfare state. Later more extended debates in the arena of a long-running parliamentary inquiry introduced more nuance, adding two 'hybrid' visions that sought to temper market liberalism and ease the tension between competitive efficiency values and social citizenship values. One hybrid vision sought to articulate an alternative vision to the public choice perspective; the other strategically manipulated its resources to translate social citizenship values into the framework of the public choice perspective.

This range of responses can be seen as reflecting the material interests of rightist, leftist and 'third way' politics, echoing themes in broader debates in political theory between liberalism, communitarianism, and various attempts to mediate between the two.[4] Australian Prime Minister Keating, whose Labour government presided over the introduction of National Competition Policy, had in fact influenced the crafting of the British 'New Labour' position which later acquired the official tag of the 'Third Way'.[5] However, any overly schematic view of links between ideas and interests should be resisted, for as Chapters Four and Five will show, when meta-regulation is implemented in specific contexts, the dialogue in which the three responses participate actually destabilises the very categories that initially constitute the possibility of conversation. But first, to turn to the vision that does most work in categorising the terrain of regulatory politics, at least in this instance of meta-regulation.

Regulatory Politics from a Public Choice Perspective

The concept of regulation at the heart of this project was defined in a deliberately inclusive and open-ended way, in order to accommodate the malleability of responses to meta-regulation's impact. Recall the definition provided in Chapter One: regulation refers to efforts by the state to address social risk, market failure or equity concerns by shaping or directing social and individual actions through the exercise of political power. This is a definition which is agnostic as to the technical means which the state uses to carry out regulatory goals, and which is inclusive as to the range of goals which the state pursues in regulating activity. It emphasises the political nature of state intervention but is otherwise capacious. This capaciousness is necessary for capturing a full spectrum of political positions within regulatory politics. It is a conception of regulation which as far as possible aims to avoid any substantive normative orientation.

But a public choice perspective on politics, which was the intellectual nexus of assumptions underpinning the introduction of National Competition Policy, did have a substantive normative orientation buried in it. At its core, under the influence of a public choice perspective, Australian meta-regulation institutionalised a presumption in favour of market governance, certainly in relation to the *means* of regulation at a general level. The constraints imposed by the reform package institutionalised scepticism about assumptions the welfare state tended not to question – the efficacy of command-and-control regulation and the positive social benefits flowing from such regulation. This preference in favour of market mechanisms or incentive-based frameworks over command-and-control frameworks of regulation sought to secure the public benefit without using prescriptive rules encoded in law.

Arguably the public choice perspective is also skewed, not only against certain techniques or means of regulation, but also against certain regulatory goals – at least at the level of practical implementation in specific sectors. That the preference for markets as a means shades in practice into a skew in favour of competitive efficiency values will become more clear in Chapters Four and Five. There, where the specifics of technical bureaucratic politics are explored, it will become evident that meta-regulation catalyses institutional reforms in particular policy sectors that tend to increase the political vulnerability of measures addressing non-efficiency values. But in this chapter, I will confine myself to articulating the assumptions of a public choice perspective at a more general level.

The logic of a public choice perspective on regulatory politics has two important implications. The first, which is built into the general design of the reform programme from the start, is an ambivalence about the appropriate role of politics in having the 'last word' on regulatory justification. Ultimately politics does retain a role but the power of the NCC is meant to 'purify' it of special interest group influence – or if that fails, to fully publicise the choices that are made under such influences. 'Purified' politics is drained of factionalism and ideally made transparent.

The second implication, which is only implicit in the general design of the reforms but emerges strongly at the implementation stage described in future chapters, is a distinction between different categories of regulation, some more justifiable than others. In this chapter, I will initially orient the discussion of regulatory categories around just two: market infrastructural and social citizenship, and then explore developments that challenge the stability of this bifurcated categorisation.

These two implications of a public choice perspective – the relevance of a *purified* politics and the categorisation of justifiable regulation – are linked to each other. What connects them is a general emphasis on technocracy and the insulation of key economic policymaking choices from democratic politics: both features typical of an expertise-based discourse.

Democratic Dialogue and Due Process

A public choice approach to regulatory politics involves a set of assumptions about the nexus between democratic politics and regulatory legislation. The most important assumption here is that much of what passes for democratic political choice is distorted by the influence of special interest groups. This builds on the observation that the winners and losers of binding political decisions are typically asymmetrically distributed, such that political decisions that will have concentrated costs and diffuse benefits are particularly difficult to secure, due to the intensity of resistance by those groups suffering the concentrated cost. As a corollary, political decision-making will tend to skew *towards* choices that award concentrated benefits to certain groups at the price of diffusely distributed costs. In the public choice schema, most regulatory legislation is precisely this: the product of a democratic process distorted by concentrated interest groups who arrogate 'rent' to their benefit by means of securing protectionist legislation.[6]

Cost-benefit analysis of regulatory choices is viewed as a possible ameliorative strategy precisely because it *is* insensitive to distributive issues. By requiring an aggregate assessment of net social welfare once winners *and* losers are taken into account, it effectively requires political decisionmakers to take into account diffuse 'losers', each of whose individual loss is small enough to lack political salience. By rendering such costs transparent, it is hoped that a political disincentive to ignore them will be created.

As we saw in Chapter Two, early forms of meta-regulation in Australia implemented a template of general cost-benefit analysis and a requirement that rules meet a standard of 'net benefit' in the context of an overall goal of maximising general social welfare. However, as an analytical constraint on policymaking, cost-benefit analysis is relatively diffuse. It amounts to a restatement, but in the language of economics, of the familiar injunction to a legislature to make laws for the "peace, welfare and good government" of the community it rules. The CPA meta-regulatory regime by contrast had a sharper focus, organised around a general presumptive (but rebuttable) goal of maximising market competition, and requiring rules to meet the standard of being the least (market)-restrictive alternative for securing the desired goal. This shift to a market-centred standard of evaluation that requires *legislative* restrictions on competition to be assessed against a least restrictive means test gives a sharper analytical edge to the economic rationality template thereby imposed on regulatory policymaking choices.

The design of the legislative review component of National Competition Policy does not entirely eliminate the political role of democratically elected officials in having the 'last word' on regulatory policy choice. Rather, it imposes an additional hurdle (a market-centred net benefit test) that constrains the making of those choices, and builds institutions and incentives around the hurdle that come close to creating an actual veto point in the political process. This hurdle/veto seeks to insulate regulatory policy choice not from politics *per se*, but from a certain kind of politics – that which reflects the disproportionate influence of concentrated interest groups. Politicians *can* ultimately choose to retain or create new regulatory policies that do not pass the market-centred public interest test as interpreted by the National Competition Council, but in doing so they must both sacrifice considerable fiscal resources and expose themselves to public criticism. The rationale of the reforms is that these disincentives will facilitate political decisions that reflect the 'true' general interest of the (diffuse) public, and not the sectional interests of a powerful or disproportionately affected few. As the National Competition Council Council asserts:

> Governments should be congratulated for their continued commitment to the NCP reform programme … This reflects a commitment to good government in the interests of all Australian, rather than the pursuit of narrow, short-term political interests.[7]

Will is tempered by reason, by the economic rationality of an intellectual framework rooted in a public choice conception of how politics can go awry.

The notion that a 'least restrictive option' test adds a sharper analytical edge to the more diffuse cost-benefit analysis approach is further illuminated by drawing an analogy with trade law,[8] also an area where public choice approaches to regulatory politics have become increasingly popular. It is apt here because federal politics were so crucial to the introduction of National Competition Policy, and the concerns with achieving greater levels of national productivity and competitiveness were to a large extent channelled into aspirations for greater market integration within the borders of Australia. In this context, the public choice line of reasoning articulated above applies as follows: concentrated interest groups secure disproportionate influence with state legislatures[9] and obtain 'rents' through regulatory legislation which benefits them at the cost of general taxpayers both in that state and in other states. The requirement for rational justification, in economic terms, of such regulatory legislation is meant to expose and distinguish a kind of covert protectionism from genuine public interest rationales.

This is increasingly presented as not simply a discipline that serves efficiency values, but also as one that enhances political legitimation. The argument here is that the constraints of processes like meta-regulation are put in place as a battle on behalf of the unrepresented, unorganised taxpayer or consumer. The underlying logic of such an argument is that due to collective action problems, diffuse and unorganised groups such as taxpayers and consumers are effectively suffering 'taxation without representation' when regulatory policies are implemented by governments.[10] Regulatory management regimes thus 'represent' a set of otherwise silenced interests, placing a political gloss on the economic perspective.

A similar vision of the function of economic rationality in regulatory policymaking was elevated in Australia to a constitutional level by a senior Treasury official:

> There is a constitutional function for Treasury which is relatively independent of the government of the day ... that doesn't mean that we pursue our agenda independently of the government of the day ... [but] I believe that my thoughts and actions stem from that set of stimuli [which make up the independent constitutional function] rather than from the government per se, although they are tempered by the policy programme of the government.[11]

This comment was not made in relation to the meta-regulatory reform explored in this book, but it captures the essence of the view also powerful in public choice theory, that economic rationality acts as a constraint on politics that serves the 'true' public interest. The institutional context of National Competition Policy, with its oversight function given to an independent federal agency, intensifies the relevance of this view. And indeed, the documentary history of the National Competition Policy reforms and interviews with key officials are all pervaded by examples of this public choice perspective, some of which follow.

Personnel in the federal Office of Regulation Review were not prepared to accept that the mere existence of political demands for legislation, either now or in the past, was sufficient justification for the continuation of any particular programme.[12] Their general approach evinced a suspicion of 'politics' (in the sense of effective interest-group pressures) visible in briefing guidelines such as the requirement that regulatory agencies not review their own programmes. In part this was motivated by a desire to make the regulatory policy choice more open, transparent and accessible to civil society, but the dominant motive was to restrain factionalism, as indicated by the fact that transparency had secondary priority: public inquiry and consultation should take place *"except if it should be likely to hinder reform"*.[13] A closed review process at arms-length was considered preferable to an open process that might catalyse a factional politics of strong sectional interest groups.

The National Competition Council, in its publication of an assessment framework for its third round of compliance oversight, stated that "[g]overnments should be congratulated for their continued commitment to the NCP reform programme ... this reflects a commitment to good government in the interests of all Australians, rather than the pursuit of narrow, short-term political interests."[14]

The defeasiblity of such 'special interests' was crucial to the architects of the reform package, who designed the membership of National Competition Council to be 'non-political' in order to facilitate this.[15] 'Independence' from politics meant in this case avoiding obviously representative structures. It also meant, in the ongoing implementation of meta-regulation that is explored in the next two chapters, ensuring that as often as possible, reviews of particular policy sectors were not controlled by the relevant government department – once again pressing for insulation from representative politics. This was a core commitment of those central agency bureaucrats with a mandate to oversee the adequacy of the review process.[16]

In insulating regulatory policy decision-making power for as long as possible[17] from representative politics, there was a double-edged emphasis in the independence thereby achieved, since it had to acquire an alternative source of legitimacy from that of democratic mandate. The tension is caught in the comment of one official who said, "At heart the NCP programme is not about economic rationalism gone mad but about a culture of transparency and reasoned justification in economic policy".[18] There is potentially significant tension between transparency and reasoned justification, particularly when the latter is heavily embedded in economic expertise, as it tended to be in this public choice perspective. More emphasis on reasoned justification tends to imply the replacement of political debate with technical expertise; on the other hand more emphasis on transparency alone promotes a more *political* conception of open civil society that counters closed bureaucratic politics. At a conceptual level, the public choice perspective emphasised both. In practice, one often had to give way to the other, and we see much variation in the following two chapters on this score.

'Purified politics', then, is strained of factionalism and rendered transparent by the application of economic rationality at arms-length from the political process, and constrained by norms of due process. The idea that this kind of 'purified' politics should ultimately have the last word under the meta-regulatory regime was important to the original design. The Independent Committee of Inquiry's final report made clear the *limits* of the centrality of economic expertise. It insisted that the reform package sought to create a set of institutions and processes that facilitate a *political* dialogue about the wisdom of specific policy choices. That dialogue, the report acknowledged, would inevitably have to grapple with conflicts between and amongst competition, efficiency and other social objectives:

> The recommended processes and institutions leave much of competition policy squarely in the political domain. While parts of competition policy ... lend themselves to administrative and at times judicial processes, most of the other areas of policy [including meta-regulation] require trade-offs between the interests of different groups in the community. Economics rarely provides clear answers to these kinds of issues, though economic analysis can and should be used to make the trade-offs more transparent.[19]

This statement focuses on the *limits* of what economic rationality can contribute to regulatory policymaking processes, and retains a role for politics. The role only comes into play, however, *after* due tempering by the discipline of economic rationality. And justification in accordance with the terms of economic rationality was, in the Australian programme, mandatory. Moreover oversight of the adequacy of such justification was enforced by hard fiscal incentives. While in theory the political process could freely select the criteria on which it would make final decisions, in practice the public choice framework of analysis provided an implicit criterion on which to base a final decision. Thus the reforms promoted not so much a free play of democratic dialogue, but rather emphasised transparency and a structured form of due process, the content of which would be filled out by key criteria from the framework of economic rationality underpinning the reforms. The next section explores the way in which the public choice perspective on regulation constructed its vision of the 'public interest' that an undistorted politics of regulation could secure.

Categorising Justifiable Regulation: Market Infrastructure and Social Citizenship

While the public choice literature harbours a built-in suspicion that regulatory legislation is often in effect a distortion of the political process, it does not seek to delegitimate all political intervention into social or individual choices, nor to suggest that undistorted social and economic exchange could take place in the absence of government infrastructure. Rather, it seeks to identify certain *categories* of rule-encoded political intervention as more prone to reflect distortions than others. I would argue that in effect public choice theory imports a distinction from economics into the legal-political sphere: that of a distorted versus an undistorted market. In particular, public choice approaches recognises that a smoothly working market requires in and of itself a structure of common rules backed by political enforcement.[20] Thus legal-political interventions that enforce property rights and contractual agreements, or that guarantee a stable currency, are crucial to creating and sustaining a market: what Anthony Ogus calls 'private facilitative law'.[21]

Much private facilitative law is embedded in the common law and enforced by courts, but some takes the form of formal legal rules and is thus regulatory in nature. Public choice theory[22] seeks to endorse this kind of regulatory law, but not others, and therefore categorises regulation with respect to the function that it performs in terms of political economy. If political intervention is aimed at facilitating efficiency or correcting market failures, then regulation is justifiable as a technical corrective, best performed by politically insulated technocrats or delegated to societal actors. A second (and rather amorphous) category of 'social' objectives (e.g. redistributing income, ameliorating social risk or fostering ecological goals) is, under this view, better addressed not by regulatory strategies, but rather by transparent political programmes administered and funded directly by the state. This approach gives a substantive normative cast to the familiar division between political and technical issues. While the facilitation of competitive or efficient markets justifies regulatory intervention as a *technical* corrective, pursuit of what could be broadly described as 'social justice' values, on the other hand, is viewed as distorting efficiency objectives if pursued through regulation, and thus best pursued explicitly (and independently) as a *political* corrective.

In effect, two different categories of regulation emerge, which could usefully be called market infrastructural regulation on the one hand and social citizenship regulation on the other hand. The former is naturalised, its status as technical corrective giving it an allegedly neutral status which does not, under the public choice perspective, appear as political in the factional sense, but rather as the product of undistorted politics serving a 'true' public interest.

The structure of legislative review in the Australian meta-regulatory programme does not preclude the justification and retention of either category of regulation. Indeed a 'checklist rationality' approach to the implementation of meta-regulation would, like a 'thin' conception of the rule of law, leave open the full range of political choice both as to means and end provided justification was transparent and adequate.

But in that slippery word 'adequate' lies the implicit distinction between market infrastructure regulation and the second category: social citizenship regulation. The implicit naturalisation of political intervention that facilitates competitive market efficiency means that justifiable regulation may face a different burden of proof, depending on whether it falls under the category of market infrastructure regulation or that of social citizenship regulation. Like 'thick' conceptions of the rule of law, the substantive import of a meta-regulatory process is highly contestable. But from the perspective of a public choice framework at least, market infrastructural regulation is easily cast as 'thinner' than social citizenship legislation. The argument might run as follows.

Market infrastructure regulation aims primarily to create a stable infrastructure for exchange and interaction between societal actors. It seeks to facilitate choice rather than direct it. This is not to say that market infrastructure regulation never constrains behaviour. Rules against fraud, or specific prohibitions of say, speculative dealings in the stock market, may also serve market infrastructural goals, even while they constrain rather than facilitate specific types of behaviour. But those constraints are put in place in order to protect a space for voluntary interactions rather than to direct the content of those interactions more closely. Market infrastructural regulation, even when it imposes constraints, imposes relatively thin constraints.

By contrast, social citizenship regulation has a 'thicker' quality to its goals, addressing specific harms that it seeks to eliminate from economic and social life. In addressing such specific harms, it may seek particular distributive outcomes or direct resources to particular uses.[23] As such, it is a category of regulation more likely to attract the public choice suspicion that substantive benefits amounting to rents for limited classes have been attained by disproportionate political influence.

The implications of a public choice perspective on regulation therefore tend to favour the retention of market infrastructural regulation and the constraint, or at the least the strict scrutiny, of social citizenship regulation. In this way, meta-regulation institutionalises a presumption in favour of market governance.

Of course, the borderline between market infrastructural regulation and social citizenship regulation in practice is not necessarily stable, even in theory but particularly in practice. That slipperiness constitutes a core facet of the politics of implementation, and its dimensions will emerge in the rest of the chapter and in Chapter Four. Nonetheless it is also true that a schematic division between competitive market values and social justice values, slippery as it is in practice, shapes the regulatory conversation. Indeed the wider the constituency participating in the conversation, the more pragmatically and loosely the conceptual framework derived from 'expert' technical models is used.

In the broader community politics at the heart of the remainder of this chapter, there is a productive intersection between participatory politics and the closed epistemic discourse of a public choice perspective on regulatory policymaking. That intersection, often jarring to the logic of the epistemic discourse, provides openings for reconfiguring the spectrum of political choices made possible under meta-regulation. In the following sections, I first locate the political reverberations of the category distinction underpinning the reforms, and then trace two of the most significant of the resulting reconfigurations within the multi-vocal politics of meta-regulation.

Legislative Debates

While the bulk of National Competition Policy was encoded in intergovernmental agreements completed by executives without parliamentary input, one aspect of the package (the extension of state anti-trust and competition laws to individuals and non-incorporated businesses) required new legislation. In the legislative debates occurring at the time of passing these bills, there were two main competing visions of the implications of the reforms. Both proceeded on the assumption that the reform package was intended to encourage sceptical questioning of social citizenship regulation while at the same time endorsing the benefits of market infrastructural regulation. Thus both critics and supporters in this initial stage reflected the category divide that I have argued provided the intellectual underpinnings of the reform package.

Supporters of the reforms emphasised the benefits of competitive markets. In rare cases, this took the form of bluntly stated ideological victory, as when the Victorian Liberal-National Coalition government declared:

> [The bill] spells an end to the opposition's socialist dreams, the managed economy and public ownership. It spells the end of what opposition members talk about now and what they have talked about in past years. The bill signals the inevitable victory of economic rationalism in Australia.[24]

However most supporters presented a less frontal endorsement of the notion that markets cause creative destruction, focusing on change and progress as positive facets of the need to mature as a nation. Thus politicians reminded readers and listeners of "the importance of change and the need to be relevant and therefore you have to test new ideas", to echo the words of the Victorian Premier, Jeff Kennett.[25] They argued that "Australia sees itself coming of age in the world market and sees itself as having to conduct itself in a fashion which places it better on the world stage",[26] and that "this bill is seen to be more than usually beneficial, placing as it does change and progress before us, and making organisations work for the betterment of Australia".[27]

This perspective characterised a welfare state focused on social citizenship as the status quo, and by insisting on the need to move forward from the status quo, justified aspects of the NCP package such as the 'reverse onus of proof' structure of the meta-regulatory regime. It celebrated the primacy of competition in a global marketplace as the only way to 'stay in the game'. In doing so, it painted the proper task of law, carefully designed and duly constrained from careless overuse, as that of the guarantor of that market infrastructure.

The contrasting vision was one primarily of loss, uncertainty and anxiety about preserving and protecting hard-won social gains. The precise nature of what was at stake was expressed, broadly speaking, as community and social cohesion. Sometimes dissenters spoke of losing a culture of tolerance and mutual helpfulness in the face of the Darwinism of unfettered competitiveness. Or, relatedly, they invoked equity across society and between generations. For the more conservative forces concerned with rural Australia and small business viability, the importance of community was expressed more through themes of nationalism and the sovereignty of sub-national levels of government, both of which were perceived as threatened by the NCP reforms. It is worth quoting at length Senator Coulter's speech in the federal Senate which weaves together several of these threads:

> The intentions [of the bill] are laudable but nonetheless dangerous and their corrosive effect on our culture and our social life is everywhere to be seen by those with eyes not blinded by the religious ecstasy of economic rationalist ideology...One cannot legislate for goodness. A government can, over time however, pass a series of laws which so undermine the fabric of society that anti-social behaviour flourishes and the moral and cultural cement that binds citizens together in a society is inexorably dissolved. The bill before us today marks one of the stages of that dissolution – just one of the stages. For over 200 years Australians have built up a culture of tolerance and mutual helpfulness. In the few short years of this Labour government, first under Prime Minister Hawke and now under Prime Minister Keating, this mutual respect and support one for the other has been steadily eroded.[28]

The social citizenship image of regulation with its emphasis on law as a force for cohesion and as primarily a moral command is vividly present here. The primary impetus is to preserve: from this perspective, the NCP reforms embody a wrong-headed view of government regulation.

Parliamentary Inquiry

The parliamentary debates explored above ended by passing the requisite legislation at all nine levels with no added amendments. The media reported that "in the end, according to Professor Hilmer, the logic of the argument overwhelmed any opposition to introducing the plan".[29] An extraordinarily unusual instance of consensus? Hardly. The lack of opposition reflected the closed nature of the policy community that had negotiated the reforms, rather than an absence of dissent. In the wake of passing these reforms, three parliamentary inquiries were conducted over the years of implementation, indicating the ongoing level of disquiet in the wider community about the implications of the reforms.

Such inquiries are a rich site for elaborating on the various justifications offered to expand or contract the scope of CPA. They illuminate the competing stories seeking to make sense of meta-regulation in different ways. By exploring in depth the first of these inquiries,[30] it is possible to perceive the emergence of evolving compromises: more nuanced visions of how regulation might try to integrate the competing values embodied in market infrastructural regulation and social citizenship regulation. In these broader community-based aspects of the regulatory conversation, the fluidity and malleability of meta-regulation's prescriptions begin to emerge. In contrast to the public choice perspective, and the relatively simplistic dichotomies of the debates in the legislative arena, malleability becomes nuanced. We begin to see what Sol Picciotto, in discussing the effects of globalisation on governance, has described as:

> a contested process of destabilisation and restructuring involving a search for new forms of synthesis between the economic and political aspects of social relations, rather than a deterministic tendency for economic pressures from an already existing world market to undermine otherwise stable political structures.[31]

The search for new forms of synthesis to which Picciotto alludes produces, in this excavation of the threads of the parliamentary inquiry, two principal reformulations of the legitimate role of the state. The two models represent variations on tempered forms of market liberalism. They are both hybrid compromises that try to integrate market infrastructure and social citizenship goals. They build on the recognition that rule-based political intervention is an essential precondition for facilitating smooth and efficient markets. But they aim to retain a role for pursuing forms of social welfare that are 'thicker' than economic productivity, requiring political leadership and public deliberation on the issue of what role non-economic goals such as equity and ecological sustainability should play in the simulated markets envisaged under the new regime of competition. Both models concede the utility and desirability of seeking alternative mechanisms to direct state provision or regulation when pursuing 'social' goals. But they insist that mechanisms like competition and markets should be marshalled not simply as an engine of economic growth, but as a means to achieve a more precisely defined conception of the public good (or a means of avoiding specific harms such as significant inequity or ecological damage).

The first of the two different hybrid models I call a community morality (CM) perspective. This was implicitly invoked by actors, both state and non-state, who called for the maintenance of key functions such as the promotion of community and cohesiveness *in tandem with* the new ones of forcing and supporting market-mimicking strategies. Other groups re-framed the goals of social justice, access and equity typical of traditional welfare state discourses in terms of the new language of competition and economic analysis, drawing on the image of the 'consumer-citizen' as the key organising concept for their arguments. This strand suggested the second perspective: a differentiated consumer sovereignty perspective (DCS). The DCS strategy was one preserving social citizenship values through strategic translation while the CM approach was an attempt to craft new avenues for expressing such values independently of economic discourse.

The first parliamentary inquiry, conducted in 1995, was located in the House Committee on Banking, Finance and Public Administration. Its terms of reference encompassed three main areas: the application of the 'public interest interpretation clause', policies relating to community service obligations, and the implications of the reform package as a whole for local government.

The first of these issues directly implicates the meta-regulatory regime and its potential impact on social citizenship. The second issue is theoretically narrower. The technical meaning of 'community service obligations' refers to the obligations of major infrastructure providers of essential services (gas, water, telecommunications, electricity) to ensure that no one section of the community is excluded from provision. When services are provided in a context where 'normal commercial practice' would not provide service, the provider is refunded by the government to the extent of that Community Service Obligation (CSO). CSOs, technically, therefore are the residual aspects of provision of essential services that would not be provided consistently under 'normal' levels of competitive efficiency. However, in the parliamentary inquiry, the phrase took on much broader, more inclusive connotations and was used in interesting ways in support of a reframed social citizenship perspective.

Thus two of the three main foci of the inquiry concerned the shadow cast over social citizenship by National Competition Policy. The third issue reflected the lack of inclusion of the sub-state levels of government in the consultation phases, and as such reiterates the general importance of the politics of federalism in the crafting of the reform package.

The pattern of responses to the call for public submissions was as follows (103 total submissions, some sources overlap more than one category):

Table 3.1   Breakdown of public responses to parliamentary inquiry

Source of submission	Net number of submissions (excluding supplementary)	% of net total submissions
Local government	26	31
Primary industry	9	11
Line (programme) depts	7	9
Social policy lobby groups (aged care, aboriginal, education, environmental, consumer, education)	7	9
Academia	6	7
Labour	6	7
State governments	6	7
Infrastructure suppliers	6	7
Central depts	3	3.5
Professions	3	3.5
Business trade groups	2	2.5
Supplementary submissions from same sources (evenly distributed across sources)	20	20 (of gross total incl. supplementary submissions)

Source: Compiled by author from Commonwealth Parliament of Australia (1995), *Submissions to Inquiry into Aspects of the National Competition Policy Reform Package*

An aggregation of this pattern of response into government, business, academia and community groups produces a distribution of 50.5% governmental sources, 23.5% business (including professions, agriculture and infrastructure suppliers), 23% civil society (7% academia, 9% community groups, 7% labour). This might seem to indicate that the issue's salience is still primarily intergovernmental. However, the figure is somewhat skewed by the presence of 30% of the submissions from local government, who were included explicitly in the inquiry's terms of reference. In several respects, local government contributions are arguably more reflective of a community perspective than of intergovernmental politics. In part, this is because local government is much closer to the electorate than state or federal government, in part because their perspective and interests in relation to NCP clearly differed from that of the state and federal governments who were parties to the actual agreement. Local government in fact contributed, in ways that complemented various community and civil groups, to a partial reframing of the emerging agenda on the appropriate reach of competition and market principles. If the response to the parliamentary inquiry disaggregates local government contributions, the picture looks more like 19.5% state, 31% local government, 23.5% business and 23% civil society.

Why disaggregate the contributors in terms of distinctions between state, market and civil society? Because if there is a tight link between material interest and broader normative commitments, then one might expect state actors to argue for a hierarchically institutionalised version of social citizenship, market actors for a market infrastructural vision, and civil society actors for a more decentralised, community-based version of social citizenship. However, the various threads that unwind in this chapter indicate a much more fragmented picture, where few generalisations can be made at the level of state/market/civil society. For instance, over a third of business submissions came from primary industry, a sector whose interpretation of meta-regulation had much more in common with certain civil society groups (especially consumer advocates) than with large trade associations or infrastructure suppliers. And even within primary industry, it is strictly not true to speak of a single monolithic position. Nonetheless, generalising with caution and despite considerable fragmentation within sectors, the trajectories discussed in the next four sections can be observed within the regulatory conversation.

Bifurcated Perspectives: Business and Labour

As stated earlier, the most interesting positions in the inquiry uncovered more nuanced hybrid interpretations of what meta-regulation meant for the overall direction of regulatory policy choice. However, not all groups moved towards such hybrids. Business and labour tended on the whole to reflect the rather starkly bifurcated position that characterised the legislative debates – i.e. that what was at stake was either support for market infrastructural regulation or a vision of social citizenship on the other hand. These positions reinforced the tendency to categorise regulation in a bright-line fashion, though business and labour took diametrically opposite positions on the desirability of constraining social citizenship regulation.

There was a relatively small proportion of submissions from business aside from primary industry. This was certainly no reflection of the regime's lack of importance to this sector. For example, 20% of the Australian Chamber of Commerce and Industry's and resource time was devoted to the CPA meta-regulatory regime.[32] Their relative absence at the inquiry was in fact a measure of their political strength at the earlier, more decisive stages of executive negotiations and agenda-setting. They had an ongoing advantage of a seat at the closed, private forums for which the parliamentary inquiry was in part precisely an antidote.

In the submissions that were made (leaving aside primary industry for the time being), business largely reiterated concerns familiar from the public choice perspective on regulation, though they focused more on the 'business impact' of regulation than on an undistorted or 'purified' conception of the public interest. Chief amongst these concerns was the determination to reverse the onus of proof in generating regulation, a reversal that would alter a precautionary culture of 'if in doubt, regulate'. The Australian Chamber of Commerce and Industry ("the ACCI") argued that "regulation should be considered the least appropriate way in which to address issues of concern to the govt i.e. it should be the last resort after education, publicity, moral suasion, industry self-regulation and other approaches have been fully assessed and considered ineffective".[33] The new onus, they argued, must privilege competitiveness above all: "it comes down to an understanding that all elements of our community, including the regulators, must contribute to competitiveness".[34] The Business Council of Australia objected to the low priority of competitiveness and efficiency on the list of factors that made up the 'public interest interpretation'. They requested that the test be reformulated in such a way as to give efficiency and competitive factors a dominant place.

Business went further than simply giving predominant emphasis to the economic factors of efficiency and competitiveness; they also sought to undermine competing factors. In private, they lobbied the newly created National Competition Council with the aim of officially narrowing the interpretation clause to exclude formally all factors other than competitiveness, efficiency and productivity.[35] In addition, some business representatives focused on translating features typical of social citizenship into economic concepts that would then impact negatively on competition. The ACCI, for example, characterised affirmative action hiring policies and government procurement policies as 'input CSOs' that burden the competitiveness of government business enterprises and must be eliminated in order to achieve competitive parity with the private sector.[36]

Although the concept of market infrastructural regulation acknowledges that pursuing competitiveness and efficiency is not always at odds with the existence of regulation, many business submissions nonetheless tended to imply that there was a sharp division between regulation that promoted competition, and regulation that promoted non-economic ends. This was a result of two linked assertions that were explicitly made. The first was that competition issues should be treated quite separately from social justice issues, the two-step approach implicit in public choice approaches to regulatory politics. The second was an assertion that when regulation has pro-competitive objectives, there is such a strong presumption that 'net community benefit' will result that an affirmative demonstration of public interest ends is not necessary.

This second assertion was made by the National Competition Council (whose members were primarily business representatives), and by the Victorian (right-wing) government.[37] By dispensing with the necessary balancing of costs and benefits for pro-competitive regulation but not for other regulation, this stance favourably distinguishes rules that are purely market infrastructural and places a burden on all others. In the process, it posits social justice as incompatible with competition, and argues for trade-offs to be made in favour of the latter.

Most sections of the union movement also assumed the basic incompatibility of social justice and competitive efficiency, and argued instead for the inverse position to be taken. The Australian Council of Trade Unions ("the ACTU") explicitly objected to the reversal of the onus of proof instantiated by the regime, arguing that the burden of proving that change is necessary should be on 'deregulators' (Inquiry 1995 v5: 639). They relied heavily on the public interest interpretation clause of the CPA for this position, arguing that "proper recognition of the public interest matters" listed in Clause 1(3) of the CPA mandates this onus. Relatedly, the unions also resisted the priority of efficiency and competitiveness as the most important goals to be pursued. Instead, as the Community and Public Sector Union argued (Inquiry 1995 v1:55), the most important goal was "universal access ... to basic human rights and economic imperatives as determined by our political community ... in ... our expressions of constitutional rights, international treaties and international benchmarks".

This insistence on the language of social citizenship, public law and human rights carried over in a general antagonism on the part of labour for 'translation' of these social goals into the concepts derived from expert economic discourses. For example, the State Public Services Federation objected to the mechanism of 'community service obligations' (CSOs), arguing first that this concept relied on targeting specific disadvantaged groups when it was preferable to aim for *universal* access to essential services and attributes of social citizenship such as education and health (Inquiry 1995 v1:55). Secondly, they continued, it was a mischaracterisation of policies such as affirmative action, government procurement, and the 'new administrative law' to view them as 'input CSOs'. Although business associations such as the ACCI had continued to insist on characterizing these policies as input costs which were over and above 'normal commercial practice' (input CSOs), the ACTU had in fact succeeded in excluding these kinds of policies from considerations of whether competitive neutrality existed between public and private sector (Inquiry 1995 v5: 640). In pursuing this end, the ACTU relied, like business, on a narrative that opposed the economic and the social (or at least efficiency and social justice): a bifurcated perspective that tried to apply different levels of cost-benefit scrutiny and presumptive legitimacy to different categories of legally-encoded regulation.

From Bifurcation to Multivocal Compromises

Business and labour were not *monolithically* for and against (respectively) market infrastructure and social citizenship regulation in inverse patterns. For example, the ACCI, which represents many small and medium-sized businesses, conceded that "a traditional regulatory approach dependent on dense black-letter law may (with improved cost-efficiency) still have some valid role in sensitive areas of public health and safety such as food". They did advocate a change of *strategy*, pleading that "hard-line policing should be replaced by risk management in all but a few critical areas of government such as quarantine, safety and the like".[38] But "sensitive areas of public health and safety" were acknowledged as legitimate bases for some sort of regulatory response.

Despite this acknowledgement, the ACCI still put a tight rein on its conception of the scope of critical public health issues. It was presumptively antagonistic to regulation in areas of retail licensing, barriers to entry into professions, and other professional regulation, as well as to affirmative action hiring policies and government procurement policies. As we shall see in Chapter Five, some groups in the migration review successfully made arguments that barriers to entry into professions can be viewed as raising issues of 'public security'; the ACCI's partially conciliatory statement would not have tolerated this definition of matters that justified regulation. Thus we can see that the stances of professionals on the scope of justifiable regulation may diverge from those of 'business', though I have loosely associated them here.

This emerging polyvocality leads at last to a more detailed consideration of the 'new syntheses' of the alleged opposition between market infrastructure and social citizenship. As stated earlier, two visions of compromise can be distinguished, both of which focus strongly on accommodating *both* goals of market infrastructure and social citizenship. They both react against a monolithic emphasis on the importance of competitive efficiency, and both seek to foster social cohesion and to some degree temper market forces. As the Australian Catholic Social Welfare Commission argued, "there should be no objection to governments withdrawing funding if efficiency or accountability is poor ... [E]fficiency is not a 'dirty word'".[39] Rather, as Craig Johnston of the Public Interest Advocacy Centre contended, NGO strategies and contributions in Australia in recent years have "allowed social justice, sustainable development and consumer issues to, not displace economic efficiency, but to acknowledge its validity, and to temper the monopoly position which economic efficiency has had in dominant sectors of public policy".[40]

Each of the two hybrid models that flesh out meta-regulation's malleability has three principal facets: the values to which they adhere, the linguistic modes and techniques they use to express these values, and the institutional mechanisms they advocate to promote these values. Since these three facets overlap, I will preface detailed exploration of each with a more integrated overview.

Community Morality Perspective

A range of groups in the parliamentary inquiry called for the maintenance of key functions such as the promotion of community and social cohesion *in tandem with* supporting and facilitating market competitiveness. I have labelled this perspective a community morality (CM) facet of the regulatory conversation. It does not deny the importance of market competitiveness, but CM advocates insisted that it should be *no more important* than a diffuse notion of shared needs. These shared needs constitute the 'community morality' and tend to posit a 'thicker' concept of the public good than a pure market infrastructure approach. They vary across groups but they share a general tenor of being expressed in non-economic terms; for example as community morality in the most direct sense (e.g. in support of regulation of brothels), as compassionate or equitable duties arising from the exposure of the vulnerable, or as the need to foster social cohesion (e.g. by not isolating rural communities).

Language resonant of public law and human rights discourses, or a more diffuse variety of social democratic welfarism, was usually used to express these values. Institutionally, there was in general little attempt to integrate the urgency and specification of CM needs into a market framework; rather the argument of these groups is focused on persuading the relevant authorities of the importance of tempering the market. The advocates often paid lip service to the co-equal importance of efficiency and competitiveness, but they did not elaborate a great deal on strategies or mechanisms that would institutionalise a compromise. Often they implicitly relied on the hierarchically organised modes of state power characteristic of the traditional welfare state, which would locate the day-to-day elaboration of the content of community morality in the expertise of professionals, whether those be teachers, doctors, social workers or civil servants. Some church-based groups, however, explicitly countered this with a more decentralised institutional imagination for elaborating community morality.

The submission of the Australian Catholic Social Welfare Commission[41] ("ACSWC") is a good example of the CM perspective on meta-regulation. ACSWC articulated 'guiding principles' to be used as a benchmark evaluating legislative and political policies: viz, "the human dignity inherent in all individuals and their right to be active participants in their national and local communities".[42] ACSWC argued that this should stand in stark contrast to the guiding principle of the CPA: to foster rules that are the least restrictive of competition. They challenged the notion that increased competition was compatible with human dignity and active participation. They argued that individualisation in the market context actually depersonalises, makes the individual a means to an end that is fungible. "People in need are seen by for-profit providers as a means to financial reward, not as ends in themselves".[43] Unit cost funding in the health sector, for example, "in fact pushed service agencies to see those clients less as individuals and more as merely the throughput that must be generated…if the organisation is to survive financially".[44]

The basis for resisting a connection between dignity and active participation on the one hand, and increased market competition on the other hand, was that ACSWC viewed participation and self-respect as socio-political values, not economic ones. They interpreted this as requiring special attention to those who are economically less well off. ACSWC criticised the notion that social cohesion is a "natural consequence of economic prosperity",[45] and expressed concern that state withdrawal from public provision of services or funds exposes the vulnerable and disadvantaged to an absence of support. The community, they argued, has a "moral duty to provide support to vulnerable and disadvantaged in need".[46] This duty is a concomitant of "the notion of rights of social citizenship, which [require] universal access to a comprehensive range of social services, as a means of enhancing social solidarity and social cohesion".[47]

It was not only church-based groups that advocated this kind of community morality approach, though most other groups were less loquacious in its defence. The Queensland Farmers' Federation, for example, expressed concern about the impact of the CPA regime on the "welfare obligations of the nation", specifically the availability of full transport and communications in rural areas as an essential prerequisite not just for the economic productivity of a rural region, but also for its social cohesion. Hawkins' Retirement Village resisted the characterisation of CSOs as 'unusual costs' that lay beyond the pale of 'normal commercial margins', arguing that they should be an expected duty: "examples of the better corporate behaviour which Australian society expects of its larger corporations" (Inquiry 1995 v1: 12). The National Tertiary Education Industry Union demanded to be formally excluded from competition policy altogether and the Australian Education Union argued that education was not analogous to a 'business service'. They invoked the value-laden nature of teaching, the significance of professional and collegial culture, and the collective rather than individual nature of the benefits flowing from education to support their contentions.

The CM model clearly builds on a direct recognition of need and vulnerability expressed in non-economic language, most notably the language of duty. At its strongest, that duty partakes of a strong redistributive ethos, captured in the notion of solidarity. The ACSWC quoted Pope John Paul II:

> Solidarity is not just a vague feeling of compassion, or shallow distress at the misfortunes of so many people, both near and far. On the contrary, it is a firm and persevering determination to commit oneself to the common good; that is to say the good of each individual, because we are all really responsible for all.[48]

For the ACSWC, "this means that the community as a whole must take responsibility for ensuring that each of its members have the resources to live in dignity and to participate actively in the economic, cultural and social life of the community".[49] This combination of strongly felt compassion and the imposition of duty was used in a very similar way by the National Anglican Caring Organisations Network (Inquiry 1995 v2:185-192) to express the values of the CM perspective. The Network, as well as various labour groups, viewed social citizenship as a moral or social obligation to the collective whole, rooted in public law and human rights values, (especially social and economic rights) rather than utilitarian cost-benefit analysis.

Did these perspectives of compassion-motivated duties and correlative rights suggest any concrete strategies for institutionalising such aspirations?

A plausible assumption might be that law and legal institutions would be an appropriate hammer to temper the cost-benefit approach to legislation. Certainly Western Australia seemed to posit law and economics as opposing analytical tools in this context (Inquiry 1995 v7:1058): "In common with other jurisdictions we have interpreted public interest as an economic and not a legal concept. Consequently we are using a benefit-cost approach to legislation reviews which are currently underway" (Inquiry 1995 v7:1058). In the UK, Prosser has argued that certain key 'public service principles' (e.g. universal service, non-discrimination) are embedded in UK utilities law and should trump economic arguments in the formulation of policy. [50]

However, the groups voicing community morality perspectives were for the most part frustratingly silent on this aspect of their approach. Only labour groups really clearly hoped that law would be a tool for enforcing the public interest interpretation clause, however, and they are not strictly within the compass of the CM model (ranging closer to the more uncompromising social citizenship perspective). Church-based groups on the other hand, and in particular the ACSWC, wanted to distance themselves from any expansion in the role of the state, probably including law. They emphasised subsidiarity, the preference that smaller groups or groups lower in the political hierarchy should preferably perform as many roles as possible in fostering human dignity and active social participation. The ACSWC was, however, also sceptical of pre-welfare state voluntarism which it regarded as paternalistic and fostering dependency. [51] It preferred to support a model that combines professional and non-judgmental care with advocacy, and to suggest that such advocacy is best achieved through a *network structure of community care providers.*

The idea of a network was invoked by ACSWC to foster the CM kinds of values already discussed. Thus, they argued for three things: "clearly defined networks of church and community organisations that will strengthen the sector's cooperative ethos"; [52] for the development of research that would lead to "a strong set of performance indicators that actually mean something and do not reduce the concept of effectiveness to one of economic efficiency"; [53] and for cross-subsidisation within organisations from the least vulnerable towards the most vulnerable – a way of institutionalising "mutual responsibility and care".

Here we see something interesting: traces of language and governance techniques from both the market infrastructure and social citizenship conceptions of the rule of law, but marshalled explicitly to serve values associated with the latter. Of course as a hybrid, this model has internal tensions. Cross-subsidies and sector-wide networks were precisely the kind of anti-competitive mechanisms that the National Competition Policy intended to target from its inception. But at the same time, ACSWC, by focusing on local-level cooperative networks, suggests that the decentralised flexibility that market governance structures provide might be valuable, so long as it does not also promote values of competitive individualism. As they argued:

> 'Consumer' is not a dirty word. But it cannot be the only word when it comes to the way community-based social service agencies operate. If they want to be more than a retail outlet for government funded services...they must offer constituents opportunities to contribute rather than just consume. Constituents must be offered opportunities to contribute to their own well-being, by being empowered to take greater responsibility for overcoming their disadvantage, and they must also be offered opportunities for contributing to the well-being of others and the well-being of the whole community.[54]

What of other submissions beyond that of the ACSCW? Labour, education, church-based groups and the poorer) sections of the aged and farming communities all focused on the kinds of matter specified in the public interest interpretation clause and built from them a story that runs parallel to the thread that emphasises market competitiveness and efficiency. It is a story that challenges its parallel thread obliquely, refusing to engage in an integrative way with it, yet also refusing to enter into combat. Most groups supporting the CM perspective refused to engage in any 'translation' exercise that would move them towards integrative engagement with the language (and even in part the goals) of the market infrastructure perspective. The National Anglican Caring Organisations Network, for example (Inquiry 1995 v2:185-192), resisted the quantification of performance targets in the social welfare sector on the grounds that they were destructive of non-material resources and outputs and especially of intrinsically shared goods such as trust, interpersonal esteem and respect. They pointed out that services such as 'meals on wheels' have multiple facets and that increased competition will highlight the economic facet (the provision of food at speed) to the detriment of the social facet (the social contact and communication with an isolated and only partially capable client).

Even though rhetorically the community morality perspective was sympathetic at least to the notional importance of efficiency goals, there is a sense in which challenging their predominance though 'parallel resistance' side-steps the trade-offs that would actually have to be made in the final analysis in individual sector reviews. For example, the ACSWC acknowledged the value of self-reliance *at the same time* that it said government had "gone too far" and had placed "unfair burdens" on the disadvantaged.[55] If the core of the complaint is unfairness, one needs a theory of substantive justice to guide selection of the threshold at which the effects of competitive markets constitute 'unfair burdens' rather than incentives for self-reliance for certain groups. Without addressing this kind of question, most of the groups promoting a community morality perspective invoke non-market values alongside market values without any concrete sense of how to achieve the compromise which is sought.

What might assist in making concrete such strategies? Given the general resistance of the community morality perspective to 'translation' of non-market values into the economic discourse, it is interesting to note one or two flickers of 'translation' in the submission of the Catholic Social Welfare Commission. Witness this brief moment in which the rhetoric of social duty is abruptly substituted, as if interchangeably, by an economic framework: supporting the vulnerable is "the expression of a social duty, or in economic terms, an investment in the common good. The social dividend of this investment is a healthy participative democracy and social harmony, both prerequisites for greater individual liberty and economic growth".[56] There is also the reference to developing 'performance indicators' that will capture more than simply economic efficiency. A hybrid strategy centred on translation is intensified in the second principal narrative in the regulatory conversation traced in this chapter: the differentiated consumer sovereignty approach.

Differentiated Consumer Sovereignty Perspective

Differentiated consumer sovereignty (DCS) approaches to resisting market spectacles were, like CM approaches, committed to fostering a relatively 'thick' conception of the public interest and similar kinds of social citizenship values. However, they tended not to recognise or specify these values *directly*. Rather, their explicit focus was the level of autonomy and personal sovereignty necessary for effective market participation. They incorporated social goals indirectly into arguments relating to the *preconditions* of such autonomy and sovereignty. Moreover, they made these arguments in a very different language from the CM advocates, using primarily an economic discourse of consumer sovereignty, information asymmetry and market failure. They aimed to 'translate' or re-frame the goals of social justice, access and equity that characterised welfare state discourses in the language of competition, drawing on the image of the 'consumer-citizen' as a key organising concept. Where groups were representing specific kinds of consumers, they naturally focused their arguments in terms of characteristics specific to that consumer (e.g. aged consumers, aboriginal consumers) – hence the appellation 'differentiated consumer sovereignty'. A cross-section of community groups – aboriginal, environmental, consumer advocacy and certain primary industry advocates – took the DCS approach.

DCS approaches, especially in comparison to CM approaches, supported the development of institutional mechanisms that insulate decision-making processes from traditional democratic politics. Whereas many CM perspectives (though less so with church-based advocates) cast political intervention in a positive light as conserving social citizenship values of equity and stability, DCS advocates seemed *equally* suspicious of both business and government. While their primary values gave priority to redressing (to use their terminology) 'market failure', they were almost equally sensitised to 'government failure', particularly groups with historical records of weak political influence such as aboriginal groups. DCS advocates were interested in the use of private power for fulfilling functions previously pursued in state arenas, or, to relate their objectives to a broader literature,[57] in impressing private power with a 'public trust'.

Now, as we saw with church-based advocates of the CM perspective, there was an element of this in their approach too. But the difference lies in their hostility to the profit-oriented market framework, to the character of the institutional recommendations they made, and to the values they harnessed to those techniques. All of these are interrelated, but we can begin by contrasting the decentralised networks that interest DCS advocates.

Whereas the network advocated by the ACSCW aimed to increase the *political* influence of a sector (social services) that would otherwise be likely to suffer from the application of the CPA regime, DCS advocates were much more suspicious of political power. As the Australian Conservation Foundation argued:

> It is important to distance the management of water and wastewater services from political interference from government, while at the same time maintaining full public accountability. Decision-making processes must therefore be distanced from the political process, and communications between government (including shareholders) and boards of management should be documented and subject to public scrutiny. (Inquiry 1995 v4:493)

Gary Moore, Director of the New South Wales Council of Social Services, indicated that in lobbying to exempt human services from the CPA regime (or at least temper the application to them of the market framework presumption) independent agencies have been a more fruitful avenue than Ministers.[58] This preference for institutional autonomy is indicative of a more formal, comprehensive idea of 'networks' than the CM approach. It implies a web of multiple formal access points to ensure that not only efficiency objectives but also social justice, equity and ecological goals will be pursued. For example, the Australian Conservation Foundation supported the following mix of strategies for ensuring that ecological integrity was integrated into a more competitive framework: independent regulators possessing strong powers of information-gathering, community and environmental representation on regulatory authority boards, the application of Freedom of Information legislation, legislatively encoded annual reporting requirements, enforcement of consumer protection legislation and the availability of an Ombudsman (Inquiry 1995 v4:489).

The Public Interest Advocacy Centre ("PIAC") moulded a similar web of institutional recommendations into a broader argument for institutionalising 'consumer protection obligations' which had four primary components: information disclosure, complaints and redress, service standards and customer contracts, and customer participation (Inquiry 1995 v5:604). The mixture of public and private law techniques in this institutional strategy formalises a network of access points where no one group possesses ultimate control over policy implementation. Exactly how this works will become clearer in the case study of the utilities sector (Chapter Five). For the moment, it is interesting to note that this suspicion of traditional politics reflected in institutional recommendations for independent, insulated bodies is something the DCS advocates share with the public choice perspective of those who crafted the original reform package.

It is also the case that DCS advocates, like the public choice perspective on regulatory politics, framed their technical strategies in the terms of economic discourse. However unlike public choice supporters, they did not embed into the use of that discourse a presumption against the goals more closely associated with social citizenship. Rather, they aimed to strategically mould the conceptual framework provided by economic analysis in order to *support* social citizenship values.

For example, the Australian Dairy Farmers' Federation emphasised the unequal bargaining power of farmers and consumers vis-à-vis retail supermarkets, as a means of justifying the retention of marketing authorities. It strategically chose to focus on lower prices for consumers rather than on the need for social cohesion in rural communities as the Queensland Farmers' Federation had done. The Council on Ageing (Inquiry 1995 v3:277) contended that a failure to provide universal and affordable access to services such as health, legal and financial advice would constitute 'market failure' because these sorts of professional services were necessary to redress "information asymmetries" between the aged and other groups, and should thus be treated analogously to essential infrastructure services such as utilities.

More thoroughly, the Public Interest Advocacy Centre demonstrated in a detailed case study of water reform exactly how specifying a 'social citizenship objective' extracted from the public interest interpretation clause would affect the analysis undertaken in a CPA review (Inquiry 1995 v5:51). They chose social welfare and equity (Clause 1(3)(e) and ecologically sustainable development (Clause 1(3)(d)). For the latter, they demonstrated how integrating this objective would give priority to demand management of water rather than supply when measuring efficiency. In regard to the former, they showed how certain technical pricing methods can accommodate social welfare and equity objectives.

Finally, the National Farmers' Federation took an interesting approach falling within the DCS camp (Inquiry 1995 v4:558). They built on the notion of 'community service obligation', arguing that "CSOs should be regarded as minimum service standards which are commonly held by the community to be a right of every member of the community". However, they widened the traditional ambit of the notion of CSOs considerably, suggesting they encompass health services, education, water, gas, garbage, electricity, telephone, quarantine, education, public transport and mail. They also cast CSOs as comprehensive and compulsory obligations, rather than residual and optional:

> A CSO is an explicit decision by the community that a given service or level of service should be available to all members of the community...that a service provider has an obligation to the community (Inquiry 1995 v4:558).

Finally, they remained steadfastly agnostic about whether CSOs were best implemented through public or private mechanisms:

> When defined as a standard, CSO delivery does not need to be the sole preserve of government business enterprises. CSOs may be delivered by private or public sector providers. Where functions are privatised or opened to competition, government will need to retain some form of control that ensures that private providers do not breach the defined CSO standard. This control may take the form of licensing or a contractual arrangement with government which provides a power of enforcement (Inquiry 1995 v4:558).

This contribution is a multi-faceted reformulation of the traditional welfare state. It redefines government functions as ensuring the delivery of services to minimum standards, via contractual techniques, as opposed to ensuring social integration via techniques of political participation. Minimum welfare rights are defined in market terms with government as a background guarantor that standards are maintained, and in this way, private power is impressed with a public trust.

It is clear that social equity and ecological integrity are values that drive much of the DCS approach described above, but there is still a striking degree to which those values are harnessed to an overriding aim of creating a fully autonomous, independent and informed consumer – the ideal market actor. The autonomous consumer is the *fundamental* goal that supports the legitimacy of the broad range of social citizenship values. As the National Farmers' Federation insisted, the ultimate aim of the public interest test embedded in the CPA regime was to give consumers more choice rather than less, and to decrease the inputs needed to create a given output (Inquiry 1995 v4:555)

But it is not always obvious what particular regulatory strategy should flow from a focus on enhancing choice and individual autonomy. This is true even within one fairly narrowly defined sector. For example, in the primary industry sector, the Grains Council of Australia argued that in order to preserve choice and the capacity to participate in the *international* market for *domestic* farmers, it was necessary to retain the anti-competitive Australian Wheat Board. Yet the Australian Grain Industry Task Force disagreed, arguing that the Wheat Board blocked the choice of certain domestic farmers to develop niche markets overseas, to invest in grain futures markets to protect themselves against risk from price fluctuations and to invest in downstream processing. The key to this difference lies in the different constituencies behind the two associations. Only fairly well-resourced and well-educated wheat farmers would be capable of exploiting the choices outlined by the Task Force; many farmers would indeed need the assistance of the Board even to maintain their traditional methods of production.

Thus we are brought face to face with the issue of whether material interests determine the link between a particular strand or narrative within the regulatory conversation and the interest group advocating that strand. This is not a question that admits of a clear answer, especially since it is my own interpretation of the parliamentary inquiry submissions that has linked a particular group with a particular narrative, and indeed shaped the extraction of the narratives themselves. Nonetheless, I would suggest that some broad patterns are observable. First, as is abundantly clear by now, there is no neat division between the perspectives advocated and the broad categories of state, market and civil society that I first used to disaggregate the results. Local government assumptions bore a closer resemblance to groups such as education unions or some of the smaller primary industry associations than they did to submissions from other parts of government. And the variety of business and civil society groups each showed signs of advocating both CM and DCS perspectives on regulation.

Although some sections of business and labour stood on opposite sides of a bifurcated argument about the welfare state, most groups were trying to mould a compromise. If there is any discernible cleavage, it happened along the line of producer/consumer interests. Groups representing a particular location in production processes (labour, primary industry, professionals) tended on the whole to adopt CM approaches, as did church groups and education lobbies. In so doing they simply argued simply for less competition to apply to their sector, and adduced a diffuse version of community morality to support their case. By contrast, arguments made on behalf of 'users' or 'consumers' of goods and services tended to be more of the DCS kind of approach, and focused on redefining an effectively functioning market, rather than simply tempering its effects. The most extended version of this argument based itself on the general category of 'consumer', but many small variations existed depending on the specific identity of a user group (the aged, aboriginal people).

But the picture is still more complex than this. Even within any of these sub-groupings, associations that had comparatively greater resources and national standing (e.g. National Farmers' Federation as opposed to the Western Australia Farmers' Federation, large urban local councils as opposed to small councils from isolated rural areas) tended to rely on DCS approaches rather than on CM ones. This could be because, possessing more resources and clout, they had less to lose by compromising more (since the DCS approach is arguably closer to a market infrastructure conception than a social citizenship conception). It may also have been that they simply had access to the technical and intellectual expertise that allowed them to perform the job of 'translating' their aspirations into the language and techniques of the presently dominant paradigm. And relatedly, the DCS perspective may have been more attractive because of the difficulty – in a secular, pluralist, liberal culture – of making substantive normative arguments in support of 'thicker' versions of the public good. Perhaps it is no surprise then that church groups, despite possessing relatively significantly resources and national organisational resources, declined to go too far down the DCS path. Their access to a more explicitly normative framework than most other actors in the political economy framework gave them the discursive resources to retain a CM perspective.

Conclusion

The overall argument of this chapter can be summed up as follows. The design of institutions of economic adjudication under meta-regulation in Australia was significantly shaped by a public choice perspective on regulation that institutionalised a suspicion of democratic politics. A public choice perspective on regulation assumes a particular version of the 'public interest' that advocates that the imposition of public rules on private actors should be restricted to the improvement of market efficiency, while 'non-market' goals are addressed by explicitly political responses. This 'two-step' approach implies a distinction between market infrastructural regulation and social citizenship regulation. In consequence, Australian meta-regulation institutionalised a presumption in favour of market governance.

However, broader community debate over the implications of meta-regulation attempted to exploit the fluidity of the distinction between social citizenship and market infrastructure and thus indicate the malleability of the political implications of meta-regulation. The debate showed that the vision of market liberalism typically implied by the public choice perspective is not the only interpretation of the cultural and political meaning of meta-regulation. Nor is the 'traditional welfare state' the only alternative. Instead, two hybrid versions of tempered market liberalism emerged. Both sought to secure a compromise between market infrastructure and social citizenship goals, and in so doing, blur the boundaries between those categories of regulation.

The community morality (CM) perspective was supported broadly by church groups and by producer groups, especially local-level ones with comparatively fewer resources. It potentially posed a more comprehensive challenge to the language of economic analysis, but provided few institutional avenues for implementing its vision. The differentiated consumer sovereignty (DCS) perspective was broadly supported by general consumer advocates and groups representing specific classes of consumers, as well as by national-level, comparatively well-resourced producer groups. It was much more adept at translating social citizenship goals into the language of economic discourse than the community morality perspective. Distrustful of both the state and of unfettered markets, it hinted at network structures monitored by independent agencies as an institutional solution to a compromise.

A more detailed contextualised sense of what these various interpretations of meta-regulation mean at the concrete policy level will emerge in Chapter Five in the course of a range of case studies. But the significance of meta-regulation is ultimately embedded in enduring institutional change, however much the implications of such change is muddied at the edges by fluid interpretive conflict at the implementation level. Thus before exploring the political malleability of meta-regulation (and its limits) at the level of implementation, the next chapter fleshes out in more detail the key routines and practices that give the culture of meta-regulation institutional solidity. The contours of those routines and practices, it will emerge, gain their institutional solidity by being understood in terms of an incipient legality.

Notes

[1] Majone (1989), *Evidence, Argument and Persuasion in the Policy Process*, Yale University Press, New Haven, Connecticut; Zedner (1995), 'In Pursuit of the Vernacular: Comparing Law and Order Discourse in Britain and Germany' *Social and Legal Studies* Vol. 4, pp.517 ff; Black (1996), 'Constitutionalizing Self-regulation' *Modern Law Review* Vol. 59, pp.24 ff; Black (1998), 'Talking About Regulation' *Public Law* Spring Vol., pp.77-105.

[2] Pildes and Sunstein (1995), 'Reinventing the Regulatory State' *University of Chicago Law Review* Vol., 62 pp.1-129.

[3] Hilmer, (2001), *Interview*, Morgan, p.2.

[4] Gutmann and Thompson (1996), *Democracy and Disagreement*, Belknap Press of Harvard University Press, Cambridge, Massachusetts; Giddens (1999), *The Third Way: the Renewal of Social Democracy*, Polity Press, Malden, Massachusetts.

[5] Pierson and Castles (2001), *Australian Antecedents of the Third Way*. Joint Sessions of the European Consortium for Political Research, Grenoble, available at http://www.essex.ac.uk/ecpr/jointsessions/grenoble/papers/ws11/piersoncastles.pdf

[6] Stigler (1971), 'The Theory of Economic Regulation' *Bell Journal of Economics and Management Science* Vol. 2, pp.1-21; Posner (1987), 'Adoption and Market Theory: the Regulation of the Market of Adoption' *Boston University Law Review* Vol. 67, pp.59-72.

[7] National Competition Council (2001), *Framework for the Third Tranche Assessment of Government's Progress with Implementing National Competition Policy and Related Reforms*, Ausinfo, Canberra, p.vi.

[8] The analogy with trade law reminds us that oversight of such issues can as easily be given to courts as to independent agencies. Indeed within the Australian polity, s92 of the constitution effectively installs a form of judicial meta-regulation in respect of inter-state trade barriers, by requiring that trade between the states be free. Just as the remit of regional trade law increasingly implicates core domestic regulatory policy choices by characterising them as indirect trade barriers (Weatherill (2000), 'New Strategies for Managing the EC's Internal Market' *Current Legal Problems* 53 595-619; Heritier (2001), *The Politics of Public Services in European Regulation*, Max-Planck-Projektgruppe Preprint No. 2001/1) and international trade law (McGinnis and Movsesian (2000), 'The World Trade Constitution' *Harvard Law Review* Vol. 114, pp.511-605), so too is the meta-regulation of National Competition Policy in part about discouraging local-level regulatory choice.

[9] Of course federal legislation is equally subject to the disciplines of the CPA meta-regulatory regime, and the fact that oversight is located in an independent national (rather than federal) agency reflects this.

10   McGinnis and Movsesian (2000), 'The World Trade Constitution' *Harvard Law Review* Vol. 114, pp.511-605.

11   Campbell and Halligan (1992), *Political Leadership in an Age of Constraint: the Australian Experience*, University of Pittsburgh Press, Pittsburgh, p.24.

12   Coghlan, Assistant Commissioner, Office of Regulation Review, Productivity Commission, Canberra (1997), *Interview*, Morgan. February 15 1997.

13   Office of Regulation Review (no date), *Guidelines for Identifying Priorities for Portfolio Review Programmes and Bodies to Undertake Reviews and Public Consultations*, p.3, emphasis added.

14   National Competition Council (2001), *Framework for the Third Tranche Assessment of Government's Progress with Implementing National Competition Policy and Related Reforms*, Ausinfo, Canberra.

15   Hilmer, (2001), *Interview*, Morgan, p.3.

16   Senior Official A, (1997), *Interview*, Morgan. February 15 1997; Senior Official F, (2001), *Interview*. Morgan, pp.2-3.

17   In the final analysis, the ultimate decision was always returned to political representatives in the Australian scheme, *provided they were willing to accept possible financial penalties as a result.*

18   Booth, Policy Analyst and Research Associate, Australian Chamber of Commerce and Industry (1997), *Interview*, Morgan. February 12 1997; Senior Official E, (1997), *Interview*, Morgan. February 12 1997; Bernauer, (2001), *Interview*, Morgan; Senior Offical D, (2001), *Interview*, Morgan; Senior Official D, (2001), *Interview*, Morgan.

19   Hilmer (1994), 'The Bases of Competition Policy', Paper given at a conference *Trade Practices: A New Regime in the Making*, Hotel Inter-Continental, Sydney, p.ix; clarification added.

20   Peltzman (1989), 'The Economic Theory of Regulation after a Decade of Deregulation', *Brookings Papers on Microeconomics*, pp.1-59.

21   Ogus (1994), *Regulation: Legal Form and Economic Theory*, Oxford University Press, Oxford.

22   Veljanovski (ed) (1991), *Regulators and the Market*, Institute of Economic Affairs, London; Spiller (1994), 'The Institutional Foundations of Regulatory Commitment' *Journal of Law, Economics and Organization* Vol. 10, pp. 201 ff; Majone (1995), *The Development of Social Regulation in the European Community: Policy Externalities, Transaction Costs, Motivational Factors*, European University Institute, Florence; Majone, (ed) (1996), *Regulating Europe*, European Public Policy Series, Routledge, London.

23   Deakin (1997), 'Private Law, Economic Rationality and the Regulatory State', in *The Classification of Obligations*, Birks (ed), Clarendon Press, Oxford.

24   Victorian Legislative Assembly (1995), *Hansard*, 11 October 1995, p.360.

25   Victorian Legislative Assembly (1995), *Hansard*, 11 October 1995, p.360.

26   Victorian Legislative Assembly (1995), *Hansard*, 11 October 1995, p.616.

27   Australian Legislative Assembly (1995), *Hansard*, 26 June 1995, p.1760.

28   Australian Legislative Assembly (1995), *Hansard*, 26 June 1995, pp.1772-1775.

29   *Sydney Morning Herald*, 12 April 1995, p.4.

30   Commonwealth Parliament of Australia (1995), *Submissions to Inquiry into Aspects of the National Competition Policy Reform Package*, House of Representatives Standing Committee on Banking, Finance and Public Administration, AGPS, Canberra (8 Volumes). Due to the very frequent reference to this inquiry, I shall reference quotations in the main text by shorthand – e.g. Inquiry 1995 v1:55 – rather

than providing full endnotes. Note that this inquiry and the one that followed failed to produce any significant policy change in National Competition Policy. Significant change was only secured in the intergovernmental negotiations of 2000, which followed a third enquiry I discuss in Chapter Six. The impact of the first inquiry was primarily bracketed by the change of government in 1996. Although the Committee held some further hearings before releasing their report, the change of government undermined confidence in the ultimate power of the Committee's recommendations to secure any changes.

[31] Picciotto (1997), 'Fragmented States and International Rules of Law', *Social and Legal Studies*, Vol. 6, p.261.

[32] Booth, Policy Analyst and Research Associate, Australian Chamber of Commerce and Industry (1997), *Interview*, Morgan. February 12 1997; Senior Official E, (1997), *Interview*, Morgan. February 12 1997.

[33] Australian Chamber of Commerce and Industry (1992), *Liberating Enterprise to Improve Competitiveness*, unpublished report obtained by author in interview with Booth, 1997, p.27.

[34] Australian Chamber of Commerce and Industry (1996), *Changing the Onus for Regulation*, p.4.

[35] Public Interest Roundtable (1997), *National Competition Policy – Legislation Review: The Reality of Hilmer and Implications for the Public Interest*, Notes on speakers taken by the author who was present.

[36] Australian Chamber of Commerce and Industry (1996), *Changing the Onus for Regulation*, p.28.

[37] Victorian Government (1995), *Guidelines for the Application of the Competition Test to New Legislative Proposals*, Melbourne, pp.32-33; Public Interest Roundtable (1997), *National Competition Policy – Legislation Review: The Reality of Hilmer and Implications for the Public Interest*, Notes on speakers taken by the author who was present.

[38] Australian Chamber of Commerce and Industry (1996), *Changing the Onus for Regulation*, p.8.

[39] de Cavalho (1996), *Competitive Care: Understanding the Implications of National Competition Policy and the COAG Agenda for the Community Services Sector*, Australian Catholic Social Welfare Commission, Canberra, p.48.

[40] Johnston (1995), 'Riding the Wild Surf: Participatory Implementation of Competition Policy in New South Wales', Paper presented at Conference *What Price Competition Policy?*, University of New South Wales, Sydney, p.14.

[41] de Cavalho (1996), *Competitive Care: Understanding the Implications of National Competition Policy and the COAG Agenda for the Community Services Sector*, Australian Catholic Social Welfare Commission, Canberra.

[42] de Cavalho (1996), *Competitive Care: Understanding the Implications of National Competition Policy and the COAG Agenda for the Community Services Sector*, Australian Catholic Social Welfare Commission, Canberra, p.i.

[43] de Cavalho (1996), *Competitive Care: Understanding the Implications of National Competition Policy and the COAG Agenda for the Community Services Sector*, Australian Catholic Social Welfare Commission, Canberra, p.55.

[44] de Cavalho (1996), *Competitive Care: Understanding the Implications of National Competition Policy and the COAG Agenda for the Community Services Sector*, Australian Catholic Social Welfare Commission, Canberra, p.51.

[45] de Cavalho (1996), *Competitive Care: Understanding the Implications of National Competition Policy and the COAG Agenda for the Community Services Sector*,

Australian Catholic Social Welfare Commission, Canberra, p.33.

[46] de Cavalho (1996), *Competitive Care: Understanding the Implications of National Competition Policy and the COAG Agenda for the Community Services Sector*, Australian Catholic Social Welfare Commission, Canberra, p.45.

[47] de Cavalho (1996), *Competitive Care: Understanding the Implications of National Competition Policy and the COAG Agenda for the Community Services Sector*, Australian Catholic Social Welfare Commission, Canberra, p.45.

[48] de Cavalho (1996), *Competitive Care: Understanding the Implications of National Competition Policy and the COAG Agenda for the Community Services Sector*, Australian Catholic Social Welfare Commission, Canberra, p.47.

[49] de Cavalho (1996), *Competitive Care: Understanding the Implications of National Competition Policy and the COAG Agenda for the Community Services Sector*, Australian Catholic Social Welfare Commission, Canberra, p.47.

[50] Prosser (1994), 'Privatization, Regulation and Public Services' *Juridical Review* Vol. 3, pp.3-17.

[51] de Cavalho (1996), *Competitive Care: Understanding the Implications of National Competition Policy and the COAG Agenda for the Community Services Sector*, Australian Catholic Social Welfare Commission, Canberra, p.46.

[52] de Cavalho (1996), *Competitive Care: Understanding the Implications of National Competition Policy and the COAG Agenda for the Community Services Sector*, Australian Catholic Social Welfare Commission, Canberra, p.52.

[53] Regarding this, see Senate Legal and Constitutional References Committee (1996), *National Well-being: A System of National Citizenship Indicators and Benchmarks*, Commonwealth Parliament of Australia, Canberra.

[54] de Cavalho (1996), *Competitive Care: Understanding the Implications of National Competition Policy and the COAG Agenda for the Community Services Sector*, Australian Catholic Social Welfare Commission, Canberra, p.61.

[55] de Cavalho (1996), *Competitive Care: Understanding the Implications of National Competition Policy and the COAG Agenda for the Community Services Sector*, Australian Catholic Social Welfare Commission, Canberra, p.46.

[56] de Cavalho (1996), *Competitive Care: Understanding the Implications of National Competition Policy and the COAG Agenda for the Community Services Sector*, Australian Catholic Social Welfare Commission, Canberra, p.47.

[57] Sax (1992), 'The Constitutional Dimensions of Property: A Debate' *Loyola of Los Angeles Law Review* Vol. 26, pp.23-37; Aman (1998), 'The Globalizing State: A Future-oriented Perspective on the Public/Private Distinction, Federalism, and Democracy', *Vanderbilt Journal of Transnational Law*, Vol. 31, pp.769-870; Wilhelmsson and Hurri (eds) (1999), *From Dissonance to Sense: Welfare State Expectations, Privatisation and Private Law*, Ashgate Publishing, Aldershot, England.

[58] Moore, Director of New South Wales Council on Social Services (NCOSS) (1997), *Interview*, Morgan. February 20 1997.

4 Agenda-setting and Bureaucratic Politics

The initial responses to meta-regulation at community-political level that have just been explored in Chapter Three did not have a significant practical impact on setting the *initial* shape of the reform agenda. The real power, particularly initially, lay in the technical-bureaucratic facets of implementing the reform package. This chapter details the institutional context, routines, practices and choices of the network of central agency officials who were key to the implementation process.[1] Consistently with the public choice perspective animating the reform package in Australia, the meta-regulatory institutions themselves were designed to be relatively insulated from democratic politics, reflecting anxiety that democratic politics are too likely to engender factionalism when operating in closed arenas. This independence accorded interpretive power to a network of economically qualified central agency officials. However the institutional autonomy of this network was only relative: politics did still play a role, both intended and unintended.

The first part of this chapter fills out the *institutional* shape of the network. It highlights three shared, relatively stable features of the overall institutional configuration, which together buttress the general argument that meta-regulation is an incipient form of non-judicial legality. The three features are: insulation from politics; the practice of 'taking words seriously'; and an emphasis on formal, neutral expertise. The chapter also, however, brings out variability, focusing particularly on the degree to which different jurisdictions drew a line between political and technical input into the process of setting the reform agenda under meta-regulation. Further implications of this variability emerge in the second half of the chapter, where the relative stability of institutional configurations is contrasted with the slippage in the actual practice of agenda-setting.

This second half compares the shapes of the agendas set by three of the seven participating governments, governed under different political colours. The juxtaposition highlights the malleability of meta-regulation, by identifying various difficulties in applying a 'market lens' to the entire policy spectrum of governmental activity. These difficulties stem in part from the conceptual problem that some government legislation can be seen as *constituting* either state or market, rather than as facilitating or distorting, as the case may be, an already existing market. In addition, in this second section, it will become evident that the messy operation of raw political interest cuts across principled agenda-setting, further intensifying malleability, though this time in contingent, unpredictable ways.

Institutional Configurations

The broad framework of the NCP intergovernmental compacts left implementation issues very widely drawn. In relation to the meta-regulation regime specifically, the Competition Principles Agreement (CPA) specified only the required outcome and the bare outlines of the review process, including deadlines and compliance incentives, leaving the institutional support and specific techniques to the discretion of the various jurisdictions.

Clause 5 of the CPA stated:

> The guiding principle is that legislation (including Acts, enactments, Ordinances or regulations) should not restrict competition unless it can be demonstrated that:
> a) the benefits of the restriction to the community as a whole outweigh the costs; and
> b)the objectives of the legislation can only be achieved by restricting competition.

To comply with this principle, each jurisdiction had to review the entire stock of its legislation by the year 2000, and – if full review applied – to positively document the evidence that would justify the continuance of that legislation. The same principle guided the enactment of new legislation. Compliance oversight would be carried out by the National Competition Council and included a requirement that each jurisdiction publish annual compliance reports. Beyond this, however, the CPA did not give any further guidance on the specifics of legislative reform; indeed it insisted that "each Party is free to determine its own agenda for the reform of legislation that restricts competition".

In pursuit, therefore, of a legislative agenda that would minimally impact competition, the several state governments together with the federal government set about building institutions and designing routines that would embed the 'guiding principle' into regulatory policy choice. In what follows, I want initially to highlight three shared, relatively stable features of the overall institutional configuration: insulation from politics, the practice of 'taking words seriously' and an emphasis on formal, neutral expertise. Together these features buttress the general argument that meta-regulation is an incipient form of non-judicial legality. In exploring them, I compare the institutional configurations established by three of the seven participating governments: the federal (Commonwealth) government and the states of New South Wales and Victoria. The choice of these three jurisdictions allows comparison across the three most well-resourced and populous jurisdictions of Australia under useful conditions of contrasting political control. The federal government was under the auspices of Labour for half the initial agenda-setting period, but then switched in March 1996 to a right-wing Coalition government which continues in power to date. New South Wales was governed by a minority Labour government which had just come into power and was deeply split internally about the wisdom of the reform package as a whole. Victoria was governed by a right-wing Coalition government which had a large stable majority in power when the reforms were established, but has been governed by Labour again since late 1999.

Insulation from Politics

Each of these three jurisdictions allocated authority to oversee the legislative review process within its central bureaucratic units. In contrasting ways, each sought to ensure that both political input and technical expertise guided the agenda-setting process for pro-competitive legislative review. While on the one hand a separation from politics was a crucial facet of the rationale offered for the reform package as a whole, at the same time a bridge back to politics was essential if the reforms were to 'bite'. Overall, what is characteristic of the institutional configuration was the emergence of a politically insulated network of central agency officials. Within the network, however, internal variation can be observed. The federal government configuration, as well as national coordination of oversight, tended to separate political and technical guidance institutionally; Victoria and New South Wales on the other hand blurred the two functions in the same group of officials. Another axis of variation saw left-wing governments generally less inclined to insulate their meta-regulatory officials from direct political influence or direct community input, as well as more likely to decentralise to some extent central control of the agenda-setting process.

Federal Government Institutions

In the federal government, technical and political input were separated. The technical actors most important to the process and outcome of the agenda-setting process at the federal level were the bureaucrats who staffed the Office of Regulation Review (ORR). In the initial agenda-setting stage when Labour was still in power, technical input was supplemented by political-community input through the formal channel of a Council on Business Regulation, which coordinated with ORR at key points.

The ORR is located in the independent statutory body now known as the Productivity Commission. The Productivity Commission, set up to promote micro-economic reform, has considerable insulation from the political process. Three particularly important facets of this are the statutory basis for the agency's powers, the five year tenure of the Chairman (election cycles are every three years) and the ability to publish sensitive policy recommendations, inquiries and reports without government clearance.

ORR not only enjoys insulation from politics, but also relatively generous resource support. The Office employs fifteen professional economists and one lawyer. The legislative review component of Competition Policy was not its sole responsibility, but forms one part of a broader objective of promoting 'quality regulation' in federal lawmaking procedures.

From the initial introduction in 1984 of regulatory impact analysis statements under the earlier weak federal version of the RIA regimes (discussed in Chapter Two) through to the early stages of CPA legislative review, ORR performed its task through dialogue, advice and recommendations, all of which occurred in closed confidential channels between departments and ORR.[2] In 1997, however, as a result of the recently-elected conservative Coalition government's inquiry into regulatory issues affecting small business, ORR acquired a more formal power to leverage its influence. Departments were required to attach 'coordination comments' from ORR to their legislative proposals, and ORR gained a reporting line to the Assistant Treasurer in relation to this, giving the office a formal channel – located in a powerful central political department – to ensure that its standards of regulatory quality were observed.[3] While this bridge back to political influence was helpful to

ORR's overall impact, it still preferred to maintain an image of "neutral independent consultant", as apolitical as possible.[4]

The Council on Business Regulation (CBR) was an advisory body, broadly corporatist in structure, whose recommendations fed into the agenda-setting process at the highest bureaucratic level. Its members were personally appointed by the Keating Labour government in order to assist it with determining the priorities of the CPA legislative review programme. The deliberations of the Council were not open to the public.[5] The CBR had eight members – three representing various business interests (small business,[6] big business,[7] professional services),[8] one representing farming interests, one representing the consumer lobby, one environmental representative, one labour representative and one from the social welfare lobby. This more or less mirrored the set of established interests who had, over the years, won a place at the bargaining table in Australian politics.

CBR advice fed into the agenda-setting process at the penultimate level: that is, immediately prior to the final political confirmation of the review agenda by Ministers. Between November 1995 and April 1996, CBR met three times with ORR staff (who acted as secretariat and prepared sample recommendation lists) in order to finalise recommendations on legislative review for feeding into the political decision-making process. In March 1996, the government changed hands after an election, and the incoming conservative government refused to call any meetings of the CBR before the June 1996 deadline for agenda-setting expired.[9] As a result, the final input of politicians was unassisted by the community representation Labour had sought to achieve through the mechanism of the CBR. The Coalition government also fast-tracked the final political approval procedures: instead of submitting each departmental schedule to individual portfolio Ministers, all the final coordination was channelled through Treasury and the Structural Adjustment Committee of Cabinet, a powerful committee prominent in micro-economic policy issues, for final political endorsement.[10] Thus the change from a left to a right wing government increased ORR's formal powers, decreased avenues for transparency and community consultation, and centralised final political decision-making in respect of the agenda for pro-competitive legislative reform.

State Government Institutions

While the two major states differed in their institutional choices to an extent, they both shared, relative to the federal government, a preference for retaining more direct political control over the agenda-setting stage and subsequent oversight. This was reflected in the governmental location of NCP officials as well as in an absence of separation between political and technical aspects of oversight. It also appeared to fluctuate slightly depending on the political party in power at the time.

Victoria established a Competition Policy Task Force under the auspices of the right-wing Kennett government in the Department of Premier and Cabinet. This task force coordinated the agenda-setting process in the early years of National Competition Policy, assisted by a Legislative Review Working Group made up of representatives from a cross-section of departmental portfolios. This location reflected the considerable central political will supporting implementation of the reform package in this government, as well as a personal enthusiasm for the tenets of the reform package on the part of the Premier.[11] Once the agenda-setting stage had passed, ongoing oversight moved to the Treasury, where a National Competition Policy Unit with a staff of between three or four economists took over the responsibility. Since the Labour government's election in 1999, the NCP unit became part of the Economic, Regulatory and Social Policy Branch of Treasury, reflecting a desire on the part of the new government to broaden oversight responsibility beyond the narrow remit of purely economic concerns.[12] Staffing levels remained stable.

In terms of formal influence, signed consent by the NCP Unit had to be obtained on reviews carried out under the Competition Principles Agreement at three separate stages: when terms of reference were set and a review team constituted, when a draft report came in, and when final recommendations were made. In giving or refusing such consent, the Unit referred to detailed centrally approved guidelines that each department had to comply with. The Unit therefore retained considerable policy control at the same time as it performed the gate-keeping function of ensuring technical compliance with meta-regulation. The location in Treasury, where economic rationality tended to dominate, made this melding of political calculus and technical expertise relatively easy to achieve. Under the right-wing government, this melding saw individual reviews structured with greater inputs from expertise and insulation from politics – using arms-length economically qualified consultants in independent review structures for the most part.[13] However this emphasis shifted as soon as Labour regained power, to a focus on returning the carriage of legislative reviews to Ministerial and departmental control, subject only to a more 'checklist rationality' oversight function by the NCP unit in Treasury.

New South Wales, under a minority Labour government, chose to retain relatively greater political input into the agenda-setting and oversight process, and secured this with a relatively decentralised institutional configuration. The government created a small unit named the Regulatory Review and Intergovernmental Affairs Unit based in the core whole-of-government department, the Cabinet Office, and reporting directly to the

Premier. As part of the Cabinet Office with this direct line to final political decisions, the Unit had considerable power influence to annotate and thus influence review recommendations. The Unit, like that in Victoria, had between three and four staff, all economists. Unlike Victoria, however, these individuals were also responsible for coordinating intergovernmental affairs on a range of policy fronts, as well as general regulatory reform issues extending beyond National Competition Policy. They were consequently under-resourced, a situation widely recognised in the network of officials at the core of National Competition Policy.[14] They compensated for this by decentralising the carriage of reviews to a large extent, allowing departments and their relevant Ministers to make initial agenda-setting choices without the constraint of centrally set guidelines, and to have final decisions on the constitution of review teams. The senior officials in New South Wales emphasised their role as facilitator of a change in bureaucratic culture from the inside, rather than as a policing gatekeeper of externally imposed criteria.[15] Consequently, and in contrast to those cleaving more closely to the public choice intellectual underpinnings of the reforms, they did not place as much weight on 'independence from politics' (meaning, usually, Ministers and the stakeholders exerting influence through Ministers).

Notwithstanding the political *location* and *structure* of NCP institutions at state level, officials in both states emphasised that the policy *content* of the reform package was dominated by 'neutral expertise'. By this they meant that as far as the role of their units was concerned, political input did not extend to making decisions on outcomes, but only to enforcing a particular approach to policymaking.[16] That approach is one that justifies regulatory policy choices in terms of positively documented market failures and in the opinion of the senior officials of the key policy network, was an approach that left room for the retention of regulatory interventions that were in some way a constraint on competition. The extent to which such regulatory policy choice did remain genuinely open to state-level governments implementing National Competition Policy was, however, significantly influenced by the national-level institutional configuration overseeing the reform package as a whole.

National Institutions

At the national level, political and technical input was, as with the federal government, institutionalised separately rather than merging the two functions within a single political unit. Instead, the National Competition Council as a statutory independent agency took the primary responsibility for technical oversight of compliance, while COAG, the federal network of senior government representatives advised by a secretariat of senior bureaucrats (the Committee on Regulatory Reform), drove policy direction.

While COAG was responsible for setting overall policy direction and the forward work programme of NCC, the implementation of the meta-regulatory regime of legislative review, fell very largely to the remit of NCC's day-to-day routines.[17] And as the overall oversight institution, NCC's institutional independence from politics was important to the development of meta-regulation in ways that foreshadow incipient legality.

The NCC is an independent agency made up of five private sector appointees from business backgrounds and supported by 20-23 staff, most of whom are economists but some of whom are lawyers. The council is appointed for a three year term, by vote of all the states and territories, from a list approved by the (non-voting) federal government – it thus represents a 'national' perspective. Many of the inaugural staff were seconded from the federal Treasury and the Productivity Commission. The inaugural Council members were from academia, law, accounting, mining and investment banking, but more recently a representative from the social welfare sector was added, as public backlash to the reform package grew.

The NCC makes annual assessments of the rate of progress of each jurisdiction in legislation review, and evaluates the justifications advanced by each state for retaining their regulatory programmes. The payment of the annual substantial 'tranches' of money to the states (the competition payments, AUS$16 billion over the first five years and recently extended) is dependent upon this assessment of the NCC. Although the Commonwealth Treasurer formally authorises the payment or non-payment of the competition payments, the NCC makes the final recommendation, in practice dispositive, as to whether any financial penalties for unsatisfactory compliance are to be levied.

NCC became a crucial node for the network of central agency officials who would, through iterated dialogue and 'technical cooperation' over the next five years, build up a fund of interpretative consensus regarding the implementation of meta-regulation.

Despite the variations in the level of insulation from politics described above, NCC's relatively strong insulation combined with its fiscal enforcement powers cast an insulating shadow over the remainder of the network, at least at the level of day-to-day operating principles. Even where NCP units were part of political decision-making environments, as with the states, the professional orientation of their staff members as economists facilitated "common understandings, good relationships and a general consensus on the main aims [of National Competition Policy]".[18] These shared commitments had space to operate relatively autonomously of the political pressures placed on the state NCP oversight decision-makers due to the triangulating impact of NCC on the incentive structure. Because the 'external, independent' judgment of the politically insulated NCC would impact the state budget, the NCP units could insist on holding departments and politicians to courses of actions that they might otherwise resist.

Taking Words Seriously

Complementing this shared feature of relative insulation from direct political pressure, the network of central agency officials shared a distinctive interpretive stance to the intergovernmental agreements that formed the basis of the reform package. That stance was one of 'taking words seriously', as one of the officials commented.[19] Indeed, another official commented that at times the text of the intergovernmental agreements seemed to have acquired the status of the being the object of quasi-biblical exegesis.[20] A particularly important development that illustrates the interpretive stance of taking words seriously was the notion that the agreements created a 'burden of proof' *against* regulatory intervention. The emphasis on this illustrates the hybrid nature of the intergovernmental compacts as something neither strictly legal[21] nor 'merely' political. Senior officials commented on the way in which building bureaucratic compliance around highly specific reliance on the meaning of particular phrases, in the context of the shared professional norms of the key officials, was an important technique for securing the kind of insulation from direct political influence I have been emphasising as constitutive of 'incipient legality'.[22]

The key words that bore the brunt of this interpretive seriousness were those in Clause 5 of the Competition Principles Agreement which laid down the "guiding principle" for the meta-regulatory regime. Clause 5 stated:

> The guiding principle is that legislation (including Acts, enactments, Ordinances or regulations) should not restrict competition unless it can be demonstrated that:
> a) the benefits of the restriction to the community as a whole outweigh the costs; and
> b) the objectives of the legislation can only be achieved by restricting competition.

The interpretive stance of the network of key central agency officials often elided a key tension. On the one hand, they emphasised that this principle had no substantive import but rather imposed a formal rationality on regulatory policymaking decisions. They frequently insisted that fleshing out this guiding principle did not dictate any particular outcome, but merely provided a set of general rules that would improve the quality of regulatory decision-making. As one official argued, "At its heart, the NCP programme is not about economic rationalism gone mad, but about a culture of transparency and reasoned justification in economic policy".[23]

At the same time, however, this due process emphasis contains a sting in the tail, which emerges clearly in the comments of key officials' interviews. Its purpose is to create a presumption that works against a decision to intervene politically into the economy, especially via command-and-control regulation. The general rules of meta-regulation may not *preclude* a decision to regulate, but they *are* intended to discourage it.

For example, the National Competition Council insisted in all of its documentation that under Clause 5, unless actual empirical evidence was provided in support of government intervention, the *presumption* would be against government intervention.[24] In theory, a final decision not to intervene would still require governments to consider the social citizenship facets of regulation listed in the hard-won 'public interest interpretation clause', Clause 1(3). But while the NCC paid lipservice to this clause, its modus operandi undermined its salience by treating the public interest factors as 'add-ons' to the core economic analysis of market failure. This approach constructed NCC oversight as concerned with the market infrastructural facet of regulation, while state governments would deal with the 'soft' public interest justifications.[25]

Since NCC, with its fiscal incentive of the competition payments, had much more enforcing power than the state government units, this in practice gave priority to economic analysis of justifiable regulation in terms of market infrastructure. So for example, NCC stated that "where the net benefit to the community from a [pro-competitive] reform measure is clear, the NCC does not see a requirement for governments to conduct a formal assessment of the public interest in terms of subclause 1(3)".[26] Moreover, leaked correspondence from the union movement (Inquiry 1995, v6:797-818) showed NCC's blunt hostility to the public interest interpretation clause, which it considered subverted the overall goals of National Competition Policy:

> The rationale underlying the competition policy agreements is the presumption that enhancing competition is generally in the public interest. As a consequence, the Council does not see a requirement for a government to formally examine the matters in clause 1(3)of the Competition Principles Agreement on every occasion that it implements reform (Inquiry 1995, v6:817).

Of course, the substantive stance of NCC on the balance between social citizenship facets and market infrastructure facets is really only properly visible in individual decisions, some of which will be explored in the next chapter. But it is clear enough from their general approach that they did not view meta-regulation in 'checklist rationality' terms. 'Inadequate progress', they insisted, might flow from "a series of flawed processes *or inadequate reform outcomes*".[27] Despite the NCC's insistence that "there may be a variety of outcomes which satisfy the requirement for adequate progress in relation to the CPA...[and that] in some areas jurisdictions are required to judge for themselves whether particular reform outcomes satisfy the spirit and intent of the NCP programme",[28] the NCC essentially regarded its job as assessing whether there is a 'rational basis' for the final outcome of review – a significantly more substantive approach than that of 'checklist rationality'.

The other members of the network of central agency officials also followed this pro-market substantive leaning in their interpretation of the 'guiding principle' of the legislative review programme. In the federal government, ORR personnel were strongly committed to the notion that the most important facet of the CPA reforms involved their challenge to the status quo through the establishment of a burden of proof that militated in favour of change.[29] Absent an 'adequate' case in favour of regulatory intervention, deregulation would be the presumptive solution. While 'adequacy' would be a standard that would incorporate 'public interest' facets such as those listed in Clause 1(3), ORR was in practice careful not to define adequacy with any precision, a tactic that made it easier to ratchet up the standard of adequate analysis from year to year.[30] While higher standards may just involve more comprehensively reasoned cases, ORR in some unpublished guidelines suggested it took a more substantive view of the matter, recommending that public inquiry and consultation should take place *"except if it should be likely to hinder reform"*.[31]

State government officials were a little more circumspect on this particular matter, perhaps no accident in view of their lower level of political insulation. The Victorian senior officials considered that at least early on in the reform process there had been a substantive skew in favour of competitive efficiency as a justification that weighed, in practice, more heavily than 'softer' dimensions of the public interest. Interestingly, they confirmed the influence of NCC's 'shadow' in this regard, suggesting that the state NCP unit itself may well have taken a looser view of the justification threshold, but it was held to a stricter view by the oversight presence of NCC.[32]

The officials in New South Wales, the least politically insulated of all those in the network, showed least indication of giving a substantive spin to the onus of proof encoded in the guiding principles. They emphasised instead a delegated, incremental approach which left the drawing of the justificatory threshold up to the relevant Minister or department, and did so in the absence of centrally produced guidelines or documentation.[33] While they encouraged the disaggregation of efficiency issues from 'softer' public interest dimensions in regulatory policy choice, they made a point of emphasising the open-endedness of final decisions on appropriate trade-offs. Thus of all the nodes in this network of officials, New South Wales was the one that most blurred the line between technical and political interpretive stances, arguably pulling meta-regulation closer back to 'politics as usual' in the process.

Neutral Expertise

The interpretive stance that taking Clause 5 seriously created a burden of proof against government intervention, was one buttressed by the expert discourse uniting the network of officials. The influence of this expertise was disseminated throughout departments and the rest of the bureaucracy by means of documents produced as 'interpretive guidance' for implementing National Competition Policy. For example, Victoria produced a centrally approved document[34] early on in the agenda-setting process and fleshed it out with a detailed template for regulatory analysis provided by independent consultants at a later stage later in the enforcement process.[35] New South Wales, while giving minimal guidance at first, later piggybacked on the CIE guidelines produced by Victoria. The ORR developed its own guidelines, and further guidelines were produced in the national arena for coordinating the review of professional services.[36]

These guidelines, all very similar in their basic conceptual approach, were in time relied upon by all the central agency NCP units overseeing the meta-regulatory regime. They articulate a conceptual template, drawn directly from neoclassical economics and thus reflecting their shared professional commitments, that acts as the background constraint for decision-making on regulatory policy choices. Victoria, for example, stated in its instruction manual:

> Each of the steps [taken in assessing legislation to determine if it comes within the review agenda] involve the application of economic concepts. It would therefore be advisable when assessing compliance with this guideline to obtain suitable economic advice. Such advice may be obtained from internal departmental resources, specialist bodies such as the Office of Regulation Reform (ORR) or economic consultants with expertise in microeconomic reform.[37]

Though more details will be given in the breakdown of agenda-setting patterns that follows in the next section, central agency guidelines all shared certain key features. They all focused on requiring policy makers to think in terms of market competition as the first option for solving social problems. Government intervention of any sort required a threshold justification, a justification that had to be framed in precise terms of addressing a market failure, and only if the failure was of significant magnitude. Further more, redressing the failure should only involve government intervention if absolutely necessary. "A command-and-control regulatory approach should be the last option. Economically they are the least efficient and may impose significant costs on the community".[38] Or, as the Victorian guidelines insisted, "market failure is a necessary but not sufficient ground for government intervention".[39] That is, *government* failure had to be disproved as well as market failure proved. As can be seen, the analytical template routinises the substantive burden of proof to which this network of officials was broadly committed.

Another shared feature of the conceptual templates provided to guide bureaucrats in implementing the reform process was an emphasis on transparent justification rather than sophisticated cost-benefit modelling of precise quantitative costs, even where that is feasible. Indeed, unfeasibility of full quantification, particularly of benefits, is readily conceded in these central guidelines. The overall approach simplified the assumptions of economic expertise and encouraged an open-textured, pragmatic approach to the application of this analytical framework. As one official said:

> We want departments to think about the objective of regulation in terms of market failure, to think through the problem from an economic perspective rather than from a heavily quantitative basis. Questions like 'what is the market failure justification? Or what is the legitimate social policy objective?' are more important than numbers, costs or benefits. [40]

Expert discourse used in this pragmatic fashion is another important bridge between technical reason and political will, that keystone of effective implementation. Its open-texturedness, however, is also key to the slippages that result in the actual day-to-day application of this conceptual template. The template underpinning the reforms, while it did not of itself require more competition *per se*, did focus attention on government in terms that required it to be classified in an either/or fashion as a restriction on competition. But political malleability and interpretive fluidity characterised the actual working through of this task, flowing in part from the pragmatic, open-textured manner in which officials sought to apply the framework of expertise and in part from the internal variation in institutional design within this network of central agency officials. The result was a mosaic of different state and federal agendas that the next part of this chapter explores.

'Market Spectacles' and Three Patterns of Agenda-Setting

Agenda-setting was the first practical step in the implementation of meta-regulation. In June 1996, in compliance with the first obligation under the intergovernmental Competition Principles Agreement (CPA), each Australian jurisdiction was required to publish a reform agenda: a list of those statutes and regulations that would be reviewed under the CPA, along with a timetable and an indication of relative priority. This involved a decision-making process, primarily carried out by the network of central agency officials described above, that reviewed the entire corpus of existing Australian government legislation at both state and federal levels, with the aim of making a prima facie assessment of whether it unjustifiably restricted competition. Such an assessment meant that decision-makers had to view government legislation through 'market spectacles', even if only to exempt that legislation from the reform agenda.

Just as judicial rationality in court proceedings codes political choices as either legal or illegal, so economic rationality in meta-regulation codes regulatory policy choice as justifiable or unjustifiable. In so doing it must draw lines, just as law draws lines. The lines drawn by setting the agenda are analogous to the line drawn by courts between justiciable and non-justiciable issues. In exploring the patterns emerging from such agenda-setting, the question arises as to whether a threshold of justifiable regulation can be clearly observed.

The overall answer to this in the Australian case is that although some general patterns can be observed, the threshold was both malleable, and also difficult to identify due to its dependence on unstated, taken-for-granted assumptions.

The malleability emerges from several sources. At times it seemed to flow from strategic interest group politics, the very kind of 'special interest lobbying' which the public choice perspective seeks to eliminate from regulatory policy decision-making. At other times the agenda was shaped by broad political considerations peripheral to the reform objectives of National Competition Policy but still of general public significance. Finally, even when the decisions were based on good faith attempts to apply neutrally the technical conceptual framework drawn from economics, some key, typically unstated, assumptions in this task led to conceptual diffuseness and unpredictability.

Before documenting the actual patterns of agenda-setting, a few more words about this conceptual slipperiness are merited. The reform agenda applies to any legislation that restricts competition. In a literal sense, all legislation could be said to restrict competition, insofar as it expresses a collective political choice in the form of a binding general rule, thus mandating limits to individual unrestricted choices. But this would be to take the notion of 'competition' to an unduly abstract level. Indeed, some of the major proponents of the reforms had not envisaged that they would ever extend to social programmes[41] and in practice, the agenda-setting process aimed to constrain the scope of reform more narrowly. However, because the intergovernmental agreements applied entirely generally (due to the political sensitivity involved in any explicit exceptions), agenda-setting thus required regulation to be characterised as relevant or not relevant to competition.

However, there is no obvious answer to the question of when regulation entails encroachment on a market or not. Consequently unstated, taken-for-granted assumptions permeate and shape the agenda decisions: in particular, assumptions regarding when government legislation is assumed to be constitutive of either state or market in the first place, rather than restrictive of competition. As we shall see in tracing three different reform agendas under governments of three different political colouring and stability, the characterisation of a piece of legislation depends on usually unstated boundary assumptions about the legitimate scope of market governance. For example, adoption can be characterised as a market for babies[42] but that does not necessarily mean that policymakers will want to treat adoption as a competitive market that should presumptively remain unrestricted. Thus in practice, the threshold between legislation subject to the pro-competitive reform agenda and legislation which is not 'market-relevant' at all is an unstable one.

The threshold becomes particularly fluid when mixed regulatory objectives exist. While the public choice perspective favoured by the network of central agency officials seeks to draw a bright-line distinction between forms of regulation that pursue competitive market efficiency on the one hand and those that pursue social justice values on the other hand, many forms of regulation are in practice hybrid in their aims. This leads, as we shall see, to variability in the scope of agendas in different jurisdictions. Despite this variability it is also possible to identify a rough sense of a 'core' conception of regulation regarded as *not* relevant to competition and markets. That core, at its smallest, consisted of legislation that constituted the very institutions of the state itself. Much more variable was the scope of the 'reform-proof' zone, especially whether or not it extended to social welfare and cultural functions carried out historically by the state, but not necessarily intrinsic to its identity as state. Speaking very broadly, conservative governments tended to expand the threshold of competition-relevant regulation more readily than Labour governments, incorporating cultural policy, welfare policy, and some of the broader 'social' types of police powers into the lens of meta-regulatory reform.

Federal Government

Agenda-setting in the federal government began in late April 1995, when each department was required to draw up a schedule of all the legislation (including regulations, or secondary legislation) which it administered and then divide that into three categories. These categories were: legislation outside the scope of the review agenda altogether (*excluded* legislation), legislation within the scope of the agenda but *exempted* from its application, and legislation subject to review. The difference between exemption and exclusion is essentially the difference between technical reasons for not reviewing a programme and policy-based reasons for not reviewing it. Exemption required the department to demonstrate that the legislation had either been recently or currently under review, or that it was not cost-effective to review it. Exclusion required a substantive argument that the terms of CPA review were not relevant to the legislation; i.e. that it simply did not fall within the purview of 'market spectacles'.

The drawing up of departmental schedules was coordinated with the ORR, whose staff continually reviewed them and discussed them with departmental executives. The ORR did the major analytical work fleshing out the review trigger i.e. the question of whether particular legislation "restricted competition". ORR briefing documents to all departments and the CBR targeted as any regulation which directly or indirectly governed the entry and exit of firms or individuals into or out of markets, controlled prices or production levels, restricted the quality level or location of goods and services available, restricted advertising and promotional activities, restricted price or type of inputs used in the production process.[43] This definition incorporated a 'boundary assumption' about what areas of social life were appropriately treated as markets, goods or services, or production processes.

It is boundary assumptions that define the outermost threshold of meta-regulation, and which reveal the most about the extent to which policy-making is dominated by an economic rationality. It is only occasionally that they emerged as self-consciously contested areas. For the most part, those boundaries were either taken-for-granted or constructed in a quiet, unnoticed way by the routinised activity of departmental classification.

Setting the agenda was part of this classification activity and involved making choices about what was viewed as a restriction on competition and what was not. Since exemptions (as opposed to exclusions) were based either on redundancy or expense considerations, it is exclusions that are more interesting for tracing the boundaries of economic rationality in conceptions of regulatory policy.

For the most part, ORR took a cross-sector stand that stressed above all the need to rethink fundamentally whether regulation or political intervention was in any particular case *necessary at all*. In other words, ORR wished precisely to unsettle boundary assumptions. This general approach put ORR into a fairly conflictual relationship with departments. Most departments (Treasury being the main exception) viewed the CPA regime in terms of the most recent analogous precedent in their experience.[44] In the federal context, that precedent was not so much the weak RIA regime, whose scope was very narrow, but a set of programme reviews that occurred as part of the 'new managerialism' described in Chapter Two. These reviews had not sought to question the general policy direction and even the mechanisms of implementation of target programmes, but rather analysed efficiency and value-for-money within that status quo framework. Departmental perspectives therefore tended to follow this approach, while the ORR insisted on its stand of 'onus of proof against the status quo'.[45] The latter stand had much more potential to bite into basic policy commitments, and was therefore contentious.

The outlines of this contentious process can be perceived through the process whereby in the early agenda-setting stage, the ORR's technical support for departmental agenda-setting became a powerful hinge shaping the decisions of the community representative mechanism of the Council on Business Regulation. The CBR-ORR dialogue provides an illuminating window into these otherwise typically unstated assumptions regarding the reach of the norm of market competition. ORR, once in possession of all departmental schedules, then appended their own recommendations to these schedules and submitted all the paperwork to the Council on Business Regulation. In what follows, I have used the agenda changes and conflicts recorded in CBR deliberations to infer the *rationales* for excluding certain policy areas altogether from the purview of CPA review: there is no existing record of actual discussion.[46] What is clear is that non-economic factors of the kind listed in the public interpretation clause played an important role in the arguments and deliberations between the ORR and the CBR. This counters the 'official interpretive stance', which paid scant attention to that clause, notwithstanding its mandatory language. Further, while most lists of excluded legislation reflected undebated consensus on boundary assumptions, debate and argument did on occasion erupt over the issue of excluding certain programmes which *had* been included. These policy areas are key flashpoints for contested areas of the boundary between market and state arenas.

In commenting on patterns of inclusion and exclusion of review, I include a sense of where departments, ORR, CBR and politicians clashed and (where possible) why. Overall, ORR exercised considerable influence on the agenda-setting stage, but its control was by no means complete. About 85% of the priorities identified by ORR as appropriate for review were supported by CBR.[47] Some of the disagreements or negotiations over the remaining 15% are covered in the sector-specific tracing that follows.

Departments can be divided roughly into three sectors for the purposes of identifying broad patterns: central coordinating departments (e.g. Treasury; Finance; Prime Minister and Cabinet), economic policy 'line' departments (e.g. Industry, Science and Technology; Primary Industry and Energy), and social policy 'line' departments (e.g. Health; Immigration; Education).

In establishing a pattern across coordinating, social and economic policy departments, it is useful to first identify a core sense of what is within CPA review and what is excluded, and afterwards turn to the contested peripheries. Treasury claimed centre stage in respect of centrality to the regulatory reform agenda. Almost 20% of the total reviews listed by the federal government were reviews of Treasury legislation and of the 19 highest priority reviews, Treasury claimed nearly a third.[48] Thus financial regulation, especially in the areas of banking, insurance and pensions, but also in relation to foreign investment rules, was viewed as critical to the overall promotion of competitiveness and a healthy market. There was some conflict over certain exempted acts, and pensions regulation appears to have been added by the politicians rather than the bureaucrats. But the exclusions, mainly in the area of taxation, were a matter of consensus.

Other departments which had a large proportion of their legislation classified as restrictive of competition were three economic policy departments: the Department of Primary Industry and Energy, the Department of Industry, Science and Technology, and the Department of Transport. Examples of the policies involved here include anti-dumping legislation, agricultural marketing schemes, tariffs and bounties, shipping registration requirements, and consumer product labelling legislation. ORR largely shared the views of Primary Industry and Energy (DPIE), but came into sharp conflict with the other two departments. In these conflicts, ORR got its way and the CBR appeared to have little to contribute. ORR's comfortable interaction with DPIE was due to the fact that extensive consultative practices were already in place, and the department had a higher than usual proportion of economists employed.[49] In other words,

ORR as a supervising body trusted process and expertise, and was not necessarily committed to a predetermined substantive policy view.

In accordance with its general commitment to unsettling the status quo, however, ORR was prepared to press departments that tended to view themselves as not affecting business or markets, and these were usually in the social policy strand. The Department of Environment, Sport and Territories was probably the most extreme example: in its entire portfolio of over 120 acts and accompanying regulations, only two ordinances and one set of regulations (all of minor importance) were identified by the department as falling within CPA spectacles. In relation to this department, as well as in respect of the Department of Health, and that of Education, (e.g. over funding frameworks for higher education that overwhelmingly favoured public universities), ORR challenged departmental judgment, generally successfully.

There were also, however, substantial areas of social policy that ORR, in consensus with the relevant department, was happy to rule outside the CPA's purview. The Department of Arts, that of Social Security and most programmes under the Department of Immigration all came into this category. Large portions of law and order policy under the Attorney-General's department were also not seen as providing or affecting potentially competitive market services, notably the provision of court and police services, legislation protecting human rights and prohibiting race and gender-based discrimination, and family law. Thus cultural policy, welfare policy, and police powers in the narrow sense were assumed to be 'non-market' areas.

The conflicts that arose over environmental, health and education legislation reflects the conceptual diffuseness of hybrid policies, policies that complicate any assumed distinctions between market infrastructural regulation and social citizenship regulation. In general, legislation in arenas of social citizenship regulation – education, communications, health, immigration, environmental policy, race and gender-based policy – tended to be susceptible to multiple classification, raising *both* market competition issues and issues of equity or protection from social risk. The ad hoc patterns in the agenda resulting from this hybridity are underpinned by the unspoken boundary assumptions of agenda-setting. There seemed to be two principal boundary assumptions in this arena.

The first, a fairly abstract criterion, was the *formal incidence* of the rules in question. If they directly affected non-state actors who provided goods or services to consumers and citizens, they were much more likely to fall within the CPA agenda than if they directly affected individuals. Indeed, ORR's private shorthand in its documentation for the trigger criterion was whether or not it 'affected business'. Thus Medicare payments, child care assistance or the provision of public schooling were not on the reform agenda, whereas the provision of home and community services for the aged and disabled, as well as private health insurance rules were included (both the latter had private providers involved).

A second, less formal and more contextual factor, was *path dependence*: whether or not the good or service had historically been provided by state resources and actors. If it had, it was more likely to escape the gaze of the meta-regulatory lens and of ORR's vigilance. Put together, these two criteria imply that direct public provision of goods and services, precisely the traditional conception of the welfare state, fell outside the ambit of CPA. Yet in practice, as the functions of the welfare state are increasingly fulfilled not by direct public provision, but by the regulation of non-state actors, there are fewer and fewer programmes that fit that description. The ORR certainly played a role in pressuring departments to alter some of their assumptions that their programmes had nothing to do with business, markets or competition. Take for example the provision of business, tourist and student visas by the Department of Immigration: this was initially excluded, but after ORR's comments (which were accepted by the CBR) these areas became subject to review in accordance with the terms of the CPA.

In addition to the tendency of economic rationality, as administered by ORR, to reconceptualise once 'public' policies as policies with implications for competitive markets, there was another unpredictable factor shaping the threshold assumptions of the CPA reform agenda: politics. Hybrid programmes by their nature provided the most leverage for the operation of politics, due to the inherent murkiness of their 'technical' character. Some of the political shaping of the agenda filtered in through the avenue of the CBR and reflected broader political considerations of general public importance, peripheral to meta-regulation's reform agenda but still of significant general public interest. For example, the Department of Environment lost a battle with the ORR to exclude many significant environmental policies from review, such as ozone protection legislation, hazardous waste regulations and world heritage properties conservation legislation. Despite the inclusion of such programmes, rules prohibiting mining in the Antarctic were successfully excluded by the Department, in the face of objections from the ORR. The Department made a technical conceptual argument that the rules had no impact on business (since mining was prohibited, they argued, there was no current 'affected' business activity). But the programme was in the end exempted from review not due to this conceptual argument, but because Australia had played a large role in the international arena in obtaining protection for the Antarctic in the first place. While the prohibition removal may well have still been retained after full review, even the act of placing the legislation on the agenda may have damaged Australia's long-term credibility in the international political sphere, and this was the ultimate factor driving this aspect of agenda-setting.[50]

Although environmental legislation in general probably attracted the most conflict, also very controversial were affirmative action rules and native title legislation. In both cases, the CBR was split down the middle with business representatives ranged against the four 'community' representatives (social welfare, consumer, environmental and labour). In the case of native title legislation, ORR won and the legislation was listed for review. A similar outcome occurred in the case of affirmative action, though CBR managed to qualify the impact of this by securing a reversal of the presumption against the status quo. That is to say, the review of affirmative action legislation only, by contrast with the standard procedure, could proceed on the basis that that the fundamental thrust of the act was not under challenge in the review.

While ORR-CBR deliberations struggled with interpretive slippage and the appropriate weight of countervailing general political considerations, political interventions from the top of government tended to illustrate straightforward strategic interest-group lobbying. Agenda changes after the right-wing Coalition government came into power in March 1996 illustrate that the new government took care of its important constituents, at a number of more or less visible levels. The most important of these moves was an extensive reform of the entire industrial relations system: they did this early and rapidly and quite separately from the CPA regime. But even within the CPA regime, they altered priorities. In some respects, political scrutiny supported ORR's choices: postal services and shipping, which they had inserted into the final schedule in defiance of the previous Labour government's position, remained on the schedule after the right-wing Coalition won power. Sometimes the alterations undercut ORR priorities: the review of the wheat marketing authority, for example, though not eliminated, was put back by four years. By contrast in the area of tariffs and manufacturing supports, the Coalition government added a large range of protective tariffs and bounties to the agenda for CPA review that ORR had allowed the department to exclude. This aspect of agenda-shaping was much more closely related to raw political calculus than to interpretive disagreement over the legitimate threshold of the reform agenda.

Agenda-setting at the federal level overall illustrates a rough sense of a core state/market distinction that is extremely hazy at its borders. It is a threshold constructed by bureaucrats whose priorities were shaped by technical considerations (especially the extent of a programme's economic scope and depth) and by inarticulate 'common-sense assumptions' regarding which areas of social and economic policy touched on markets. Although the existing patterns of the traditional welfare state appeared to shade some areas from the glare of market spectacles, the economically trained bureaucrats in ORR frequently secured a widening of the zone of competition-relevant regulation, particularly in education, health and the environment. Politics altered these conceptually-shaped choices at the margins, and hybrid regulation presented the most scope for such politics. From the left (through the influence of the CBR), concessions were won on affirmative action and high visibility environmental issues. From the right (through the influence of the incoming Coalition government), the shape of the agenda shifted in hybrid areas to lean against inclusion of politically sensitive agricultural regulatory programmes and in favour of inclusion of key industrial regulatory policies.

Victoria

Victoria was governed in the agenda-setting stage by a majority rightwing Coalition government. The centrally provided instruction manual shows how economic rationality shaped boundary assumptions about the legitimate scope of reform. Key types of rules were defined as *automatically* restrictive of competition and therefore at the core of the CPA agenda.[51] These include: allowing only one company or person to supply a good or service (monopoly); requiring producers to sell to a single company or person (monopsony); limiting the number of producers of goods and services to less than four (duopoly or oligopoly); limiting the output of an industry or individual producers; limiting the number of persons engaged in an occupation. Thus quantitative restrictions on buyers, sellers or products in a market setting constituted the core of CPA review.

A second category of effects also triggered a strong *presumption* of potential reform. These included rules that limited entry into a market, made entry more costly or more difficult (e.g. through registration fees, educational standards, occupational standards, product standards or licensing), rules that reduced the number of firms, or reduced product innovation or product differentiation, rules that increased vertical integration. However, the presumption that such rules should be on the reform agenda could be rebutted in these cases, if a demonstrable connection could be made between the purpose of the rule and one of four kinds of 'market failure': absence of public goods, externalities, information asymmetry and undue market power. No explicit reference was made to the public interest interpretation clause to justify exclusions from the CPA agenda. Rather, the Victorian government relied on technical economic definitions of redressing market failures.

While the close linkage between these criteria and the discipline of economics is obvious, the boundary assumption governing their application was not easy to apply in practice. As with the federal government, the threshold of reform was shaped by assumptions about which regulatory policies are appropriately viewed in terms of a market framework. Unlike the federal government, though, Victoria actually defined a market, as "the field of actual and potential transactions between buyers and sellers amongst whom there can be strong substitution, at least in the long run, if given sufficient price incentive".[52] It also outlined a list of broad categories of exclusion, and an examination of this list may tell us something about assumptions on the limits of what can be conceived of in terms of buying and selling, and the limits to people or products being regarded as *substitutable.*

One interesting category of exclusion was anti-discrimination laws. This raises the issues explored in the federal agenda-setting process regarding regulation subject to hybrid categorisation. The Victorian government explicitly relied on the multiple objectives of anti-discrimination legislation in justifying its general exclusion. On the one hand, it characterised anti-discrimination legislation as efficiency-enhancing because it enforces employment on merit. It also stressed, however, that these rules enforce "rights to social participation, some of which will not have economic consequences". The fact that no attempt was made to demonstrate any connection between rights to social participation and some way in which they redressed market failure could be interpreted in two different ways. On the one hand, it could suggest that anti-discrimination legislation would not have been excluded from the reform agenda if it not also been regarded as efficiency-enhancing. On the other hand, it may reflect a view that 'rights to social participation' are non-substitutable and should not be treated as capable of being bought and sold. The availability of two very different ways of characterising such legislation expands the range of arguments that can justify exclusion. The resulting interpretive slippage blurs the distinction between social citizenship regulation and market infrastructural regulation.

Victoria also excluded, on a general basis, law and order legislation and state revenue laws. These types of rules were described as constitutive of state power and consequently not in themselves a restriction on competition. Like the federal government, then, revenue-raising and law enforcement are still regarded as core governmental activities. Overall, though, the Victorian government's agenda drew a wider spectrum of legislative and regulatory activities into the arena of competition and market spectacles than did the federal government. For example, even in relation to law and order, taxation and narrow police powers, areas also excluded by the federal government, Victoria was more insistent on marketising what it calls the 'operational support' aspects of these core areas, i.e. administrative support, corporate services, information gathering, reporting, and inspection. The guidelines insisted that these did not fall within the general exclusionary categories, and can therefore appropriately be contracted out to the private sector and subjected to the discipline of a competitive market. Moreover, the ambit of the reform agenda included prison services legislation, a wide range of programmes under the Department of Police and Emergency Services and a substantial portion of the internal regulation of the public sector itself (audit, superannuation and salary provision). It also encompassed the provision of most educational services by both public and private sector as well as the regulation of museums and of adoption, all disparate areas of 'hybrid' social policy and ones which were in the main left alone by the federal government.

Whether the breadth of the Victorian agenda as compared to that of the federal government was shaped by the political context in which the agenda-setting occurred might be inferred by looking at the scope of the agenda of New South Wales, which was governed by Labour at the agenda-setting stage.

New South Wales

New South Wales used 'triggers' to catalyse inclusion of legislation for priority review. Drawn like other states' triggers from the conceptual resources of economics, the CPA agenda prioritised legislation that established statutory marketing bodies, restricted market entry or exit, created a competitive advantage for public or private market participants, or reduced the contestability of a market or inhibited innovation. There was also an additional unique priority: legislation that created excessive delay or complexity in land use and planning approvals.[53]

Once again, these criteria are all grounded on boundary assumptions about the 'market' nature of a policy arena in the first place. There are both similarities and disjunctures with Victoria's overall approach to the scope of the review agenda. Some areas common to both New South Wales and Victoria fell equally heavily under the CPA lens. The two main areas of commonality were the regulation of a wide variety of health professionals, of small businesses (estate agents, second-hand dealers, etc.) and of agricultural activities. Also of shared significance was the provision of major utilities services, a sector which was a prime target of the overall competition policy guidelines.

Absent from both agendas were criminal law, anti-discrimination legislation and much provision of community services (such as child care and disability). It should be noted, however, that community services was in fact being 'marketised', not so much through reform of legislatively-backed rules, but through reform of funding policies, especially the imposition of competitive tendering processes on local government, and in this respect Victoria had gone further than New South Wales. In addition, Victoria included cultural policy, education and many aspects of law and order policy, where New South Wales did not. Thus it would appear that the presence of a right-wing administration supervising the agenda-setting process opened the meta-regulatory lens wider, drawing in culture, education, aspects of police and security powers and aspects of welfare provision, where leftwing governments at both federal and state level were more reluctant to tread.

Conclusion

The conceptual schema of economic rationality imposed by the reform programme onto regulatory policy choice was interpreted by bureaucrats under a range of political contexts in such a way that *up to a point* a core of common-sense boundary assumptions about the legitimate scope of potential pro-competitive reform emerged. This was, broadly speaking, legislation that constrained the individual and social choices of non-state actors performing activities historically conceived of as relevant to market competitiveness.

At a later stage of oversight the National Competition Council crafted a number of priority legislation review areas that were, in their view, uncontentiously 'competition-relevant' (although of course the specific nature of desirable reform in each of these areas was highly contentious).[54] The scope of the priority areas focused mainly on agricultural and primary industry marketing arrangements, transport and communication policy, financial regulation (banks and pensions), retail and trading regulation, and professions in general (especially but not exclusively all legal and health professions).

In the main, NCC priority areas did not touch on the welfare, law and order or social policy that had proved troublesome 'hybrid' zones in setting reform agendas: legislation that, whatever impacts it may have on market competition in those areas, also had substantial purposes of fostering protection from social risk, distributing public services, or redistributing resources. However, they did include requirements to review gambling legislation, child care legislation and education-related legislation. These were precisely the kinds of areas that had generated conflict at the federal level in the Council on Business Regulation, and upon which New South

Wales and Victoria had differed in the more peripheral boundary assumptions about the threshold of appropriate review. They were also areas that caused conflict within the network of central agency officials, with some jurisdictions of the view that such policy areas were beyond the legitimate purview of competition policy.[55]

The NCC's decision to focus mainly on priority areas that avoided the blurry regions of law and order, welfare and other public provision, and most social policy, was one that emphasised as little contention as was feasible in defining the scope of the regulatory reform agenda that it had the responsibility to oversee and enforce. This was in keeping with the trajectory of incipient legality that I am arguing characterises the development of meta-regulation in Australia, where politically insulated arms-length institutions shaped the reform programme according to neutral expertise-based criteria, relying heavily on an interpretive strategy of taking words seriously. Maintaining the impetus of this trajectory meant trying to minimise the effects of the fact that as implementation unfolded, those criteria failed at the margins to draw bright technical lines between reform-sensitive and reform-proof areas of regulatory policy.

Despite attempts to maintain a patina of consensus and technical clarity around the application of meta-regulatory criteria, the patterns of agenda-setting that emerged in the early stages of reform show significant malleability in the threshold defining the scope of reform. This malleability provided room for the operation of political influence on the scope of the agenda. That political influence was sometimes narrow interest-group lobbying in relation to specific pieces of legislation, but a broader influence was also perceptible. This was that left-wing governments were more likely to draw the threshold of the reform agenda in such a way that the public sector, the welfare state and at least some social policy remained outside the lens of 'market spectacles'. Similarly left-wing governments were rather more likely than right-wing governments to lessen the political insulation of the key institutions in meta-regulation, encouraging community-political input at a centralised level, or decentralised decision-making within the bureaucratic structure that increased Ministerial influence.

Nonetheless, the malleability of the conceptual framework of economic rationality is, in the agenda-setting stage, relatively peripheral. The routines and strategies adopted by the network of central agency officials still primarily institutionalise a substantive presumption in favour of market liberalism, even though the full reach of this presumption is influenced by the political context in which meta-regulation operates. The possibilities for tempering market liberalism appear to operate only at the outer edges of the 'common sense' assumptions imported by economic rationality. The next chapter, however, shows that the malleability can be pushed deeper into the heart of the categories established by the meta-regulatory regime, expanding opportunities to pursue social citizenship outcomes notwithstanding the presumption in favour of market governance built into the analytical framework.

Notes

1   In this chapter, interviews with seven of the top central agency officials of the three jurisdictions explored form an important source of my information. In order to protect the confidentiality of these officials I have anonymised their actual names though their departmental and territorial locations are still made clear.

2   Coghlan, Assistant Commissioner, Office of Regulation Review, Productivity Commission, Canberra (1997), *Interview*, Morgan. February 15 1997; Senior Official A, Office of Regulation Review, Productivity Commission, Canberra (1997), *Interview*, Morgan. February 15 1997.

3   Senior Official A, Office of Regulation Review, Productivity Commission, Canberra (2001), *Interview*, Morgan.

4   Senior Official A, Office of Regulation Review, Productivity Commission, Canberra (1997), *Interview*, Morgan. February 15 1997.

5   The following account is based on copies of the records of the outcome of the meetings and very brief minutes (there were no transcripts of discussion taken).

6   Mr. Chris Peters, Printing and Allied Trades Employers' Federation of Australia.

7   Mr. Bill Page-Hanify, Chairman, Alcatel Australia Ltd.

8   Mr. Fergus Ryan, Managing Partner, Arthur Andersen, Melbourne.

9   Later, in August 1996 after the deadline had passed, and the schedules were published, the new Treasurer disbanded the CBR altogether.

10   Braithwaite, Professor of Law, Research School of Social Sciences and Member of Business Council of Australia (1997), *Interview*, Morgan. February 16 1997.

11   Senior Official B and Senior Official C, Department of Treasury and Finance, Victorian Government (2001), *Interview*, Morgan. 2 April 2001; Senior Official C, Department of Treasury and Finance, Victorian Government (2001), *Interview*, Morgan. 2 April 2001.

12   Senior Official B and Senior Official C, Department of Treasury and Finance, Victorian Government (2001), *Interview*, Morgan. 2 April 2001; Senior Official C, Department of Treasury and Finance, Victorian Government (2001), *Interview*, Morgan. 2 April 2001.

13   Senior Official D and Senior Official E, New South Wales Department of the Premier and Cabinet (2001), Morgan. 9 March 2001.

14   Senior Official A, Office of Regulation Review, Productivity Commission, Canberra (2001), *Interview*, Morgan.

15   Senior Official D and Senior Official E, New South Wales Department of the Premier and Cabinet (2001), Morgan. 9 March 2001.

16   Senior Official B and Senior Official C, Department of Treasury and Finance, Victorian Government (2001), *Interview*, Morgan. 2 April 2001; Senior Official D and Senior Official E, New South Wales Department of the Premier and Cabinet (2001), Morgan. 9 March 2001.

17   There is an important exception to this flowing from an intervention by COAG in 2000 which led to an amendment of the intergovernmental agreements which

directly affects NCC's oversight powers. This will be discussed in Chapter Five in more detail, as it did not influence the agenda-setting stage of the reform package.

[18] Senior Official F, (2001), Morgan. 3 April 2001.

[19] Senior Official F, (2001), Morgan. 3 April 2001, p. 3.

[20] Hilmer, Chairman of Fairfax and Former Chairman of the National Competition Policy Review (2001), *Interview*, Morgan. 9 April 2001, p.3.

[21] My interview questions about the possible judicial enforcement or relevance of the intergovernmental agreements repeatedly met with a response that courts were not salient, at least not to the meta-regulation put in place under the auspices of the legislation review programme. (By contrast, certain gas companies obtained legal advice from highly regarded attorneys to the effect that Clause 6 of the CPA, which details the conditions under which states must provide access by third parties to monopoly infrastructures such as gas pipelines, electricity grids etc, may constitute legally enforceable 'binding principles' (Interview, Lim 1997).) That meta-regulation is treated in Australia at least as non-judicial territory, is also buttressed by the fact that judicial supervision of the earlier state-based regulatory impact analysis schemes (which are embodied in formal legislation and thus more formally subject to judicial review) has been almost non-existent. In over a decade of operation in Victoria and almost a decade in New South Wales, only one case was ever brought. In *Phillip Morris v State of Victoria* [1988] VR 825, a judge agreed to hear a case challenging regulations that restricted tobacco advertising, but before it came to trial, the Department of Health withdrew the offending regulations, and terminated the employment of the relevant policy employee, who had failed to prepare an adequate analysis of the impact of different options for regulation.

[22] Senior Official F, (2001), Morgan. 3 April 2001, p.3, p.9; Senior Official B and Senior Official C, Department of Treasury and Finance, Victorian Government (2001), *Interview*, Morgan, 2 April 2001.

[23] Senior Official D, New South Wales Department of the Premier and Cabinet (2001), *Interview*, Morgan, p.7.

[24] National Competition Council (1996), *Considering the Public Interest under National Competition Policy*, p.4.

[25] See Daniels 1996; and note the NCC policy of insisting that Ministers formally attest in second reading speeches that competition review principles have been followed, while at the same time indicating NCC will not itself check on whether Clause 1(3) matters have been considered.

[26] National Competition Council (1996), *Considering the Public Interest under National Competition Policy*, p.10.

[27] National Competition Council (1997), *Assessment of State and Territory Progress with Implementing National Competition Policy and Related Reforms*, p.17, emphasis added.

[28] National Competition Council (1997), *Assessment of State and Territory Progress with Implementing National Competition Policy and Related Reforms*, p.16.

[29] Senior Official A, Office of Regulation Review, Productivity Commission, Canberra (1997), *Interview*, Morgan. February 15 1997.

[30] Senior Official A, Office of Regulation Review, Productivity Commission, Canberra (2001), *Interview*, Morgan.

[31] Office of Regulation Review (no date), *Guidelines for Identifying Priorities for Portfolio Review Programmes and Bodies to Undertake Reviews and Public Consultations*, p.3, emphasis added.

[32] Senior Official B and Senior Official C, Department of Treasury and Finance,

Victorian Government (2001), *Interview*, Morgan, 2 April 2001, p.6.

33 Senior Official D and Senior Official E, New South Wales Department of the Premier and Cabinet (2001), *Interview*, Morgan. 9 March 2001.

34 Victorian Government (1995), *Guidelines for the Application of the Competition Test to New Legislative Proposals*; Victorian Government (1995), *National Competition Policy: Steps to Assist Agencies in Complying with the Guidelines for the Application of the Competition Test to New Legislative Proposals.*

35 Centre for International Economics (1999), *Guidelines for National Competition Policy Legislation Reviews*, Centre for International Economics, www.intecon.com.au, (on file with author).

36 Council of Australian Governments (1997), *Principles and Guidelines for National Standard Setting and Regulatory Action by Ministerial Councils and Standard-Setting Bodies*, on file with author.

37 Victorian Government (1995), *Guidelines for the Application of the Competition Test to New Legislative Proposals.*

38 Council of Australian Governments (1997), *Principles and Guidelines for National Standard Setting and Regulatory Action by Ministerial Councils and Standard-Setting Bodies*, on file with author, p.24.

39 Victorian Government (1995), *National Competition Policy: Steps to Assist Agencies in Complying with the Guidelines for the Application of the Competition Test to New Legislative Proposals*, Point 5 of Step 3.

40 Senior Official D and Senior Official E, New South Wales Department of the Premier and Cabinet (2001), *Interview*, Morgan, 9 March 2001, p.4.

41 Australian Legislative Assembly (1995), *Hansard*, Senate, 22 June 1995. Labour Federal Treasurer's speech, pp. 1695-1707. Hilmer, Chairman of Fairfax and Former Chairman of the National Competition Policy Review (2001), *Interview*, Morgan. 9 April 2001, p.3.

42 Posner, 'Adoption and Market Theory: the Regulation of the Market in Adoption' (1987) *Boston University Law Review* Vol. 67, pp.59-72.

43 Office of Regulation Review (no date), *Guidelines for Identifying Priorities for Portfolio Review Programmes and Bodies to Undertake Reviews and Public Consultations.*

44 Senior Official A, Office of Regulation Review, Productivity Commission, Canberra (1997), *Interview*, Morgan, February 15 1997.

45 Senior Official A, Office of Regulation Review, Productivity Commission, Canberra (1997), *Interview*, Morgan, February 15 1997.

46 No transcript was ever made of the deliberations and therefore the precise content had to be gleaned from accounts given to me in interviews, brief minutes of the meetings, and most importantly the changes visible across the various meetings in terms of which programmes were added and which exempted or excluded.

47 Senior Official A, Office of Regulation Review, Productivity Commission, Canberra (1997), *Interview*, Morgan, February 15 1997.

48 Commonwealth Parliament of Australia (1996), *National Well-being: A System of National Citizenship Indicators and Benchmarks*, Senate Legal and Constitutional References Committee, Canberra.

49 Senior Official A, Office of Regulation Review, Productivity Commission, Canberra (1997), *Interview*, Morgan, February 15 1997.

50 Braithwaite, Professor of Law, Research School of Social Sciences and Member of Business Council of Australia (2001), *Personal Communication*, Morgan.

51   Victorian Government (1995), *Guidelines for the Application of the Competition Test to New Legislative Proposals.*

52   Victorian Government (1995), *National Competition Policy: Steps to Assist Agencies in Complying with the Guidelines for the Application of the Competition Test to New Legislative Proposals*, p.1.

53   New South Wales Government (1996), *Legislation Review Schedule*, p.3.

54   National Competition Council (2001), *Framework for the Third Tranche Assessment of Government's Progress with Implementing National Competition Policy and Related Reforms*, Ausinfo, Canberra.

55   Senior Official D and Senior Official E, New South Wales Department of the Premier and Cabinet (2001), *Interview*, Morgan, 9 March 2001.

5 Implementation in Competition's Shadow

Overview

This part of the book aims to anchor the various threads of the previous chapters in the detailed context of case studies of particular sectors that were subjected to the discipline of meta-regulation. Throughout, the overall concern has been to explore the question of meta-regulation's impact on social citizenship while at the same time fleshing out the features of meta-regulation that can be interpreted as a mode of incipient legality. These issues have been approached from a range of perspectives: conceptual (Chapter One), historical (Chapter Two), and interpretive empirical elaboration of general trends in community-political (Chapter Three) and bureaucratic-technical (Chapter Four) responses to the initial agenda-setting stage of reform. These various perspectives all contain within them a tension between presenting meta-regulation from a standpoint of institutional solidity on the one hand, and on the other hand with a focus on the interpretive fluidity of its categories and, sometimes, institutional location.

This chapter traces more precisely how and when fluid interpretive conflict over regulatory policy choice in specific instances leads to enduring institutional and policy change. The deeper form of malleability identified in these four case studies suggests that at least some means of tempering market liberalism can – via translation strategies – be pursued within the heart of the framework of economic rationality. Despite this, key facets of tempered market liberalism, in particular those that would foster redistributive values, are cut off and silenced by that framework. Thus while in Chapter Three at the level of community dialogue and political debate we saw two different responses to meta-regulation that sought to be inclusive of social citizenship values – the 'differentiated consumer sovereignty' perspective and the 'community morality' perspective – at this level of technical implementation the latter perspective is mostly silenced.

Taken together, the four case studies that follow indicate a strong tendency to 'translate' the social benefits of regulation into the language of market failure and consumer sovereignty. In this translation, redistributive equity values were most at risk, though environmental values were also vulnerable. But even where social citizenship values were translated and taken into account, the *institutional* responses to pursuing them can render them politically more vulnerable. Political vulnerability is closely related to institutional design, and specifically to whether policy outcomes that are important to the disadvantaged groups that seek inclusive social citizenship are exposed to hierarchical or network structures of control.

The organisational possibilities for policy outcomes in particular reviews can be mapped as a function of prescriptiveness of rules and degree of discretion accorded to the principal policy-implementing institution:

Figure 5.1   Organisational possibilities for policy outcomes

high

Discretion of principal policy implement-ing institution	STATE PLANNING	BUREAUCRACY
	MARKET	NETWORK

low   Prescriptiveness of rules   high

Hierarchical control centralises control from the top-down and retains discretion to alter the policies implemented through them. A network structure has weak central top-down direction but also constrains quite heavily the degree of discretion dispersed throughout the system. This constraint, which locks in the consideration of social citizenship values, comes from giving dispositive power over policy direction to multiple actors, any one of which can veto or constrain behaviour of the others. Networks explicitly articulate rules that co-ordinate the actors' preferences (rather than leaving it to the actors). The consequently greater density of prescriptiveness in the rules of a network structure (as compared to a market structure) gives a voice to interests that may otherwise have been marginalised. Vulnerability occurs when network structures fail to crystallise, leaving social citizenship values subject to hierarchical political control.

Once institutional considerations are taken into account, we will see that the analytical and conceptual malleability of meta-regulation does not necessarily protect social citizenship from erosion, notwithstanding the strategic potential of translating social citizenship values into the language of economic discourse. Just as the network of central agency officials gradually accrued power to shape the regulatory reform agenda by virtue of its institutional positioning, so too the institutional form of social citizenship values is an important facet of their staying power under meta-regulation.

Following on from the case studies, the last section of this Chapter turns to general enforcement patterns and oversight by the National Competition Council. This body was the target of widespread public discontent because of its relatively visible role in the complex network of techniques, strategies and routines that together made meta-regulation a structural barrier to the pursuit of social citizenship values. The chapter will conclude with an exploration of how the institutional strength of the NCC contributed to this barrier, linking it to an interesting political backlash that actually intensified meta-regulation's incipient legality.

Case Selection Principles

The four case studies explore the implementation of the Competition Principles Agreement in four different policy sectors: the social policy dimensions of utility services, agricultural marketing services, immigration advice services, and public sector auditing. The basis for selecting these case studies was two-fold. One limb of the selection principles aimed to try and isolate the effect of politics – in the sense of the ideological commitments of the government in power at the time of reform – upon the outcome of review. The second limb of selection principles aimed to secure a good spread of different types of policy sector. Here the goal was to include not only policy areas that were conceptually and politically at the heart of the reform agenda in a relatively uncontentious way, but also 'limit' cases that tested the boundaries of the reform agenda's scope.

In order to test for political influence, three jurisdictions were chosen: the Commonwealth (federal) government and the states of New South Wales and Victoria. Not only are these the three most populous and powerful jurisdictions in National Competition Policy, thus heightening the political salience of regulatory reform, but they also provided a useful spectrum of political control. During the period of research, Victoria was governed by the right with a comfortable majority, New South Wales by the left via a minority government and two key independents, and the federal government underwent a switch of administration from left to right (both with comfortable majorities) in March 1996, a year after the adoption of National Competition Policy. We saw in the last chapter that political considerations, both of general importance and of a narrower lobbying kind, could affect the scope of the reform agenda, and these cases will enable similar considerations to be explored a little more systematically at the sector-specific policy level.

In terms of substance, the four reviews concern the restructuring of utilities (primarily focusing on electricity) in New South Wales and Victoria, the Rice Marketing Board's functions in New South Wales, the registration of immigration advice agents by the Commonwealth government, and the auditing function of the Victorian Auditor-General. All these different kinds of regulatory arrangements are important to the emerging contours of the 'reinvented state', the boundaries of which were so much at issue in the agenda-setting exercise explored in Chapter Four.

Utility restructuring was one of the primary goals of the reform package as a whole, and its dimensions were in fact considerably broader than legislative review, as will emerge in the discussion below.

The Rice Marketing Board is one instance of statutory marketing arrangements in the agricultural sector. Such arrangements were a major target of the National Competition Policy as originally designed, and were targeted by the original architects of the reform package as central examples of the kind of anti-competitive arrangements that have prevented Australia from adapting appropriately to a global economy. Their political priority was more recently enforced by their central place on the National Competition Council's list of priority areas.[1]

The regulation of the provision of immigration advice is in part analogous to the regulation of professions generally, another priority area identified by the National Competition Council. In addition, however, it focuses on extremely vulnerable clients and has embedded in it explicitly redistributive aims, which makes it a good example of the hybrid regulatory concerns emerging in the unbundling of the welfare state.[2]

Finally, the audit review has two related features that make it interesting as a 'limit case'. First, it involves consideration of the 'purchaser/provider split', whereby regulatory and service delivery functions are institutionally separated: a common technique of introducing market discipline into public service provision previously thought of as 'social' or non-economic. Secondly, this reform logic was applied in the unusual instance of an institution that is *itself* an oversight mechanism. As we shall see, this directly pitted a logic of accountability embedded in markets and competition *against* a logic of accountability grounded in the rule of law. As such, it directly enacted, as a part of the review itself, the normative conflicts underpinning the implementation of the CPA, and became a kind of 'test case' for the appropriate scope and impact of the reform package.

All the reviews explored in this chapter were conducted in the early stages of National Competition Policy, under the direct auspices of the Competition Principles Agreement (CPA). The basic task was as follows. Once reform agendas had been set by all the various jurisdictions (Chapter Four), the CPA required that all regulatory programmes listed on state and federal agendas be fully reviewed and analysed to determine if they impose restrictions on market competition. To the extent that any regulatory programme was found to restrict competition, the CPA required either reform or elimination unless the programme demonstrably did two things. The relevant department had to show *both* that the programme generates a net public benefit *and* that there was no alternative way, less restrictive of competition, way of arriving at the same beneficial outcome.

The reforms in the utility sector, however, had a somewhat broader remit than the precise application of the above test. This is in part because most of the regulatory context for utility services provision did not exist in legislative form, precisely because the industries were state-owned and state-operated. Thus the narrower meta-regulatory regime did not apply neatly to utilities, and this sector was subject to a raft of specific agreements of a rather broader nature. These agreements were still encoded in the CPA and still reflected the conceptual frameworks underpinning the more narrowly tailored reform criteria, thus making the use of the utility sector as a case study an appropriate test of the dynamics of meta-regulation under the CPA.

Utilities Sector: New South Wales and Victoria

The main goals of the utility-related reforms were to establish a national framework for the transmission of electricity and gas, and to introduce competition into the sale of electricity, gas and water. In this section, I first compare the broad institutional forms chosen by New South Wales and Victoria (governed by left and right parties respectively), in order to test the influence of partisanship on the ways in which market infrastructure is institutionalised. Secondly, I compare strategies that developed early on in the reform period in New South Wales and Victoria to incorporate equity-related values into that newly emerging market infrastructure. This is a more specific focus on how liberalisation of the utility sector affects the redistributive facet of social citizenship.

Three principal effects are noticeable. First, the 'translation' of social citizenship goals into the discourse of economic analysis is extensive, reflecting the fact that in practice, the bite of the differentiated consumer sovereignty (DCS) perspective identified in Chapter Three as one possible response to meta-regulation is stronger than that of the community morality (CM) approach.

Secondly, however, the *practical effectiveness* of that discursive reframing depends on institutional context. Where relatively transparent network structures developed, there was more scope for institutional innovation to incorporate social citizenship in new ways.

Thirdly, political ideology influenced institutional design choices. New South Wales under the leadership of a left-governed administration introduced relatively transparent network structures in the utility sector. Victoria, governed by the right during the initial period of research, developed a much more hierarchically centralised and closed institutional governance structure, which made the pursuit of social citizenship values much more dependent on political discretion (and thus, under the right-wing government, more vulnerable).

The second and third effects are difficult to disentangle: network structures facilitate protection of social citizenship values, as does the presence of a left-wing government. Whether there is any causal relation between political partisanship and the emergence of network structures is much more difficult to tell.

Background and Context

Australian utilities – telecommunications, water and electricity – have always been economically significant portions of the production process, accounting for 10% of GDP in the late 1980s,[3] and functioning as a critical input to most other types of economic and industrial activity. This explained their importance for National Competition Policy goals. Historically these infrastructure industries were structured as state-owned monopolies[4] and run as political behemoths by Ministers who intervened frequently on a political basis in the day-to-day workings of the enterprises. Over time, utility provision has become increasingly subject to the application of private sector principles and strategies. The rising intensity of such application is commonly portrayed as happening in three stages: commercialisation, corporatisation and privatisation.[5]

Commercialisation involved the limited application of business principles to public organisations, with an emphasis on meeting cost-cutting targets in a context of ceilings on public borrowings. The spread of rules mandating a commercialisation orientation began at the Commonwealth level in the mid-1980s. It took early shape during the 1984 Hawke government's overhaul of broad budgetary and civil service procedures,[6] when the Industry Minister John Dawkins manoeuvred a set of *Policy Guidelines for Statutory Authorities and Government Business Enterprises* (GBEs) through the requisite political avenues over the course of three years. The final White Paper reduced direct control on GBEs as a result of complaints over political interference, and concentrated on requiring corporate plans with explicit financial targets and increased public and political monitoring of annual reports. Thus transparency increased and political control began to be supplanted by financial control.

Corporatisation intensified these tendencies by imposing the legal structure of private companies on GBEs while retaining their public ownership. Importantly, this meant utility companies were now legally bound to pursue maximum returns for shareholders, although the shareholders were nominated Ministers who held them on behalf of the public fisc. Privatisation, involving the sale of assets to private corporations (e.g. water in Victoria) removed the last vestiges of public ownership from the structure of utility provision, although regulatory control was not necessarily ceded as we shall see in examining the Victorian utility reforms. New South Wales has not (as yet) proceeded to the third stage, but prefers, under a Labour government, to retain the corporatised structures and residual political control of the second stage.

The basic thrust of the movement across the three stages has been to dilute responsiveness to electoral signals and intensify responsiveness to market signals.[7] Consistently with this trajectory, much of the legislation and policy directives directly affecting utility provision over the last ten to fifteen years has been pro-competitive regulation, or at least regulation that aims to instil and mimic private sector practices, rather than impose politically-mandated objectives on the industry (such as the subsidisation of disadvantaged citizens). Politics does continue to impose some social citizenship values on utilities, primarily in requiring them to develop a programme to fulfil universal service obligations and in imposing some price controls on them. These are not always achieved through formal legal regulation, though, and the different institutional responses to this mix of market infrastructure and social citizenship goals will be discussed in more detail in future sections. First, I outline the main shape of the changes in institutional design sparked by pro-competitive regulation.

Very broadly, the changes have created an additional layer of institutions in the utility sector, and two layers of formal rules governing the connections between different layers. To explain what I mean, consider the matter diagrammatically. When utility services were provided by government monopolies, all users had a direct relationship with the state in the provision of essential services. This created a bilateral relationship:

Figure 5.2   Organisational relationship prior to corporatisation

State ------------ end-users (business, local government, residential etc.)

The introduction of competition inserts a new layer into the bilateral relationship, which becomes mediated by a middle layer of providers (generators and distributors) who can each form relationships with discrete groups of like consumers:

Figure 5.3   Organisational relationships post-corporatisation

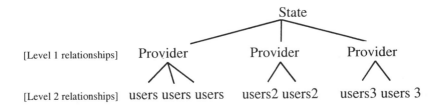

The bulk of the formal rules applying to utilities that have proliferated in the last decade have been market-constituting, rather than market-tempering. Price regulation, however, was a major rule-generating area that was addressed simultaneously, and one that tempered the dynamics of a free market. Rules addressing equity issues through universal service obligations have taken longer to emerge, and are being written and devised in much less transparent fashion than price regulation. In what follows, I explore the main features of the 'rules of the game' that provide the framework for the above institutional structure. There are two levels of rules. First-order rules structure the relationship between state and providers (Level 1 in Figure 5.3). Second-order rules define relations between end-users and the providers (Level 2 in Figure 5.3). First-order rules typically cover property rights and pricing issues, and may include environmental and equity obligations imposed by the government upon providers. Second-order rules provide accountability for consumers of utility services, either through general consumer protection mechanisms or through specific programmes targeted to benefit disadvantaged groups of consumers.

As we shall see, second-order rules tend to be less transparent, less formal, and more vulnerable to political discretion or private provider discretion, while first-order rules are more formal and legal. This reflects the two-step conception of justifiable regulation which underpins the public choice perspective driving meta-regulation (see Chapter Three): formal legal intervention is an appropriate mode of protecting property rights and general efficiency questions, while equity and social issues are better redressed through direct political intervention, or left to the discretion and choice of the relevant social actors.

But there is a degree to which this neat distinction between the character of first and second order rules is complicated by politics. To explore this, first I compare first-order rules in Victoria and New South Wales, which were governed by right-wing and left wing governments respectively in the agenda-setting stage of utility reform. Secondly, I explore accountability strategies for end-users in the two states, looking at both substantive equity issues (focused on Community Service Obligations) and legal process issues (focused on Consumer Protection Obligations).

First-order Rules of the Game: Comparative Institutional Responses in New South Wales and Victoria

In New South Wales and Victoria,[8] gas, water and electricity were all corporatised during the period leading up to and just after inception of National Competition Policy in April 1995. In Victoria, the government in power in all three cases was a right-wing coalition. In New South Wales, a right-wing coalition presided over the corporatisation of Sydney Water, but a Labour government was in power for the corporatisation of gas and electricity. Ironically, the basic framework of corporatisation for the three sectors of utility services did not end up looking significantly different, notwithstanding fervent criticism of the two parties of each other's approaches.[9] This is probably at least partly because the Coalition held power under a minority government and two non-aligned Independents held the balance of power until Labour's victory in 1995. The Independents were often a sympathetic ear for green, consumer and social welfare groups, and they forced through significant amendments to all three corporatisation templates.

Both Victoria and New South Wales share some commonalties in the structures they chose. Both moved away from closed monopolies controlled entirely by political authority. Both designed structures that applied commercial and market discipline to the delivery of electricity and water. Both states separated regulatory functions from provider and operator functions, and both opted for general regulatory bodies who target a range of essential utility services (rather than sector-specific bodies, as for example in the UK). Both New South Wales and Victoria are ultimately subject to the jurisdiction of the national independent agency, the Australian Competition and Consumer Council, which will over time work towards uniform cross-state arrangements for access to monopoly infrastructure such as pipelines and electricity cables. In addition, at a broad level (though the details differ as outlined below), both New South Wales and Victoria preferred to regulate through neutral, expert bodies who operate relatively openly. Both stated their intent to shield regulating bodies as much as feasible from 'politics', in the sense of vulnerability to the demands of powerful vested interests. Trade-offs that were previously made politically *within* the government monopoly thus became more transparent in the sense that they were secured and monitored through external regulatory pressures from other agencies. Overall, then, enhanced transparency, institutional disaggregation, dilution of political control, and an increase in the use of expert technical frameworks for high-level decisions are all features that characterise both the New South Wales and Victorian regimes.

Differences do persist, however, between the two state regimes. Although both right and left-wing governments applied some form of market discipline to the delivery of essential services, Victoria went further. Under the conservative Kennett government, it privatised its electric power industry in the generation and distribution areas, a policy which met with vociferous but ultimately ineffective opposition. Water provision, although retained within government, has been substantially restructured in the direction of ultimate operation on a full cost-recovery basis. In New South Wales, both electricity and water utilities have remained public in line with the ideological commitment of the Labour government to retain public ownership. Market discipline consisted of the introduction of competition within the framework of public ownership (the monopoly generator of electricity, Pacific Power, has been split into several competing generators) or application of the corporate form to public bodies (monopoly water boards have been corporatised).

Further, although both states have separated regulatory functions from provider functions, different arrangements subsist between regulator and provider. The differences primarily affect the degree of hierarchical political control exercisable over regulatory policy. They also affect the points of access for the consideration of non-economic values. In brief, the set of institutions and rules in New South Wales gives more scope for the consideration of non-economic values, and puts in place a fragmented, 'network' structure of regulation: multiple bodies with overlapping jurisdiction and no clear political hierarchy. Victoria initially constrains the consideration of non-economic factors while retaining relatively more central political hierarchical control and a lower degree of transparency and formality than New South Wales.[10] In what follows, I elaborate a little more on these differences between the two states.

In New South Wales,[11] a regulatory role has been given to multiple bodies each of which has a different mandate, and no one of which has priority over the other regulatory mandates. The major concession wrung by the Independents in the political situation in New South Wales was to secure co-equal multiple mandates in the legislative framework. The utility providers must give equal weight to commercial efficiency, social responsibility and ecological sustainability. To achieve the co-equal importance of multiple mandates, the three functions were disaggregated institutionally. The main providers were to focus their own governance structure primarily on commercial efficiency (supervised by the Licence Regulator, which oversees compliance with licence conditions governing distribution of electricity and water). Social responsibility (public health standards, fair pricing, universal service obligations) and ecological sustainability were made the responsibility of separate agencies such as the Department of Health, the Independent Pricing and Regulatory Tribunal (IPART) and the Environmental Protection Authority (EPA).[12]

These various regulatory agencies do not all provide comparable levels of protection for the goals they are charged with securing, and to a certain degree, social citizenship goals are dealt with more informally and flexibly than market infrastructure goals. The Health Department uses the least amount of transparency and formality: its regulatory role is encoded in Memoranda of Understanding drawn up on an interdepartmental basis and not legally enforceable. The Licence Regulator operates with medium transparency and formality. EPA is a mixture: it relies on Memoranda of Understanding, but many of its regulatory roles must incorporate extensive and transparent consultation procedures laid down by separate, pre-existing legislation (Planning and Environment Act (NSW) 1987). IPART is essentially a quasi-judicial body, using formal rule-based strategies and a significant degree of transparent, formally structured consultation. IPART has the power to take into account social equity, consumer and environmental protection when setting prices, to hold public hearings and to compel agencies to provide information. It utilises the greatest degree of formality in procedure when deciding property rights issues, usually involving access to pipelines or cables by the provider companies. Even in pricing issues, however, it is a relatively formal independent body with a limited amount of cross-policy (environmental-consumer-property rights) coordinating power.

Victoria,[13] by contrast with New South Wales and at least during the period of the right-wing Kennet government, instituted a much more centralised structure regulatory governance for utilities, and one that paid significantly less formal attention to citizenship goals, giving major priority to facilitating market infrastructure. The Kennett government's regulatory structure had no independent quasi-judicial tribunal in its regulatory structure, nor did it have a separate Licence Regulator. It located regulatory responsibility for monitoring the provision of water and electricity in the separate Office of the Regulator-General (ORG). Initially, ORG's statutory framework explicitly stated a wide variety of situations in which it was required to have regard to government policy. Although legislation was passed to guarantee the Office independence from government policy,[14] ORG overall bore the hallmarks of an executive rather than a quasi-judicial body.

One important effect of this was that most regulatory issues in the Victorian restructuring were addressed through significantly more informal and closed routines than in New South Wales. ORG is advised by a customer consultative committee which, although it has strong community representation, has only recommendatory powers. ORG's mandate was to look at pricing, service standards, market conduct and licensing but it had no clear power to examine issues of social equity raised by the elimination of internal cross-subsidies. Rather, its objectives were primarily pro-competitive, and indeed duplicated the economic regulatory objectives of the ACCC to a considerable degree.[15] Thus unlike New South Wales (where IPART has a mandate for considering social equity in pricing issues), strategies affecting certain classes of consumer in a discriminatory manner will remain a policy issue decided behind closed doors, if at all. Similarly, ORG has no explicit power to take into account environmental issues whereas they are explicitly relevant to IPART's decision-making procedure.

Thus the Victorian government retained a higher degree of central political control over regulatory issues than New South Wales, and at the same New South Wales places much more weight overall on accommodating social citizenship goals. The co-existence in Victoria of strong political control and a high priority for market infrastructure goals undercuts the claims made by the architects of meta-regulation that facilitating competitive efficiency is primarily a technical manoeuvre.

A summary of the comparative institutional choices made in New South Wales and Victoria, then, would emphasise that in both states, there was a general move towards reliance upon expert neutral bodies, using primarily economic expertise and insulated to a degree from the political process. The left-wing government created a greater number of fragmented institutions, with greater insulation from central political control, and greater scope for consideration of non-economic values. The right-wing government, by contrast, combined tight constraints on the consideration of non-economic factors with a significantly higher degree of central political hierarchical control and, by corollary, less proliferation of 'network' structures.[16]

Second-order Rules of the Game: End-user Accountability Mechanisms in New South Wales and Victoria

When provision of utility services was channelled entirely though public-owned state entities, first order rules of property rights, pricing structures and possible social obligations on providers were, like second-order rules addressing end-user issues, all internal state issues politically determined by informal procedures inside government bureaucracies. The unbundling of service provision to non-state players necessitated the development of formal rules governing first-order issues, but in theory end-user issues could have been left entirely to the discretion of the new non-state providers. In fact, however, new routines, strategies and even institutions (all aimed at maintaining accountability to these end-users) have developed, constituting the second-order rules applying to the Level 2 relationship between providers and end-users (see Figure 5.3 at page 152).

The strategies developed to address accountability issues for end-users of essential services such as water and electricity are of two main types, both primarily informal. That is to say, neither approach is typically embodied in legislation nor by formally promulgated rules. The first strategy turns to the corporations providing essential services, and leaves it to them to design programmes addressed to the needs of specific groups of disadvantaged consumers, thus sending equity concerns 'in-house', as it were. It combines private decision-making with public funding, and is essentially a *substantive equity* strategy. The main embodiment of this strategy has been the requirement for the corporate providers to address Community Service Obligations (CSOs) in their overall level of provision.

The second principal type of strategy is primarily a *process-based* strategy. It relies on informal co-regulatory models, such as voluntary industry agreements or codes, industry ombudsmen schemes, and customer councils or similar consultation mechanisms with consumer advocacy networks. A shorthand term for this strategy, which was used in practice by some (though not all) of those lobbying in this arena, is "consumer protection obligations" (CPOs).

Community Service Obligations

Prior to the introduction of competitive or market-based provision of essential services, the various utility sectors had two principal mechanisms in place for protecting disadvantaged consumers. The most common method was internal cross-subsidisation factored directly into prices, an approach which was highly non-transparent and primarily an outcome of political decision-making. Secondly, there were also schemes of direct government relief targeted at specific groups. Administrative structures in this direct targeted relief varied. In water provision in New South Wales, for example, targeted relief was administered centrally by Sydney Water itself. In the New South Wales electricity sector, by contrast, the community services sector distributed payment relief to end-users.

Direct targeted relief was usually funded by cross-subsidisation too, although not always. Victoria's Energy Relief Grant Scheme resembled in many respects the scheme of Sydney Water, with the state monopoly (Victorian SEC) centrally managing the distribution of payment relief to disadvantaged customers in danger of being disconnected for inability to pay an account. But this scheme was funded not by internal cross-subsidies but directly out of the state budget. And one utility sector, gas, had a different structure altogether, due to the fact that it had always been privately owned. For the gas industry, subsidies were required by law as a licence condition of their government authorisation. The form of the equity obligation was therefore regulatory rather than publicly provided – but the funding was once again through cross-subsidies.

CSOs reconfigure these collective equity obligations by combining two features that were not (except in the case of gas) previously combined: state-stipulated private provision and direct budget funding.[17] The way that substantive equity issues in the delivery of essential services now works is as follows. The providers of service are now either private or must operate in accordance with the market discipline imposed by the corporate form. Within the constraints of market discipline, the providers decide what returns a reasonable market actor in a purely commercial context would expect. To the extent that providing social programmes will undercut those returns, they are to be regarded as 'community service obligations' (CSOs) which the state will compensate. That compensation will no longer come from hidden cross-subsidies, but directly from the state budget, and will therefore have to pass the open political hurdles of parliamentary debate and justification. Budget compensation for social programmes will not exceed the difference between the provider's reasonable commercial expectations and its actual returns.

The technical negotiations and strategies around CSOs in the utilities sector reveal a set of assumptions that reframe social citizenship. Social equity is explicitly characterised as a burden on commercial efficacy and funded on that basis. The routines established by the introduction of CSOs effectively define the welfare obligations of a community against the baseline of a 'reasonable' market actor. This makes the social justice responsibilities characteristic of a welfare state model like something akin to a 'negative tort'. Just as unreasonably negligent individual citizen action leads to the imposition of a penalty (punishment or liability), so too does unreasonably generous corporate action lead to the imposition of a penalty: in this case, lack of budget compensation for the action. The 'social responsibility' of corporate citizens, under this view, is a question of obligation or civic duty, but the scope of civic duty is delegated to the decisions of private actors. Moreover, this 'privatised' decision-making power lies not with the end-user but with the provider. The only constraint on the scope of the obligation is negative: maximum assistance from budget funds will never *exceed* the state's judgment of what 'reasonable' assistance would entail. The state has privatised the decision-making procedures for distribution under the limits of social justice, *and* at the same time, effectively privatised the risk.

One consequence of this new set of routines is that political bargaining continues to be important in shaping the outcomes, but in a way that is displaced away from the end-users who are intended to benefit from the programmes. The pricing and delivery of CSOs is a matter between the government and the providers and the bargaining during the research period was been highly contentious and intensely secret. In particular, it was closed to the groups that would benefit from the social programmes (the disabled, low-income, isolated rural, pensioner, homeless etc). This was true both of New South Wales[18] and of Victoria.[19]

A second consequence concerns the impact of moving from indirect funding and state provision, to direct funding and private provision required by law. It is difficult to be precise, but it is notable that the subsidies in the gas sector were historically much narrower in scope than those applying in electricity and water, tending only to accrue to pensioners as opposed to low-income, youth at risk and aboriginal communities. Data on exact subsidy levels prior to the competitive break-up of electricity and water is extraordinarily difficult even to calculate, and also to obtain. But one can point to the fact that despite the continuation in Victoria of the Energy Relief Grant Scheme, the introduction in 1993 of competitive provision by several private companies led to a situation where disconnection rates more than doubled and yet the Energy Relief Grant Scheme was substantially underspending its budget.[20] This contradictory impact seems to have resulted from the administrative reorganisation attendant upon privatisation. Responsibility for the safety net scheme was transferred to the Department of Health and Community Services and the resulting fragmentation of responsibilities has made communication between customer and provider difficult and clumsy.

A third issue so far mainly dormant is the enforcement of CSOs. There is little incentive for private and even corporatised companies to provide essential services to unprofitable customers. Even if formal regulation requires them to do so and undertakes to refund the cost from the budget, it is costly and time-consuming for the companies. This issue was dormant at the time of research because the rules defining the extent of the CSO obligation were still in the process of being hammered out. But a quick comparison with the telecommunications sector, which is much further forward with the process of competitive break-up, is useful. There, companies have indeed shirked obligations which were statutorily encoded. Attempts to enforce these in the courts, for example on behalf of aboriginal people,[21] have very rarely been successful. As in other utility sectors in other countries such as New Zealand and the United Kingdom, the courts frequently disclaim judicial review powers over statutory duties to provide essential services in particular ways.[22] The one successful case to date in telecommunications CSOs concerned profoundly deaf people[23] who sought to have CSOs enforced in their favour. The reason for their success was the existence of the Disability Discrimination Act 1992 (Cth) which gave deaf people a formal right against discrimination. This existence of a legally-encoded right as a leverage point is happenstance here: in most utility contexts, no such formal rights exist.

What, then, is the overall picture of the nature of the institutions and routines introduced in the newly competitive utility sector to address issues of substantive equity? One can observe significant fragmentation of institutions and a proliferation of rules governing CSOs. These proliferating rules, however, are not transparent. There is also relatively little development of separate and independent enforcing institutions. Judicial developments indicate that the notion of a "class of consumers" to whom special obligations are owed has little legal force so far, notwithstanding its presence as a specific sub-clause of the 'public interest interpretation clause' in the Competition Principles Agreement. These features together make the pursuit of substantive equity in the delivery of utility services noticeably subject to political discretion and flexibility. Although this has historically been true of many traditional welfare state functions, the difference is that the terrain of dispute will now become a question of the *scope of the contract* under which the government indemnifies providers for social programmes. Thus technical issues of pricing will likely dominate. Even if political issues of fairness leak into this technical discussion, the dialogue will not directly include the beneficiaries of social programmes. Thus in this case the reframing of social citizenship goals has put the redistributive facet of social citizenship regulation at risk, a situation apparently unameliorated by a left-wing administration.

The potential implications of this reframing go further than the practical, concrete outcomes indicated above. At the expressive level, the structure of CSOs redefines governmental functions as ensuring the delivery of services to minimum standards, via contractual techniques, as opposed to ensuring social integration via techniques of political participation. Minimum welfare rights are defined in market terms with government as the regulator of lowest common denominator. The exercise of private power is imprinted with a dimension of public purpose, but that dimension is marginal to its central purpose of commercial efficacy. By instantiating 'normal commercial practice' as the central norm, rather than any notion of social justice, however inchoately that may have been defined in the past, the common sense assumptions underpinning social citizenship are shifted. Instead of social citizenship constituting a core right, expressive of collective obligations amongst members of society, it becomes a discretionary surplus peripheral to a core goal of maximising commercial efficacy and competitive efficiency. The effects of this kind of 'structural bias' will become clearer in the case studies that follow. In the meantime, I consider whether the second kind of strategy, rooted in legal process, has any greater chance of success in securing the protection of social citizenship goals.

Consumer Protection Obligation Strategies

CSOs address substantive equity issues but in some respects, the changes induced by the competitive break-up of utilities have had a greater impact on process-based accountability strategies. This may be because there were virtually no process-based strategies, at least not ones encoded in any kind of formal or semi-formal framework, prior to the break-up. Two main developments can be perceived. The first concerned efforts to lobby the federal government for a fully-blown 'public service' dimension to utility provision, a dimension that included both public-law-like legal processes and social equity objectives.

The second development, which was sparked in part by a change of federal government from left to right-wing,[24] involved a focus on the industry itself and to a subsidiary degree on state governments, relative de-emphasis of social equity strategies and a legal process emphasis which *blended* private and public values and strategies. Arguably, what is emerging is a hybrid regime of accountability that seeks to protect both social citizenship goals and market infrastructure goals through a 'network' structure of bargaining relations. In this network structure, law (or law-like forms) shape private bargaining relations, but rather than constraining the outcome of the actual substance of bargains made (a 'pure' social citizenship approach), they foster a compromise approach which ensures merely that the voices of those groups who support social citizenship goals are heard.

In the next few paragraphs, I chart the trajectory from the initial efforts to impose a 'public service' dimension upon utility provision to the hybrid network strategy that ultimately emerged. Before the change of Federal government in 1996 from Labour to the right-wing Coalition, the then Minister for Consumer Affairs, Jeanette McHugh, was a strong advocate of the need for formal encoding of "Consumer Protection Obligations" (CPOs) which would apply to the restructured providers of utility services in the new competition era. The stated aim of the proposed CPOs was to "ensure that utilities providing essential goods and services operate in a proper social context".[25] A series of discussion papers was released by her Department and a key conference was held to garner stakeholder support for these policy proposals.

CPOs would have required utilities not to discriminate against customers suffering financial, geographical or physical disadvantage, to ensure that customers are properly informed, to provide accessible and impartial dispute resolution procedures and to guarantee customer privacy.[26] CPOs, under a Labour government, sought therefore to expand the goals of utility restructuring beyond market infrastructure (increased efficiency and lower prices) in two directions. One direction would have supplemented market infrastructure with protections of the kind familiar to the 'new administrative law' (see Chapter Two): freedom of information and merit-based review of decisions. The second direction sought to encompass social equity objectives through more substantive redistributive obligations of the kind previously fulfilled by internal cross-subsidies (and now commonly addressed by the CSOs already discussed in the previous section).

The demise in March 1996 of that Labour government, however, ended the nascent emergence of CPOs at the federal level, not least because the right-wing Coalition regarded such issues as properly within the domain of state government jurisdiction. Accordingly, efforts to secure CPO-like processes were now focused at state government level and in some respects on the utility industries themselves. The main proponents of consumer accountability strategies are peak bodies such as the Australian Consumers' Association and the New South Wales Public Interest Advocacy Centre.

These are the same bodies who broadly advocated a differentiated consumer sovereignty (DCS) perspective in the general parliamentary inquiry explored in Chapter Three.

To a certain degree, these organisations built on the earlier work of the nascent CPOs, lobbying for public-law-like procedural rights such as freedom of information and ombudsman access. The strategy has shifted in four main ways, however. First, the emphasis of these peak community groups was more on procedural rights rather than on substantive redistribution.[27] In this respect, process-based strategies have expanded beyond public-law-like rights to private-law-like mechanisms such as customer contracts imposing service standards.

Secondly, the form of the social citizenship strategy altered. Rather than seeking federal legislation or formal regulation, the aspiration now is to embed CPOs in codes of conduct that govern the conduct and policies of the utility industry. This reflected the preference of the then Minister for Small Business and Consumer Affairs, who promoted industry-based dispute resolution mechanisms in preference to schemes mandated by formal government rules.[28]

Thirdly, the level of intervention is changing. Licence conditions, statutory obligations and pro forma contracts are all rule-based mechanisms that govern the provider-citizen relationship *only once the framework of rules* is set. Public interest groups, especially those representing traditionally marginal end-users, feel that a more effective strategy would focus on 'getting a seat at the table' in order to influence those framework rules. Thus they have begun to focus more and more on systemic strategies, rather than individual accountability strategies. Systemic strategies are intended to provide disadvantaged consumer groups with a collective voice in order to equalise their capacity for participation in the market.

The fourth change in strategy also has to do with level of intervention: not only has strategy moved from individual accountability mechanisms to systemic approaches, but also from federal to state level. Like the other changes in strategy, this is a shift caused by the change of government at the federal level from left to right wing. Perhaps it is not surprising then that it is New South Wales, still governed by a left-wing government at the time of research, where a relatively extensive network strategy developed. It is therefore New South Wales that I describe in more detail in the next section.[29]

Network Strategies of Consumer Protection in New South Wales

Network Strategies of Consumer Protection in New South Wales had two principal elements: a consumer advocacy network and consumer aggregation structures. The advocates of these moves labelled these as 'market-based strategies' to distinguish them from 'top-down' rule-based strategies.[30] This was meant to capture the fact that rule-based intervention, where it exists in such strategies, is aimed at shaping private bargaining processes rather than dictating their outcomes. Because the shaping is aimed not just at facilitating a market infrastructure, but also at opening up or preserving possibilities for securing social citizenship goals, it is a good example of a hybrid model of the kind envisaged by the differentiated consumer sovereignty perspective discussed in Chapter Three. As we shall see, its development focused strongly on bolstering the autonomous voice of specific segmented interests that would otherwise not have had much, if any, influence in the processes of changing the rules.

Consumer advocacy network   Public interest groups and community groups in New South Wales, coordinated by the Public Interest Advocacy Centre (PIAC), were concerned that in the emerging new utility structures, industry initiation overly constrained agenda-setting power. Large utilities had set up various consumer consultative groups, but they had excluded a number of significantly affected groups from that process. Those groups included credit advice services, community housing organisations, tenancy advice, community legal services, pensioner organisations, neighbourhood centres, women's centres, disability services and aboriginal services.[31] Led by PIAC, these groups began to design a mechanism which explicitly set out to *redress the power balance* that typically prevails in a co-regulatory model: the Utility Consumer Advocacy Network (UCAN).

In 1997, the above groups were successful in obtaining funding to establish UCAN in at least the electricity industry, and possibly water and gas as well, in New South Wales.[32] The consortium supports a vision of consumer-based advocacy networks that represent "the interests of people who are disadvantaged in the market place".[33] The basic aim of UCAN is to establish "an independent organisation as a voice for utilities consumers in New South Wales to redress the imbalances in the exercise of control in the market between utilities and consumers".[34] Thus it is a strategy explicitly addressed at *power relations* through the acquisition of *collective voice*. "Fundamentally, what is being asked for is an organisational structure which gives to consumers some real power to take into the market place".[35]

The break-up of utilities for the purposes of promoting competition was therefore providing an opportunity for hitherto unarticulated interests to find a voice in the policymaking procedure. The community organisations who were canvassed by PIAC to survey the feasibility of UCAN all noted that utility policies and procedures had not previously been a focus of their work, and most expressed the view that there was currently no avenue for a voice on policies and systemic procedural issues (with the possible exception of the Combined Pensioners and Superannuants Association and the Country Women's Association).[36]

Of course, the inclusion of new interests in policymaking procedures often meets with resistance from entrenched interests, and resistance certainly existed in this instance. The principal objectors were the utilities themselves, but extended also to Treasury and the Department of Energy ('hard-line' economically oriented government departments who typically supported a pure market infrastructure perspective in the agenda-setting period discussed in Chapter Four). The state itself was not a monolithic entity, though, and both the Department of Fair Trading and IPART (the Independent Pricing and Regulatory Tribunal) were supportive of the idea.

The main objections (from the utilities, Treasury and the Department of Energy) turned on fears that the proposal would foster adversarial 'special interest' politics (the kind of politics which was characterised as illegitimate rent-seeking). The utilities insisted that a legitimate consumer advocacy network must have a wide representative base to maintain credibility, and Treasury went so far as to say that only representation of the "full spectrum of consumer interests" would be legitimate. Both groups felt that disaggregating the general class of 'consumers' into specifically identified smaller groups of 'disadvantaged consumers' leads to 'special interest politics'.

The way in which UCAN proponents met this objection was to emphasise ways in which *adversarialism* was a baseless fear (clearly they did feel that the representation of narrow classes of consumers – who would otherwise be ignored – was legitimate). The objectors were wary of adversarial advocacy. Treasury, for example, expressed the view that a network such as UCAN might not have the 'maturity' to accept the overall direction of current changes, and the utilities insisted on advocates who had technical expertise and a co-operative approach. In the end, UCAN proponents agreed to support a partnership approach: on the part of utilities, an acceptance "that the network must maintain a critical eye on policies and practices" and on the part of UCAN, "a constructive approach to systemic advocacy, one that minimises the use of adversarial processes and favours consultative and cooperative processes".[37] With the support of the Department of Fair Trading, and based on this compromise, the go-ahead was given for UCAN to form.

UCAN represents the emergence of a 'hybrid' model of governance that blurs the line between political voice and market participation. It draws on state support to foster a context in which all market participants affected by competitive restructuring can have an equal voice. The network downplays social equity concerns and frames its issues almost entirely in the language of consumer sovereignty – yet by the nature of its constituency (disadvantaged consumers), it still plays a role in addressing social equity issues. It is an example of the differentiated consumer sovereignty perspective explored in Chapter Four.

Consumer aggregation approaches   Hybridity is also evident in the second primary strategy being developed in New South Wales, consumer aggregation approaches. Consumer aggregation approaches, like UCAN, seek to locate power in 'small consumers' rather than industry and are premised on a 'market-based approach' rather than the application of general government rules. The strategy focuses on aggregation of residential consumers through non-profit retail cooperatives and draws on similar initiatives undertaken in recent years in Southern California.[38] Non-profit cooperatives (or alternatively local governments) purchase electricity in bulk in order to reap the benefit of the competitive market for small consumers by pooling their purchasing power.

Aggregation of consumer purchasing power through cooperatives at present aims primarily at securing discounted prices. A study on the feasibility of energy co-operatives, the Norco Energy Co-operative Feasibility Study, funded jointly by the New South Wales Sustainable Energy Development Authority and the New South Wales Department of Fair Trading confirmed that the "significant benefits to small consumers" that energy co-operatives could offer are price reductions of 20-30% for co-ops with 1,000 to 5,000 members.[39] Although presented as a way of equalising power and providing a forum for collective voice, the main aim of this strategy is therefore to pursue the redistributive facet of social citizenship.

The fact that it focuses entirely on material gains for disadvantaged groups may reflect the limits of aggregating diverse preferences that weaken the community morality approach and give more strategic bite to the differentiated consumer sovereignty perspective. When the acquisition of political voice is directly pursued, as with the consumer advocacy network, differential representation of a variety of interests works well. When sheer market power is the aim, the only non-contentious 'community morality' is higher purchasing power – and this may provide a weak bulwark to arguments from proponents of deregulation that increased efficiency will bring costs down.

Summary

In Victoria, then, market infrastructure goals had greater priority in restructuring utility provision than they did in New South Wales, and a two-track system of shaping the relationships in the newly structured utilities developed. The final consumers of utility services (especially residential consumers) fell, during the right-wing government's administration, under the umbrella of informal accountability mechanisms that are not embedded in formal law, while in contrast, providers and investors received the protection of full judicial property rights regimes. End-users in Victoria were therefore vulnerable to the discretion of utility providers or of the government in power at the time. In New South Wales, disadvantaged end-users had more of a voice because the network structure of IPART locks in their capacity to participate in the policymaking procedure even if the Labour government loses power.

In both states, the only way for disadvantaged groups to secure some consideration was to frame their claims in the language of consumer sovereignty. Arguments that social equity should be pursued through substantive redistribution of fiscal resources were less popular or pervasive than advocacy of procedural mechanisms that would 'level the playing field'. The institutional implication of this strategy is the emergence of a hybrid mode of governance consistent with the differentiated consumer sovereignty (DCS) perspective described in Chapter Three. UCAN represents a typical hybrid strategy: an informal, consultative negotiating mechanism with small numbers of open-textured 'framework rules' backed by state power. These mechanisms permit groups that previously had no formal 'seat at the table' to participate. They represent a new avenue that has opened up as a result of rewriting the rules, but one that is only secured through 'translating' social citizenship goals into the dominant discourse shaped by economic analysis.

This shows that the kind of approach envisioned by a differentiated consumer sovereignty perspective *can* incorporate and protect social citizenship goals, even ones that concern redistributive regulation. In part, whether this occurs is influenced by partisan politics, or at least by the institutional development of 'network' structures, which appear to be introduced more readily by a left-wing governing party. Left-wing governments may do this because the broader context of international pressures to become more competitive (as well as direct pressure from business) make it difficult for them to address social citizenship issues through direct political action; whereas incorporating social citizenship concerns into the agenda of independent institutions staffed by relatively neutral experts allows them both to 'lock in' the opportunity for those goals to be addressed, and to depoliticise the issue.

The positive opportunities to pursue social citizenship in this broader context of National Competition Policy are not only connected to partisan politics but also to timing. The institutional innovation that developed in utility policy in New South Wales to protect equity values occurred on a macro-structural level at an early stage of policy development. In those circumstances (and possibly only with the extra aid of a left-wing government), the logic of National Competition Policy remained open enough not to narrow social citizenship goals appreciably. As we shall see in the next case studies, however, that logic can also catalyse changes in institutional strategy and policy goals that bite much harder, creating a structural bias against social citizenship legislation that is much more difficult to counter.

Rice Marketing Board Review: New South Wales

The rice review was conducted in late 1995 and a series of recommendations were sent to the New South Wales Labour Government in early 1996 in the form of a "Final Report".[40] It was the first review of regulatory arrangements concerning agricultural marketing boards to be undertaken in the NCP process. Agricultural marketing boards were a major target of the review process under the CPA. The original architects of the reform package such as Professor Hilmer and key Treasury personnel regarded them as a 'core instance' of the kind of regulatory intervention that required explicit justification if it was to be retained by the 'competition state' to which the reforms aspired.

From the analytical standpoint, this was a clear case of falling well within the reform agenda of reviewing 'restrictions on competition'. The legislation essentially *replaced* the market for rice with administratively managed buying and selling of rice. All rice was deemed to be owned by ("vested in") the Rice Marketing Board, and all rice (both domestic and export) was sold by the Ricegrowers' Co-operative Limited. The Rice Marketing Board was thus a device of regulatory intervention that created a monopoly in place of a decentralised market. The basic arrangement will be referred to hereafter as the "monopoly vesting arrangements".

Rice was not only clearly a target for CPA review by virtue of the monopoly vesting arrangements, but also by virtue of the kind of benefit accruing from the arrangements. CPA review aimed to retain anti-competitive arrangements only where the "public benefit" was clear and documented. As the Final Report noted, agricultural boards have largely fostered *industry* benefits rather than public benefits.[41] Indeed, in the case of the Rice Marketing Board, no secret was made of this, as the second reading speech in Parliament when the original legislation was passed in 1983 referred to the objectives of the legislation as being to "facilitate the commercial and efficient marketing of agricultural commodities *in the best long term interests of producers*".[42] It was thus a natural early target of the meta-regulatory regime.

Historically, Australia's economy has been significantly dependent on primary industry, and the agricultural boards have been the source of many rural support policies such as buying surplus provision and stockpiling and maintaining floor prices for crops. Marketing boards have also frequently co-ordinated many 'value-added' processes which have improved the quality of the final product. In the case of rice, examples of such processes were the production of stock feed, cereal and snack foods, marketing services, refining processes, and transport and freight . In other words, the monopoly vesting arrangements not only increased market power but also added value through the provision of ancillary services. Of course, in so doing, they replaced the markets for those ancillary services with a monopoly too. Still, the division between the core activity of selling rice, and services ancillary to that core function, turned out to be important to the approach of the Review Group. Before turning to an explanation of the substance of reasoning in the review, though, it is useful to outline briefly the personnel and procedures.

The review was conducted fairly transparently and was centred in the Department of Agriculture. Representatives on the Review Group consisted mostly of central agency bureaucrats and the groups affected most directly by the legislation. The Rice Marketing Board itself, the Cabinet Office, the Treasury and the Department of Agriculture, which chaired the Group, were all represented. There were no non-governmental representatives of diffuse interests such as consumer groups or and environmental groups. The analytical work which was critical to the conduct of the review was performed by private consultants hired by the Rice Marketing Board, civil servants in the Department of Agriculture, and an academic: all three of these sources of expert advice were economists.

Public consultation consisted of a widely released issues paper inviting public comment, as well as five workshops focused on this issues paper. The Review Group also made field trips to rice growing regions. Ninety-five percent of the 256 submissions came from individual rice growers, who almost all supported the status quo. There was little or no input from consumer lobbies, despite the fact that retail prices were definitely a significant issue. Apart from rice growers, local governments in rice-growing areas made submissions, as did the New South Wales Environmental Protection Agency, the Commonwealth Bank, the Australian Manufacturers Workers' Union and the National Union of Workers.

Procedurally, then, the review was transparent and semi-autonomous from politics, in the sense that governmental interests beyond the

Department of Agriculture were represented, though the review was still based within government. Participation was almost wholly producer-centred (union contributions were worried about workers' interests in the rice mills and storage facilities) and review personnel were either representing producer groups or the perspective of professional economists. The terms of reference for the review mentioned the main "guiding principle" of the CPA (the requirement to achieve net public benefit in the manner least restrictive of competition) and required the Review group to "identify any issues of market failure which need to be addressed by the Rice Marketing Board".[43] They did not refer to the public interest interpretation clause. Apart from the one submission by the EPA, then, the review was initially framed very much as an issue where market infrastructure and economic analysis were the most germane facets.

Despite this initial framing, the process as it spun out did not in fact restrict itself wholly to market failure issues nor only to quantitative economic analysis, though both certainly dominated the Final Report. But the Final Report opened with a full quotation of both the guiding principles of the CPA and the full text of the public interest interpretation clause. The Review Group explicitly identified[44] regional development and impacts on the environment as two factors from the public interest interpretation clause that needed to be taken into account. They requested that evidence be developed in relation to both these factors, and also addressed at the end of the report some aspects of public accountability.

In all three of these areas, the Review Group relied on some qualitative evidence and non-technical assessment of costs and benefits (to be elaborated in due course), thus indicating that the review process reached beyond quantitative economic analysis. It was also a process that reached beyond the specific interests represented on the Review Group, insofar as consumer interests were given significant attention despite the absence of consumer representatives. At least procedurally, then, the review demonstrated autonomy from politics without relying wholly on technocratic economic discourse in order to do so.

But to delve further into the kinds of values and goals fostered by the review, we must explore in more detail the substantive reasoning and decisions of the Review Group. Essentially these proceeded in two steps, as envisaged by the CPA meta-regulatory regime. First, the efficiency of the monopoly vesting arrangements was considered, followed secondly by analysing the justifications that might be offered for any inefficiencies thus discovered. The outcome of this two-step analysis was that the Review Group decided the inefficiencies of monopoly vesting were partially justified *in relation to the export market only,* and thus in this area, continuing intervention was acceptable. In relation to the *domestic* rice market, and in relation to peripheral services (transport, storage, processing, marketing etc.) for both export and domestic rice, the inefficiencies were not justified, and the Review Group recommended deregulation. In order to achieve this mixed result, the Group suggested dismantling the state monopoly vesting arrangements altogether, and establishing export licensing controls at *federal* level – for export rice only.

In what follows, I explain how the Group came to these conclusions, the fate of efficiency, environmental, regional development and public accountability values along the way, and the institutional implications of the final recommendations.

Value Outcomes

The economic analysis of monopoly vesting arrangements indicated that a welfare transfer from consumers to producers occurred in both export and domestic markets that would not occur in an unregulated market. This subsidisation of ricegrowers by consumers was therefore inefficient. In considering what could justify this distortion, the growers had argued that the monopoly vesting arrangements secured "countervailing power" for rice growers in a market where wholesalers and processors had enough market power to force down prices. The Board was thus a device to 'level the playing field', the growers contended. However, the Review Group was reluctant to accept this argument. It stated that several factors limited the abuse of market power by wholesalers: the existence of an export market which the growers could use as an alternative to selling on the domestic market, the existence of anti-trust provisions which could be used against the wholesalers, and the possibility of growers investing directly in the existing wholesaling sector. The Review Group thus favoured market responses, or post-hoc regulatory responses, and expressed a wish to "avoid the efficiency losses which can arise when pre-emptive regulation [such as establishing a marketing board] is used".[45]

Despite this general stance, the Review Group accepted the resultant efficiency loss for the export market, and not for the domestic market. In relation to the latter, it stated, "providing the Rice Board with the ability to derive above normal returns from *domestic* consumers goes beyond the powers required to offset potentially anti-competitive activities of wholesalers".[46] But for the export market, it considered that the "ability to obtain above normal returns from export markets [might] offset the efficiency costs associated with the arrangement".[47] In reasoning like this, it treated the capacity to obtain "above normal returns" differently in the export and domestic markets. It effectively allowed 'industry benefit' to count as 'public benefit' where foreign consumers were concerned, but when the trade-off was against *Australian* consumers, 'industry benefit' was regarded as incompatible with 'public benefit'. The Group noted that the analytical framework of the CPA regime had not been well-defined for circumstances involving export markets, but apart from this notation, it did not offer any rationale for why it discounted the welfare losses to foreign consumers. Instead, it relied on a 1991 Productivity Commission Report on Statutory Marketing Arrangements which assumed the relevant community seeking to benefit from regulatory reform was "Australia".

The 'public benefit', in the context of the export market for rice, was therefore the amount of the price premium that a single export seller could garner over and above what a market consisting of several or many rice exporters would gain. Here the private consultants employed by the Board agreed with the Department of Agriculture's economists that *some* premium existed, but the latter refused to quantify it, saying there was no evidence that would ground a sound conclusion. The private consultants employed by the Board, however, estimated the premium to be in the order of AUS$36-47 million. The academic employed to monitor this dispute over the evidence agreed broadly with the government economists.

The Review Group "noted the concerns made about the Board's approach" but emphasised that all the experts agreed that there was "*some* price premium" and asserted that it was "probable" that premiums of the size that the Board estimated would result in the next five years. Therefore, it concluded, "there are clear benefits from single desk export selling".[48] Essentially, because the welfare loss to foreign consumers did not count, the amount of the price premium was not important, only its existence. And that price premium, whatever its amount, justified the retention of the anti-competitive arrangements for exported rice. Since over 85% of Australian rice is exported, this was obviously a major aspect of the Review Group's overall decision.

Within the domestic community, however, the Review Group invested more resources in quantifying the trade-offs involved. Once again, the experts differed, and once again the private consultants' assessment favoured retention of the status quo more than the government economists' evaluation. The private consultants hired by the Board estimated that consumers subsidised growers (through paying higher prices than they otherwise would) to the tune of AUS$2million. The government economists, by contrast, put the level at AUS$12 million. The Review Group ultimately focused not on the difference in quantification but on the commonality of the result: the existence of a transfer in welfare from consumers to producers. This transfer had no justification, they argued, reiterating their earlier views that market power abuse by wholesalers, if it existed, should be addressed by post-hoc use of anti-trust laws, rather than pre-empting it by constructing a marketing board. "Competitive market forces should determine the socially optimal level of domestic consumption of Australian rice and associated prices".[49]

So far, one justification for regulatory-induced inefficiencies in the rice review had been rejected – to redress an imbalance in market power – while a second had been accepted more or less implicitly – via a threshold assumption that the boundaries of the relevant market or community are those of the nation-state. To this point, then, either efficiency values were given priority, or wealth creation for the nation-state as a whole.

When redistributive trade-offs arose *within* the rice-growing community, efficiency once again won out. This was clear in the fate of the cost-pooling arrangements carried out by the Board. The costs of services peripheral to the actual selling of rice (transport, storage, milling, operation and maintenance, marketing, some processing) were pooled among growers, and deducted on an average basis. This resulted in cross-subsidisation by growers close to major storage and processing centres to growers in remote locations. There was also some cross-subsidisation from large growers to small growers. The Review Group was concerned that these cross-subsidies would encourage rice farms to locate in inefficiently distant areas and to retain inefficiently small sizes, resulting in resource misallocation.

The economic experts in the review calculated the size of the cross-subsidies and specified precisely who won and lost within the farming community. Once again, the Board's experts disagreed with government (Treasury) experts, the former maintaining that the net cross-subsidies were negligible (approx. 2% of average return) and the latter arguing they were significant (7.4% of average costs). Once again the independent academic umpire agreed with the government, although she or he was not prepared to conclude that the cross-subsidies were sufficient by themselves to cause resource misallocation. The Review Group chose to agree with the Treasury estimates and concluded that "these inefficiencies should be eliminated...by the removal of the current [monopoly] vesting arrangements [which] should encourage greater competition in the supply of these services".[50] Once again, competition was given priority, despite the fact that growers unanimously supported the cross-subsidisation within their community and regarded this very strongly as a purely internal issue.

This last aspect of the rice review seems to raise rather directly the value of regional development. Although overall levels of economic activity and employment in a particular area are one way of assessing regional development, social cohesion and cooperation between stronger and weaker individuals in a particular community (e.g. that achieved by cost-pooling) are precisely the kind of values advocated by the community morality perspective on regulation explored in the last chapter. As the Review Group acknowledged, regional development values were invoked by the rice growers as one of the primary justifications for retaining the marketing board arrangements.

Broadly speaking the benefits were put in the form of various public goods – infrastructure investments, the development of value-adding activities that cost a lot upfront to kick-start, generation of loyalty to national brand names. The Review Group addressed these submissions by saying that in recognising the public benefit flowing from single seller restrictions on *export* rice, they had already taken into account most of the regional development benefits advocated by the grower community. When regional development was pitted against the monopoly pricing practice on the domestic market, it lost: "where the benefits of one sector of the Australian economy are at the expense of another",[51] regional benefits alone are not sufficient to justify statutory marketing arrangements. The Review Group argued:

> [We] believe that the use of ... interventions which distort market signals or create consumer transfers are not efficient means of achieving regional development objectives. Instead, the development of appropriate frameworks and policies which facilitate self-reliance and entrepreneurship are the means which Governments are using to further their regional development objectives.[52]

In fact, the main casualty of the Review Group's approach was the internal redistribution within the producer community: the burden of reform would most likely be borne by the smaller, poorer farms in the rice-growing area. Thus equity within the producer community suffered: equity was a public interest clause factor, but was nowhere referred to by the Review. *Overall* local employment and economic activity would not suffer a great deal, given that single seller restrictions for the *export* market were being retained. Arguably, this retention, which was justified officially by the wealth creation it fostered for the "Australian community as a whole", was in reality justified by regional development values. Or perhaps it is fairer to say simply that they overlapped in the context of an export market and an assumption that the CPA regime took the nation-state as its referent community. But this overlap was not made much of; the Review Group preferred to construct its recommendations as based on quantifiable public benefit to Australia as a whole rather than on diffuse benefit to the ricegrowing region of New South Wales.

The final factor taken into account by the Review Group in assessing the justifiability of regulatory inefficiency was environmental impact. They considered the EPA's arguments about the degradation of downstream water quality and the counter-arguments of growers that rice production created marshlands with recreational and ecological benefits for the community. Growers also argued that the producer surplus they gained from monopoly pricing made it affordable for them to invest in Land Water Management Plans, and therefore functioned as an 'environmental levy'. Thus they were trying to balance the cost to efficiency and burden on consumer prices with the environmental benefits that the extra money could be used to foster. EPA, however, was of the opinion that more environmental benefits would flow from *less* rice production, and that the current monopoly arrangements subsidised extra production. Thus pro-competitive reforms would in this case *dovetail* with the promotion of environmental values.

In response to the environmental levy argument, the Review Group maintained that just as pursuing regional development goals through pooling costs and cross-subsidisation was a "distorting mechanism", so too pursuing environmental benefits through commodity pricing was a "distorting mechanism". They suggested that environmental goals were better facilitated through "community/region based projects".[53] They did not actually examine any evidence to see whether the grower community were in fact funnelling their producer surplus into environmental projects. They did, however, adduce evidence that the net cost of water table degradation was AUS$76,000 per annum, and that this was "extremely slight" in view of the public benefit in increased wealth and regional development.[54] It appears, however, that this figure relates only to the environmental impact of the extra rice produced for the *domestic* market.[55] Yet the increased wealth for Australia and regional development flowed from the existence of the entire rice market, both for domestic sales *and for export*. The environmental costs of that export production were not actually counted.

The Review Group's overall approach, then, seems to have bracketed off their initial decision to retain single seller restrictions for the export market. By doing this, they counted regional development more than they appeared to, and they discounted environmental costs more than they appeared to. But this did not appear to be a strategic manipulation: rather, it flowed from the two-step analysis of the meta-regulatory regime. The structure of analysis only considered these 'non-market' kinds of issues *after* efficiency had been analysed.

In this respect, the framework of CPA analysis gave a start-up advantage to consumer sovereignty values. Consumer sovereignty was part of the original framework of the CPA regime. The general imperative to remove restrictions on competition and maximise efficiency was precisely aimed at enhancing the welfare of consumers generally. Ensuring that other values such as environmental harm or regional development were taken into account was an aspect of the CPA regime that had been 'tacked on' to the Competition Principles Agreement by dissenting groups, and, as we have seen, was the subject of ongoing contestation, secret lobbying and political dispute. *Does* the rice review bear out the fears of the Consumer Advocacy Centre[56] that the public interest clause factors would never receive more than lip service?

The answer to that question is not obvious. There is no glaring neglect in this case study. Factors beyond market competitiveness and cost-benefit quantification were certainly taken into account. Evidence was adduced for several of the public interest clause factors, and reasonable consideration was given to those issues, although in terms of space they did command only 10% of the Final Report. The empirical evidence was not conclusive but neither were there deep empirical fissures. The participants disagreed at the margins on the quantity of costs and benefits, but consensus on the main trends were clear. All of the 'public interest' issues 'counted', but not enough to outweigh domestic consumer sovereignty. The exclusion of *foreign* consumer interests from the analysis meant that regional development probably counted more than the report was willing to admit while environmental issues counted less. Equity values did not receive explicit consideration, and definitely lost out within the rice-growing community. But clearly any reform will generate losers and it is no surprise that those responsible for recommending reform will minimise the visibility of those losers. Certainly the review did not ignore wider values beyond economic efficiency and consumer sovereignty.

Nonetheless, there is still a way in which the structure of the analysis remains one which has only a precarious place for those broader values. This is because the Review Group used the 'two-step' process of the meta-regulatory regime not only as an analytical tool, but as an actual programmatic assumption. That is, the reviewers assumed not only that efficiency issues should be *analysed* separately from social justice, equity and social risk issues, but also that they should be resolved by separate institutional responses. The environmental levy response is an example of this. The Review Group rejected the proposal that the price mechanism for selling rice incorporate a premium that would enable pursuit of environmental values. Instead, it recommended that this was better pursued through "community/regional-based projects".

By refusing to bundle together the pursuit of multiple values within the market infrastructure recommended by CPA reforms, this approach does not ignore non-market values, but it makes their pursuit more *politically* vulnerable. Small remote growers must seek direct subsidies from government, eco-sensitive growers must gain funding to create a region-based project to reverse land and water degradation. These are politically vulnerable projects. In contrast, DCS advocates might well support the growers' environmental levy argument. They might argue that the rice market, in order to provide a structure that includes resources and incentives for environmental goals as well as efficiency goals, should include the capacity to price the sale of rice at a level that would fund participation in environmental management projects. They might insist that the relevant funds go into a 'tagged fund' to ensure proper use of the money. But the Review Group's approach in the rice review would label this suggestion a 'distorting mechanism'. The 'two-step' analysis prevents it being characterised as a market-based method of addressing environmental externalities.

Institutional Outcomes

To what extent did the Review Group's recommended reforms intensify network relations between institutions and/or increase institutional autonomy? First, it is necessary to characterise the status quo. The status quo was a monopoly marketing board that had extensive discretion to set prices, pool costs and order the affairs of ricegrowers as it saw fit. The Board did owe some reporting and accountability obligations to Parliament. But in practice, it contracted out all its substantive functions to the Ricegrowers' Cooperative Council that had unrestricted top-down control and discretion. In addition, Board membership and Council membership substantially overlapped and both were under the control of ricegrowers. Thus the status quo was highly discretionary and significantly hierarchical, in the mode of state planning and low reliance on formal rules (see Figure 5.1 at page 146).

How would this hierarchical state planning mode change if the Review Group's recommendations were adopted? The Review Group had two separate recommendations, distinguishing export rice production from domestic rice production. For export rice production, it had, as discussed, recommended that government continue to require that sales of rice all proceed through a single point. However, this was not a straightforward retention of state planning, but a complex shift towards structures that were still hierarchical, but more bureaucratic than before (i.e. more formal, and with greater elements of institutional autonomy).

The Review Group, while it wanted to retain single-desk selling, did not consider that the Rice Marketing Board was the "least restrictive form of regulation" available to do this. Rather, a request for the *federal* government to issue a single export licence for Australian rice was the least restrictive option. This would retain government control, but reduce cross-state duplication[57] of institutions, and would also 'slim' down the degree of intervention since one licence involves less personnel and resources than an entire Board. Although the report did not go into further detail, an export licence option would clearly require some significant number of formal substantive rules to be drafted. This would shift the institutional result closer towards a bureaucratic one rather than a state planning one.

The licence would not, however, address the 'peripheral services' (transport, processing, milling, storage) which the current Board did deal with, but would leave these aspects to decentralised market competition. The location of power in the federal government would also decrease the extent to which ricegrowers were represented at the locus of dispositive power: thus institutional autonomy (in the sense of independence from stakeholders) would increase. This was important to the Review Group: they stressed that if the federal government did not take over export responsibility, the current overlapping membership between the Board and the Co-operative should at the very least be altered to an "arm's length and fully commercial" relationship.[58]

Overall, the export recommendations therefore shifted institutional strategies towards 'slimmed down bureaucracy' complemented by markets in peripheral services, and with discretion constrained – to a greater extent than previously – by the institutional autonomy of those enforcing and administering the relevant rules.

For the domestic rice market, the Review Group's institutional recommendations would definitely move organisational structures even further away from the status quo 'state planning' mode. As has been seen, the recommendation to deregulate the selling, pricing and peripheral services of domestic rice would leave all aspects of domestic rice production to be decided by competitive market mechanisms. To the extent that individual growers would face cartels of buyers, the Review Group considered *ex post* solutions such as anti-trust laws to be preferable to pre-emptive regulation. Anti-trust laws would constrain the discretion of wholesaler actors in the markets to some degree but only if invoked by growers, thus this is more of a decentralised network structure.

Though largely moving away from a hierarchical mode of organising rice sales towards networks and markets, the Review Group also made a passing suggestion that a quasi-hierarchical strategy could address some of the redistributive issues raised by deregulating the domestic market. As noted before, the cost-pooling arrangements of the Rice Marketing Board effectively provided cross-subsidies in the provision of peripheral services that favoured the more remote growers. In addition, the monopoly provision on marketing and processing services effectively subsidised the smaller, less educated growers who did not have access to the skills and knowledge necessary to 'add value' to their basic rice crop on their own. The Review Group considered suggesting that government intervention could authorise the collection of a compulsory levy by an industry body, in order to finance the provision of market information services for the community of growers.[59] This 'information levy' proposal would remove hierarchical intervention in the direct provision of services and limit it to the provision of information, in a manner aimed at facilitating self-help. This particular strategy of facilitating choice by sanctioning government intervention to address a market failure of *informational asymmetry* is one we shall see again (more strongly) in the next case study (the migration regulation review). In the instant case, it was not incorporated into the official final recommendations of the Group.

Initially, the Review Group's recommendations to repeal state vesting arrangements but retain, at *federal* level, an export monopoly, were not adopted by the state Labour government to whom they were submitted. While no reasons were publicly given for this decision, it appears that politics gave greater weight to internal social cohesion and equity within the rice community than to securing greater competitive efficiency in the context of the broader Australian community. The National Competition Council, however, viewed this decision as one where politicians had been captured by rent-seeking producer interests who illegitimately trumped the even-handed technical analysis of the Review Group.

Two years of political negotiations behind the scenes followed, mainly in the confines of a Working Party comprising federal and state official, industry representatives and National Competition Council staff. The original recommendations were reinforced, and indeed even further liberalisation was recommended (in the form of the possibility of third party export licences supplementing the proposed federal 'single desk' selling arrangements). Continued failure by New South Wales to respond to the recommendations led to the NCC recommending a reduction in competition payments of AUS\$10 million in the second tranche assessment regime for the CPA, on the grounds of "insufficient progress".[60] Consequently, on 31 August 2000, the New South Wales Premier gave in and accepted the recommendation for regulatory reform, five years after the initial report had been issued. This result, albeit slow and hard-wrung, indicates that the structural barrier posed by the framework of meta-regulatory analysis to the pursuit of social citizenship goals is real.

Migration Agents' Registration Review: Commonwealth

The contribution of professionals to the conversation about the limits of justifiable regulation provided an interesting variation on the community morality perspective. Although generally allied loosely with business perspectives, many professional groups argued strenuously that they made a non-economic contribution to social and economic relations, a contribution that justified any barriers to entry that might exist. However, the nature of this non-economic contribution was more process-based (rather than rooted in some substantive value such as preventing harm to the vulnerable or fostering ecological sustainability). Professional groups were in fact rather vague about just what their surplus contribution is, but structured it around the words 'quality' and 'value'. Groups such as the Institute of Engineers, the Dental Board of Victoria, or the Australian Council of Building Design Professionals argued that where considerations of danger, harm or security are involved for the public, ethical standards of due diligence and technical standards shored up by specialist expertise are necessary to protect those users from harm. The arguments of professionals occupy something of a no-man's land between market infrastructure, community morality and differentiated consumer sovereignty perspectives on regulation. This demonstrates the slippery nature of classifying legislation under the lens of meta-regulation. Its implications are made more vivid in the specific context of a focused case study

This case study concerns a review conducted at the federal level, in the Department of Immigration, initially under the auspices of a Labour government but after March 1995, subject to the ultimate control of the incoming right-wing Coalition government.[61] The review concerned the functions of a government-appointed board known as the Migration Agents' Registration Board (the MAR Board). Unlike the Rice Marketing Board, the MAR Board had no power over property rights, but instead had the power to restrict entry into the business of giving immigration advice. Such advice can be given not only by professional lawyers in Australia, but also by anyone purporting to be a migration advice specialist. Prior to late 1992, the non-lawyer segment of the immigration advice industry (approximately 40%) had been unregulated, and incompetent and unscrupulous practitioners had proliferated. In response to widespread complaints about this from MPs contacted by individual members of the electorate, government officials and non-profit bodies, a registration scheme for 'migration agents' was established with strong bipartisan support.[62] The MAR Board also had a dispute resolution function, which was triggered by complaints from consumers or from the Department of Immigration.

Unlike the rice review where regulation was the result of demands from a concentrated producer group, the catalyst for regulation in this case study was the protection of a relatively diffuse group of end-users or consumers. The dilemma here was a classically typical case of the regulation of many other kinds of professional services: did the legislation provide "unnecessary protection" for those consumers? The objective of the original scheme was "to improve standards of professional conduct and quality of service".[63] The reason this was particularly necessary in the migration advice industry was due to the "vulnerability of the migration agent's client group: a high proportion are unable to speak English, were fearful of authority and had meagre financial resources".[64] At the same time, regulation posed barriers to entry into the business of giving migration advice, and thus constituted a restraint on competition. Entry barriers enforced by the MAR Board included substantive knowledge of migration law (either through a law degree or passing an exam approved by the Industry body), Australian citizenship and a demonstration of moral integrity. Were these requirements "necessary" in order to protect vulnerable immigrants? This was the question at the heart of the review process.

That process was somewhat less independently structured than the rice review in New South Wales, insofar as the Review Group was entirely internal to the Department of Immigration. It was, however, advised and assisted by a Reference Group with an independent Chair and various industry and consumer representatives. Furthermore, the Review Group built on the work of a Parliamentary Select Committee that had reviewed the scheme two years earlier with the aim of assessing whether migration agents were ready for self-regulation. That review had concluded that they were not, and the current CPA review would reconsider that conclusion, taking into account the intergovernmental agreements that gave priority to maximising competition. The personnel working on the review were not in the main economists, but rather immigration policy analysts. The Office of Regulation Review submitted material that included a significant degree of economic analysis, and some of this was incorporated into the Review Group's report ("the Migration Report"), along with data from the Department's records which was used on occasion to cross-check the predictions and assumptions of the economic analysis.

Although the way in which the process was set up was slightly more political, less independent and less dominated by economists than the rice review, the actual analysis was formally framed largely in terms of competitive efficiency and market infrastructure improvement. The terms of reference required the Review Group to report on "the nature, intent and impact of the legislation and regulations on the migration advice industry, consumers and the community", and to consider the options for regulation including self-regulation or alternatives for consumer redress if deregulation was recommended. They were required to take into account "the effects of the Scheme on consumer interests, the competitiveness of businesses seeking to provide migration advice and efficient resource allocation".[65] There was no reference to the public interest interpretation clause, even though the client vulnerability that had been the explicit catalyst for regulation in the first place might have been expected to raise issues of social welfare and equity, which the public interest interpretation clause required CPA reviews to take into account.

Value Outcomes

Notwithstanding the absence of formal reference to these matters, they did get incorporated into the analysis of the Review Group. Broadly speaking, the Migration Report blended two frames of discourse, in a way that suggested that the translation of concerns from one linguistic framework to another was eminently possible. Thus the welfare state's protective obligations of integrity towards vulnerable citizens were translated into the resolution of market failures in respect of information asymmetries that denied consumers the precondition of fully informed and autonomous choice necessary to participate in the market for migration advice. The maximisation of consumer choice functioned to protect the vulnerable. Indeed, the Review Group in large measure took the issues raised by the previous parliamentary review (in their report aptly titled *Protecting the Vulnerable*) and translated them into the analytical framework of the CPA meta-regulatory regime.

For example, the Review Group argued that regulation of migration advice "addresses a 'market failure' that leaves the consumer vulnerable to exploitation".[66] That market failure arose from several factors, the most important of which was "inadequate consumer information and an imbalance of knowledge between consumers and agents". This central market failure flowed from a number of features about migration advice – its technical nature, the long-term nature of the contract for advice, the fact that a distant outcome makes it difficult to evaluate the quality of service for a long period of time, and the fact that its recipients are often not proficient in English or may be fearful of challenging the agent's authority due to uncertainty about the legality of their status.

Having established that there was a legitimate market failure that needed addressing (information asymmetry) the Review Group then had to decide whether the regulation went 'too far' in restricting entry into the business of giving migration advice. It noted two relevant factors. First, it considered the severity of the consequences for recipients of negligent or incorrect advice, which could be as dire as the loss of personal liberty and often involved "considerable personal and financial cost and disruption to a client's working and family life".[67]

Secondly the Group considered the ORR's contention that agents would pass the costs of regulation onto consumers through higher fees. They acknowledged that the industry was less competitive than it would be with no entry restrictions, but was it *unduly* so? They evaluated empirical data showing that fees for migration advice ranged between AUS$500 and AUS$5,000 on average, with 66% of agents charging less than AUS$2,000 and the Department of Immigration and voluntary advice agencies providing a supplementary free alternative avenue. They concluded that the industry, even with the barriers to entry, was "sufficiently competitive to ensure that fees charged by agents fall within a reasonable range".[68] But they also noted that registration fees (roughly AUS$1,000/year) were high compared to comparable professional advisors such as tax agents or securities advisors and that the agents themselves received few benefits in return (such as legislation updates or priority processing or Departmental liaison contacts).

This last point raised a value often invoked in tandem with the value of consumer protection, especially by industry advisors themselves in their submissions: the quality of professional standards. Here, what the Review Group did was to shift the focus of this kind of argument away from the provider/professional and towards the consumer/user. For example, they evaluated the provision of migration advice against benchmarks prepared by the Federal Bureau of Consumer Affairs. These benchmarks were independence, fairness, accessibility, efficiency and effectiveness.

What is notable about the Review Group's evaluation of these is the degree to which they were all interpreted procedurally. Professional quality was more a matter of the manner in which clients were dealt with, rather than the substance of the advice they received. In fact, one of the main concerns of the Review Group in this respect was the limited number of avenues of redress that consumers could obtain under the complaints and discipline aspect of the MARS scheme. The MARS scheme, in focusing on formal hearings that upheld ethical standards of the profession, left consumers often unable to have access to mediation or informal dispute resolution. Similarly, because MARS focused on expelling agents from their business, consumers were unable to pursue remedies such as compensation or reconsideration of their visa application.

Thus the Review Group pursued an approach that aimed to shift the focus of 'net public benefit' from producer to consumer. Although the framework of analysis remained one of process and voice rather than the more market-oriented framework of entry, exit and price level, the consumer focus ensured that professionals only retained barriers to entry that were justified by concomitant benefits for the users of their services. In this way the structure of analysis was vigilant in preventing 'rent-seeking' from producers occurring.

There was, however, one group of citizens or consumers that did not fare so well in the translation from 'security for the vulnerable' to 'redress of market failure': those with "meagre financial resources", a factor that had been instrumental in the original motivation for regulation. Under the welfare state model, security for the vulnerable was the main focus, and this was provided for, in the case of those too poor to pay for it, by voluntary advice agencies. From the perspective of market infrastructure regulation, the emphasis on maximising choice meant that price levels *were* of concern to the Review Group, but it was competitive efficiency that was important in keeping prices down. This did not mean provision of free advice by voluntary service agencies was irrelevant, for the Review Group acknowledged[69] that voluntary advice agencies provided significant competition for migration advice agents, thus keeping fees down. Voluntary advice agencies provided 16% of the 'market' for immigration advice.[70] In this sense their contribution to a competitive market was 'counted'.

But the equitable redistribution of affordable immigration advice through provision of free advice by voluntary non-profit agencies did come under fire from the Review Group in a separate portion of the Migration Report. For the agencies were funded by the registration fee collected by the MAR Board, and the fee was deliberately set higher than the minimum needed to break even on the costs of administering registration and dispute resolution. Here the Review Group's discussion enacted a translation from social citizenship language to market infrastructure frameworks of analysis, but in the process, a critical aspect of the free provision of advice was recharacterised as a cost rather than a benefit. It is worth quoting the translation in full:

> Access and equity concerns prompted the decision to fund voluntary advice agencies to provide migration advice. The purpose was to assist the disadvantaged and vulnerable in obtaining advice from a qualified person in circumstances where they were not able to pay for that service or were disadvantaged in gaining access for social, cultural or language reasons. However the funding of voluntary advice from revenue generated by the Scheme creates a cross-subsidy which distorts the migration advice market, raising the costs to industry of registration and ultimately the price paid by the clients of fee-charging agents. If such an arrangement is in the public interest, i.e. delivers a public good, it should be publicly funded.[71]

It is not that this framework of analysis denies the possible public benefit of free advice, but it insists that this is a goal that should not be addressed by adjusting the market infrastructure. Rather, it requires a separate institutional response – direct public funding. As with the cost-pooling arrangements that existed in the rice industry, this makes the ongoing provision of free migration advice politically vulnerable. The clients most likely to take advantage of the voluntary advice agencies do not have much electoral clout, almost by definition since few would be eligible to vote.

But in any event, the desirability of direct public funding was conditional upon empirical demonstration of some concrete public benefit.[72] And the benefit that indigent citizens might receive from the continuation of the 'cross-subsidies' did not count for the Review Group. A social citizenship justification might have argued, for example, that the fulfilment of a community duty to protect the vulnerable counted as a public benefit. But the Review Group seemed to look for a different kind of "public interest argument" to justify regulation and made no further mention of the 'access and equity' advantages once it had translated them into the language of 'market distortion'.

Instead, they looked at much broader benefits accruing to the community *as a whole* and drew on comparative analogies from the regulation of tax agents and securities advice agents. They identified what they considered to be strong public benefits in these cases: the risk to stable government revenue if tax advice were unregulated, or the risk for investor confidence if securities advice were unregulated.[73] By contrast in the migration advice case, they argued, the public benefit flowing from reduction of immigration fraud or malpractice was "difficult to demonstrate empirically".[74] This was so even though the impact of immigration fraud on discrete classes of consumers (particularly those who could not afford to go elsewhere) was severe and concrete and had been acknowledged as a cost to those consumers elsewhere in the Migration Report.

Overall, then, the Review Group *did* recognise a range of harm to consumers to which regulation was a legitimate response. But what happened in this review is that the framework of analysis was sensitive to inequities in information but not to inequities in fiscal resources. It addressed an "imbalance of power" in information but not in money. No arguments were made or addressed that a particular class of consumer (poor ones) had not been taken into account by this approach.

The Review Group concluded that the overall evidence was mixed. There was some benefit for both industry and consumers under the current scheme, and there were "economic arguments for regulation of the industry relating to the imbalance of information between consumers and agents which makes this consumer group vulnerable to exploitation".[75] But for both industry and consumers the Review acknowledged explicit downsides (the cost burden on industry was too great given the level of benefits they received in return, the dispute resolution process was not flexible enough to consumer needs). Overall, the framework of the review promoted primarily a consumer protection framework of values, motivated by a desire to redress market failures of informational asymmetry – but not inequity of economic resources. Despite the apparent inattention to social citizenship issues built into the formal terms of reference, most relevant non-efficiency objectives were at least considered. But the redistributive facet of regulation turned out to be vulnerable to elimination once translation into the discourse of economic analysis occurred.

Institutional Outcomes

The scheme as it stood at the time of review was a version of hierarchical state regulation in the bureaucratic mode. The MAR Board was independent of the Department, but was chaired by the head of the Department and depended on it for administrative support. The rules regulating entry and dispute resolution were embodied in a detailed prescriptive Code of Conduct given the force of law by the Migration Agents Regulations to which it was appended.

Having identified a number of flaws in the values served by the current scheme, but still concluding that a legitimate basis for some intervention did still exist (to maintain professional standards), the Review Group surveyed a range of options for change. The options can be compared along two main axes: the degree and scope of control exercised over migration advisors, and the location of that control.

The options for *location* of control were to give power to a statutory board, to the industry itself or to a combination of government and industry. The option of least *degree* of control was deregulation and that of most control was the status quo. The Review Group favoured a compromise option that they labelled *co-regulation*. This compromised on the degree of control by separating the functions of regulation into two different categories and giving one set to government and the other to the industry. To industry, the Review Group would delegate functions of dispute resolution and the definition of the content of professional standards. Government, through an institution like the current MAR board, would retain responsibility for disciplinary and licensing functions of regulation. This division effectively would give government the control over the entry and exit to the market for migration advice, but devolve control to industry when it concerned the articulation and interpretation of professional standards.

The overall level of control over any particular migration agent would not really decrease, but the degree of government intervention (and probably of the amount of formal legal rules in the policy area) would likely decrease slightly. The structure of regulation however, would be slightly more networked rather than hierarchical, because the profession controls application of professional standards vis-à-vis consumers, but the government controls their final effects vis-à-vis the disciplinary effects on the producers of advice, thus creating parallel veto points over closely linked issues. At the same time, the complex layering of public and private control, and the intertwining of dispute resolution functions with ethical disciplinary functions, would make likely a proliferation of quite complex rules, albeit some of which would be at a more informalf and flexible level than encoded in law (Industry Codes rather than formal legislation).

It is worth noting the microscopic effects of taken-for-granted assumptions, by pointing out links and differences between the approach of the Review Group and that of the Office of Regulation Review. The latter body regarded itself as more strongly committed to a rigorous application of the economic framework of cost-benefit analysis than internal departmental review groups.[76] Both the ORR and the Review Group agreed that there were market failures in the migration advice industry that warranted an interventionist response. Every option that was canvassed included some reference to the need to rebalance the information asymmetry between producer and consumer, and to maintain some framework for disciplinary enforcement of professional standards.

But the ORR and the Review Group disagreed on the technique that would best address these problems. The primary option competing with co-regulation was 'negative licensing'. This was supported strongly by the Office of Regulation Review on the basis that it was the "least restrictive avenue" for securing consumer protection. In a system of negative licensing, there is no requirement to register as a migration advice agent, and the regulator's functions are restricted to detecting and removing from the industry only the 'bad eggs' who fail to comply with industry standards. In terms of degree of control, negative licensing was even less restrictive an option than co-regulation. It also, importantly, avoided inclusion of any element at all of industry self-regulation.

The different recommendations (co-regulation by the Review Group and negative licensing by the ORR) flow from assumptions about 'government failure' and the assumptions about the inevitability of regulatory capture that are embodied in the ORR's public choice perspective. The Review Group, by contrast tends to trust government to a greater extent. This is not to say it ignored possible trajectories of capture in any naïve way. Indeed, it shared with the ORR a concern that producers' control over their own market threshold would lead to rent-seeking behaviour. As the Review Group averred, there was not sufficient "maturity of a regulating industry body ... to look beyond the immediate commercial interests of its members".[77]

But although both ORR and the Review Group were concerned about capture, the Review Group assumed only that the industry body, and not the government body, would be susceptible to capture. The ORR by contrast was cautious about both kinds of institutions. In addition, the ORR regarded any pre-emptive solution to market failures as prima facie more inefficient than a decentralised, post-hoc response. As a result of these two different assumptions, they suggested that since negative licensing established considerably less pre-emptive intervention into the activities of migration agents, and avoided the creation of an institution susceptible to capture, it was likely to be more efficient. Unfair trading claims brought by aggrieved consumers could, the ORR argued, address the problem of 'bad egg' agents.

The Review Group noted this concern of the ORR[78] but expressed reverse concerns that without registration the flow of complaints would increase to the point where any increased efficiency would be lost. They examined empirical evidence to compare the 'cost per outcome' of post-hoc complaint resolution as compared with the screening effect of a registration scheme. They found that the cost per unqualified agent screened out by registration was AUS\$183 whereas the cost of resolving a complaint against an unqualified agent was AUS\$1,678.

Thus in this migration review the ORR's assumption about the increased efficiency of post-hoc responses to market failures was not borne out; in the rice review, however, with a Review Group staffed to a much greater degree by economists, a similar assumption had been made without any empirical checking. This was partly due to empirical difficulty: competition complaints had never been brought against rice wholesalers, whereas a complaints scheme against unscrupulous agents did already operate and provided cost data to compare.

But the outcome suggests that the economistic analytical framework, especially where it is essentially unverifiable, affects the outcome of a review team's recommendations. It is reasonably clear that the ORR, in choosing negative licensing as the most appropriate option, gave greater weight to the benefit of increased industry competitiveness than the Review Group did, even though both acknowledged that there were trade-offs to be made in securing that competitiveness. By comparison, the Review Group valued the average consumer's lack of information sufficiently to focus on a more restrictive form of intervention: co-regulation. However they both left open-ended and vulnerable the fate of the consumer who was both resource-poor and information-poor.

The final recommendation of the Review Group was to move towards a light-touch regulatory framework by establishing initially co-regulation (government-backed regulation) and then moving towards industry self-regulation. This was implemented by the right-wing government in the Migration Legislation Amendment (Migration Agents) Bill 1997, which sets up the basic regulatory framework, including the entry standards, the continuing imposition of registration charges (recently increased in July 2001 from $1180 to $1800), and a skeletal disciplinary framework that is fleshed out by an industry code of conduct. Anxieties about industry capture expressed by ORR were overturned, and the Migration Institute of Australia, the relevant industry body, was appointed as the regulator. As yet, the final move to industry self-regulation has not been made: on 23 August 1999 the government agreed that the current statutory self-regulation arrangements should be continued for a further three years from March 2000.[79] This result reflects not so much a network structure but, given the delegation to industry of the day-to-day administration of regulation, a decrease in hierarchical governance towards a less restrictive option, though not the least restrictive available.

Both the rice review and the migration review demonstrate genuine efforts to measure the costs and benefits of regulatory programmes, and to take into account values beyond efficiency and competitiveness. In the main, these values are taken into account by translating them into the framework of economic analysis with a preference for maximising market competition. This translation, while it does take account of non-efficiency values, has two effects which undermine them: it recommends institutional responses which tend to increase the political vulnerability of measures to address non-efficiency values, and it is relatively insensitive to redistributive equity issues. At the same time, the attempt to compromise on the competing political goals tends to increase the complexity and density of rules, and the extent to which network rather than hierarchical structures govern the policy space in question.

The final case study raises some analogous issues but is distinct insofar as it created a significant amount of public debate and therefore became embedded in a broader political dynamic than the two case studies already discussed. This intensified politicisation ironically took the form of a competition between two different mechanisms (competitive pressures and legal insulation) for institutionalising *autonomy from politics* in a manner that raised directly the conflict at the heart of meta-regulation: how should politics be 'tamed'?

Auditor-General Review: Victoria

In late 1996, the Premier of Victoria, Jeff Kennett, the head of a right-wing coalition state government, ordered that the review of the Auditor-General's functions under National Competition Policy[80] be brought forward on the review agenda. The review had been listed as one of some 400 reviews to be carried out under the Competition Principles Agreement (CPA), but Kennett had decided that it was now of some urgency. This decision brought criticism from the start and the change in the agenda was cited as evidence of the political expediency which critics regarded as the primary motivation for the review. The criticism came mainly from the media, some professional accountants, some academics, many lawyers, most of the Labour party and many members of the general public. The nub of the criticism was that the Premier was trying to weaken and even cripple the sole remaining institution that was willing to direct fierce criticism at his policies. The method of 'attack' was to catalyse regulatory reform that would contract out the auditing responsibilities of the Auditor-General to private accounting firms.

The Auditor-General in Victoria was responsible for auditing the activities of all government departments and public statutory bodies (some 139), as well as 35 educational institutions, 106 hospitals and nursing homes, 14 pension funds, 108 government companies and joint ventures, 78 local councils, 10 libraries and 40 water authorities.[81] Its potential influence was thus extremely significant, and in fact the Auditor-General *had* often been highly critical of the impact of various market-based reforms that the Kennett government had already made to the provision of government services. For example, one of his recent reports had revealed that much of the money government had spent on 'marketing and promotion' of the delivery of services was essentially being spent on party-political advertising – AUS$130 million of taxpayers' funds. He had also recently released a damning report on child protection services. Much of his then current work programme[82] focused on aspects of government policy and service provision which had already been subjected to reforms like privatisation, contracting-out or compulsory competitive tendering (for example, public transport, emergency services, utilities, certain aspects of health funding, high school education). The quality of, and equitable access to, these services did not always emerge with a glowing report from the Auditor-General's audit.[83] It was therefore somewhat ironic that the Auditor-General himself was now threatened with the imposition of analogous reforms.

Like the migration review (and in fact, many of the early scheduled reviews under the CPA agendas in various states), the Auditor-General had been through two recent substantive reviews of its performance, and these had a certain effect of path-dependency on the CPA review. The earlier reviews, carried out by professional accountants, had noted the preponderance of performance audits focusing on social and environmental considerations, and queried whether the department should not be developing more expertise in contemporary techniques of strategic risk management across *all* areas of risk exposure in government departments.[84] The earlier reviews thus revealed a certain amount of anxiety about the value priorities of the Auditor-General's office. In particular, they considered that greater attention should be paid to matters of risk management strategies and fiscal discipline rather than to social or environmental values. Relatedly, they criticised the way in which the Auditor-General selected the key criteria against which to measure performance audits. On the matter of integrity, expertise and efficiency, however, these earlier reviews were almost wholly complimentary. The troubles seemed to concern substantive policy orientation: very broadly, the earlier reviews urged a greater focus on market infrastructure aspects of government agencies and less on social citizenship factors.

Many of the participants in the debate were suspicious that the Review Committee was also rigidly committed to similar policy preferences. The Review Committee had three members: an academic economist (the chair), a private sector lawyer and a private sector accountant. Economic expertise therefore dominated the Review Committee's outlook. It also appeared to be autonomous from political influences, to a greater degree than the structure of Review Committees in the other two cases in this chapter. It was formally independent of government and contained no representation from the Auditor-General's department.

However, critics of the proposed reforms were doubtful about the true level of independence in the Review. The back-up Secretariat for the Review Committee was provided by the Department of Premier and Cabinet, assisted by Treasury and Finance. This at the very least indicated that there was strong political will behind the Review. It also drew accusations of *undue* political influence from many aggrieved critics of the Review, who considered that Treasury and Cabinet shared the antagonism of earlier reviews for the Auditor-General's focus on the social and environmental impact of policies.

The participants in the debate fell into two main groups. Supporting the Review Committee's preference for contracting-out government audits to private firms were the economic Ministers of the then current government (the Premier, the Deputy Leader, the Finance Minister, the Treasurer), an ex-Labour Minister turned Independent (Steve Crabb), a management academic and a number of utilities. Critics included aggrieved general citizens, political columnists, politicians, lawyers, accountants, and broader groups such as civil liberties groups and the social welfare lobby.

Despite the obvious political contentiousness of the issue, the advocates of reform relied on strategies that presented the matter as simply a neutral, technical question of what was required to implement the CPA regime. The question of whether the Auditor-General was performing his job well or not was ostensibly not at issue. Rather, what was at issue was the allegedly technical matter of whether or not more competitive arrangements would work equally well. The Kennett government and the Review Committee argued that it was a simple matter of falling squarely within the CPA terms of reference: since the Auditor-General currently held a monopoly over the provision of all auditing services in respect of government departments, it was an arrangement that 'restricted competition' and thus had to be reviewed.

Although this was logically appealing, it was passionately contested. This 'jurisdictional' fight is interesting, since it reveals much about 'boundary assumptions' of the appropriate scope of the CPA agenda. The assertion that Kennett had made a kind of fundamental 'category mistake' in subjecting the Auditor-General to NCP review in fact went to the heart of the question of just how far the NCP agenda legitimately extended. As the reforms were drafted, they applied to *all* legislation, at least where 'market restrictions' existed. As we saw in Chapter Four, however, there is no obvious answer to the question of when regulation entails encroachment on a market or not. This was precisely one of the limit cases – opponents of the review argued that audit had nothing to do with a market for any service.

The Australasian Council of Auditors, for example, argued that audit functions were analogous to the functions of the criminal justice system, or the constitutional and legal systems – non-market functions that were never intended to fall under the meta-regulatory lens of the CPA.[85] The director of the Monash University Graduate School of Management remarked acidly:

> To say that the Audit Act is monopolistic in providing for a single auditor-general is like saying the Catholic Church is monopolistic in having only one Pope. The auditor-general is the apex, the watchdog, the scrutineer and the spokesman for public audit.[86]

Gradually, there developed an organised view that the Auditor-General was *legally* beyond the scope of the CPA. Various reasons were given for this – mostly based on an argument that the Auditor-General was separate from the government (and thus implicitly, that the CPA only applied to government activities). For example, a media columnist pointed out that the Auditor-General was not bound by the Public Sector Management Act, and was therefore intended to fall outside the scope of 'public administration' generally. Precedent was frequently invoked, with another columnist arguing:

> No other state government has interpreted the scope of the national competition policy as applying to a parliamentary function. The auditor-general is simply not part of government.[87]

This lack of precedent was also noted by many parliamentarians, including the Public Accounts Committee, which went as far as requesting independent legal advice on the question of whether the review was within the jurisdiction of the CPA intergovernmental agreement. Although that advice never emerged into the public eye (the Public Accounts Committee ultimately dropped their resistance, apparently under strong pressure from the Premier),[88] it intensified suspicions that Premier Kennett was using CPA review as a smokescreen for ulterior political motives. The 'real' politics were about silencing a critical Auditor-General: the rational analysis was invoked as a distracting illusion.

Whether or not the Review was intended to mask an uglier game of politics, it still raised basic issues of how far the 'shadow of competition' should legitimately fall. Audit was a 'limit case': a case that threw up sharply the limits of defining good government with primary reference to efficiency values and the maximisation of market competition. As Shane Green, the political editor of Melbourne's most respected broadsheet, put it:

> [Kennett is] setting up national competition principles as the Ten Commandments of government. Forget all other principles underpinning parliamentary democracy and good government, competition policy rules.[89]

In order to understand how "other principles" would frame the issue with a different emphasis (and possibly a different outcome), we need to engage the details of the review at closer range.

Value Outcomes

The overall objective of the Auditor-General legislation was construed as providing accountability to the taxpayer through oversight of the "appropriate (legal, efficient, effective) use of public monies".[90] The question as framed by the CPA regime was therefore whether monopoly provision of accountability (a restraint on competition by definition) was the only way to secure the benefits of accountability. The question was complicated by the fact that 'accountability' through audit actually had two dimensions: discipline and feedback. In other words, audit of a government department was intended not only to deter misspending of public monies, but also to facilitate ways in which the money could be put to better use. The second aspect is more in the nature of an advisory, educative function, a 'management consultant' role; the first is a checking, constraining function, a 'policeman' role.

What effectively happened in the debate over this Review was that the advocates of reform focused strongly on the 'management consultant' facet of auditing. With this focus, audit could be characterised primarily as a service to a client, and the notion of the client as a consumer for whom efficiency was paramount made sense. When looked at from the perspective of the 'policeman' role, however, the consumer-focused, service orientation of audit was less obvious. Discipline of a client was more in the nature of an oversight obligation than a service. A consumer chooses a service (bottom-up); but an oversight agency chooses its targets (top-down). The appropriate location of discretion is different, depending on whether discipline or feedback is emphasised. By focusing primarily on the service provision aspects of auditing, the Auditor-General's monopoly of control over the 'who, when and how' of audits, was effectively framed as a cost. Similarly, the lack of scope for the auditee to exercise any *choice* in the process of selecting an auditor was also framed as a cost, reflecting the service provision focus but not the oversight perspective.[91]

In other words, what counted as a cost and what as a benefit depended on one's frame of reference, and in particular how the frame of reference defined the relevant client. Critics of reform insisted that the true client of the Auditor-General was Parliament. The Review Committee on the other hand maintained that the Auditor-General had multiple clients: Parliament was the primary client but the public agency auditee and its responsible Minister were also significant and important clients.[92] By including the Executive in the array of 'clients', and by emphasising the desirability of providing choice to those clients, the Review Committee was able to characterise the status quo monopoly provision of audit as an overly 'binding constraint'; one which limited contestability, competition and plural sources of audit expertise.

But for the critics of reform, this 'binding constraint' was precisely what was *beneficial* about the status quo structure. Parliamentary backbenchers, political columnists, the general public and even professional accountants' associations all insisted on the importance of having a 'single voice' reporting on the appropriate use of public monies. Not only did this ensure coherent and consistent standards of assessment that took into account a 'whole-of-government' perspective on the interrelated policy functions of different departments, but it also prevented a conflict of interest. The Auditor-General was part of the mechanism of responsible government, of holding the Executive to account on behalf of the Parliament. A web of providers of audit services combined with a duty owed to the Executive would directly dilute that primary function, since fear of losing the audit contract and the need to cater to the Executive would dampen the disciplinary enthusiasm of the audits.

The cleavage emerging in this debate rested on two rather different sets of assumptions about the meaning of accountability. One vision, preferred by the Review Committee, emphasised efficiency and responsiveness in service provision and, through market competition, a guarantee of exit on the part of the (executive) client if quality was not assured. The competing vision gave priority to independent and spirited criticism and, though legal insulation of the office, its funding and its discretionary powers, a guarantee of voice on the part of the (parliamentary) client. Both visions stressed the necessity for 'independence', which seemed to mean loosely, insulation from politics. But the independence emphasised by the critics of reform had at its core the *absence* of mutual interests linking specific government departments and their auditor. The fact that as sole auditor of government departments, he was "neither friend nor enemy", made him independent. By contrast, the market-focused view of accountability saw independence as secured by multiplying the possible range of 'friend' auditors, by providing choice and competition.[93]

Advocates of reform did acknowledge the need for the Auditor-General to have some independence from the Executive, but also maintained that it should secure independence from service delivery *of its own functions*. "There is a risk of regulatory capture", the Review Committee argued, "in that the effectiveness of the regulatory regime may be undermined by the [fact that] audit methodology, standards, and scope are established by the same body that conducts the audits".[94] This approach to independence creates yet a further layer of insulation from politics: the content and scope of particular audits must be decided at a decentralised level rather than hierarchically organised by a single state agency. The difference between the 'market' vision of accountability and the 'constitutional' one emerges in the detail of the institutional responses recommended by the Review Committee.

Institutional Outcomes

Onus of proof effects   Like both the rice review and the migration review,[95] taken-for-granted assumptions exercise a shaping influence upon the trajectory of recommendations in the audit review. Here the assumptions are underpinned by the strength of the presumption in favour of greater competition in this case study. The case had many arguments both for and against reform, and it seemed that the presumption had a concrete effect in encouraging pro-competitive reform despite the uncertainty of the benefits. To illustrate this point, consider the methodological approach taken by the Review Committee in the cost-benefit analysis. No figures were provided in the Audit Report. A comparison of the alternative options was carried out in tabular, qualitative form. Each model had a list of costs and benefits next to it which was summarised in brief narrative form with an appended comment. This approach fragmented the comparison to a significant degree: even for each individual model it was difficult to get an overall sense of the trade-offs involved, and to compare the multi-faceted dimensions of competing options was even more difficult. Instead, what seemed to happen is that the Review Committee had a preconceived opinion as to what the result of the balancing process should be, and it invoked vague assessments of probable costs and standard predictions from economic analyses to support this. It did so, however, without any data against which to test its assumptions.

For example, in assessing cost-effectiveness, the Review Committee often referred to discussions with the New Zealand Auditor-General as evidence without further elaboration: "In discussions with the NZ Auditor-General, it was suggested that even though the costs of the new system were probably greater than the old, the improvement in quality more than outweighed any increase in costs".[96] A little later, the report acknowledges (without quantifying) the existence of start-up costs associated with the contract monitoring skills that the Auditor-General will have to develop. It discounts them in the following way: "While these costs may be considered significant, the benefits of change to more competitive arrangements have generally been shown to outweigh these costs".[97]

This kind of vagueness is pervasive: in other parts of the Audit Report there is a sense that formulaic justifications are being used without great thought as to their applicability. For example, many submissions argued that performance audits of policy agencies were too complex to be amenable to precise specification in a contract. To counter this, the Review Committee argued that the enhancement of accountability through contract specification "has been a general benefit which has emerged in contracting situations. Information requirements necessary for the consumer to make an informed choice provide transparency to assess performance in delivering outcomes".[98] This response did not engage directly with the point made by the critics; it merely asserted that contracting-out services generally enhanced transparency and thus accountability. But the point of the critics was that when outcomes are too complex to be specified and broken down effectively, contract specifications will remain obscure even if they are explicit.

The effect of the pro-competitive presumption, then, increased the diffuseness of assessing costs and benefits in what would admittedly never be a precise task in any event. Given such differences, the general pervasiveness of a pro-competitive presumption tipped the balance, as the following description shows.

The Review Committee insisted emphatically on the importance of taking into account the burden of proof structure of the CPA regime. The CPA regime, the Committee reminded readers in its report, made it clear that reform in the direction of more competition was presumptively preferred. The official documentation of the review makes this quite clear, both at initial discussion stage and at final report stage. The Committee stressed[99] that even if an arrangement that restricts competition produces a net benefit, there must still, *in addition*, be no alternative way of achieving that benefit. It went on to say that current effectiveness in and of itself was not sufficient for retaining the status quo. Rather, NCP "involves a commitment to review all existing legislation *shifting the status quo* in favour of achieving competitive outcomes. The onus is on those wishing to retain existing arrangements to demonstrate why those arrangements are superior to alternative, more competitive arrangements".[100] Moreover, "it is generally inappropriate to reject outright the introduction of competition into areas which there was previously no competition",[101] for "the Committee notes and supports ... that irrespective of any preference for a particular form of ownership, cost and quality of performance of any service provider will be improved where competitive pressure is present".[102] Finally, and most bluntly:

> The Committee believes that on the whole, increasing competition delivers better outcomes to consumer, the government and the taxpayer. That is, more extensive use of competition is in the public interest.[103]

Overall, then, the substantive standard of maximising market competition was central to the analytical framework of the audit review, both at a general level and at a micro-level. On the other hand, there was no mention at any point, either in the terms of reference or the final recommendations, of the public interest interpretation clause. Yet it seems that non-market competitiveness aspects were taken into account in the final recommendations, to an extent.

Uneasy compromise   When making final recommendations, the Review Committee refused to accept the contention that the Executive and/or the audited bodies were not clients of the Auditor-General. They considered a model that would maximise the kind of 'market accountability' they wished to promote between auditor and auditee. That model, a 'decentralised model', would put the Auditor-General in the same position as any private sector firm capable of auditing a third party. However, based on unmodified market infrastructure principles, it would leave the choice of auditor wholly up to the auditee, and the Committee recognised that although this would maximise market accountability, it would compromise constitutional accountability. On this basis, they rejected the decentralised model.

Since the Committee had conceded that Parliament was also an important client of the Auditor-General, they proposed a model that was a compromise between the status quo monopoly and a decentralised model. They called it a segmented model, since it involved two layers of institutions. It would split the Auditor-General's office into two sections. One section – a fully commercial and independent unit – would undertake audits, and would compete on a tender basis for public sector audits in competition with the private sector. The other section would monitor the contracts and set the overall policy for the scope and target of audits – but would do so under the advice and supervision of a three-person tender selection panel. This panel would be chaired by a representative from the accounting profession or from the business community, and would have a third "independent person", as well as a representative from the Auditor-General's office.

This model, which was accepted by the Kennett Government in April 1997, increased the degree of private sector expertise and institutional autonomy that shaped the choices of auditing decisions. Two layers implemented two kinds of accountability: a market for public and private sector auditors would keep an eye on government bodies, while the Auditor-General would keep an eye on the auditors. The Auditor-General's responsibilities would be almost wholly confined to "regulatory responsibilities" rather than also providing "service delivery".[104] But in order for this to work, and to resolve the conflicting responsibilities of service to clients and disciplinary oversight of clients, the segmented model required a dizzying range of new and highly prescriptive rules to be written.

In this respect, this model was a good example of a network structure with its high degree of prescriptive rules and the dilution of discretion currently possessed by the Auditor-General. When significant non-market benefits are involved in an area of regulation and are taken into account by the analytical framework, network structures tend to result.

The rules recommended as necessary for securing such non-market benefits included the following: extensive rules to regulate the flow of information from private sector auditors to the Auditor-General, so that he or she could continue to report fully back to Parliament; formal regulations to structure the operation and powers of tender selection panels; contract management manuals to provide "information relating to the specification of the service, criteria for evaluation and measurement of performance".[105] Rules would also be needed to impose 'firewalls' between auditing work and consulting work done by private sector auditors for auditees. Some of these rules could be copied from current private sector standards, but performance audits of sensitive policy areas were quite different from financial audits of private corporations and would need to be thought through independently. Institutionally, then, in retaining both market and constitutional frameworks, the review created a complex network structure replete with proliferating formal rules, and a notable increase in institutional autonomy.

The uneasy compromise that resulted did not eliminate the constitutional accountability framework altogether – nor did it 'translate it' but left them in uneasy narrative tension with other. Nonetheless the overall package swung significantly towards greater maximisation of market competition. This result, it has been argued, occurred at least in part because of the bite of the CPA framework.

Whether it in fact produced a 'net benefit' to the community is more doubtful. Early on, strong doubts were expressed as to the likelihood of this.[106] Later political developments are also interesting in this respect. In 1999, a hung parliament meant the fate of the Kennett government depended on three independents, who presented him with a charter for good government that included as a prominent feature the reversal of his policy changes on audit in Victoria. Ultimately, a minority coalition government with Labour was formed instead, and Labour immediately not only reversed the introduction of private sector competition into public audit, but strengthened its accountability to Parliament as the client, in consequence insulating it further from both market and political-executive influence.[107] At no point has the National Competition Council questioned this policy reversal, showing deference to the threshold between state and market that the Victorian political debate supported.

Summary of Case Studies

These case studies have painted a picture of the effects of meta-regulation on a range of areas where government typically intervenes in the economy. They show a strong tendency to reframe or 'translate' aspects of social welfare that previously may have been expressed in the language of need, vulnerability or harm into the language of market failures or market distortion. Imbalances in information count as market failures, and merit some kind of institutional response. Imbalances in material resources, however, tend to get discounted and solutions to them to be characterised as market distortions.

There is also a tendency to recommend separate institutional responses to address non-market values, most particularly those of redistributive equity or political accountability. This can have one of two effects, depending on the institutional strategy recommended. If a hierarchical strategy, such as the response to environmental problems and the subsidisation of remote farmers in the rice industry, is recommended, then political risk is intensified for actors advocating those goals, even though analytically they have been 'counted'. If a network strategy is recommended, such as the response to constitutional accountability issues in the audit review, then complexity and proliferation of rules result.

National Competition Council Enforcement: Political Ramifications

To fully appreciate the political dynamics of implementing the meta-regulatory regime requires us to look upwards from the detail of departmental implementation to the general oversight infrastructure. This chapter therefore closes with a look at the nature of National Competition Council (NCC) enforcement, particularly its implications for viewing meta-regulation as a development of incipient (non-judicial) legality.

NCC enforcement built on the patterns of technical cooperation developed by the 'network' of central agency officials whose routines were explored in Chapter Four. Compliance was initially encouraged through political negotiation but ultimately enforced via the threat of significant financial loss. The NCC defined three tiers of non-compliance that would attract escalating penalties. The mildest kind of non-compliance was remediable if the offending government had a positive and open attitude to "meaningful discussion with the NCC on the prospect of change within the next 12 months".[108] More substantial non-compliance (i.e. action that would require a formal change in policy to bring that government into line with the CPA's requirements) attracted a 'floating penalty': suspension of competition payments until that policy change occurs. Finally, a refusal to change policy or reconsider an outcome would attract a straight forfeiture of a portion of the relevant tranche of competition payments.[109] The size of the penalty would reflect the estimated net loss flowing from a decision to maintain a restriction on competition.[110]

The NCC's response to reform of the New South Wales statutory marketing authority for rice reflected this layered approach quite precisely. As reviewed in the detailed case study, the NCC escalated its response, in combination with facilitating political dialogue and negotiations, with each of the three assessment points in 1997, 1999 and the special supplementary assessment in June 2000, and secured compliance at the final point of recommending a penalty of AUS$10 million.

While the actual levying of penalties has been relatively rare, NCC's enforcement approach has nonetheless garnered significant backlash from political executives. This has stemmed from its growing willingness over time to openly criticise many regulatory policy choices in its annual reports, and to attach conditions of further progress in specific areas to continuation of the competition payments. Such further conditions have been themselves enforced by more frequent 'supplementary assessments' carried out sometimes as often as quarterly.

One of the most public examples of backlash occurred in July 1999, when the NCC in its second tranche assessment withheld AUS$15 million from Queensland for its decision to authorise the building of a dam in the southern part of the state. They also recommended the withholding of a further AUS$98 million due to Queensland's refusal to deregulate dairy milk prices. These recommendations totalled 25% of what Queensland would otherwise have received in annual competition payments. In the wake of the emergence of One Nation, these were inflammatory moves. The Queensland Premier called in the national press for the NCC to be abolished, explicitly characterising its decisions as "punishment for failure to impose economic rationalism". Queensland Treasurer David Hammill said:

> Queensland won't be forced into deregulation for deregulation's sake ...
> If you own an asset, you're supposed to sell it. If you have a regulation you're supposed to do away with it and providing you deregulate everything, flog off every asset you've got you get a big, fat tick from the National Competition Council.[111]

This backlash showed specifically that meta-regulation *was* viewed as providing a salient constraint on regulatory policymaking of the nature of an institutionalised partial veto point, since the hostility was explicitly directed towards the notion that NCC was "second-guessing" legitimate political balancing decisions.

As the Queensland Treasurer, once again, said in a different forum:

> The NCC has fundamentally exceeded its legitimate role and responsibilities, as provided for under the COAG Agreements. Inappropriately, the Council has sought to question the validity of Community Service Obligations (CSOs) and to 'second guess' the outcomes of public benefit tests. Effectively, the NCC is an umpire which is seeking to determine the outcome of the game, rather than just enforcing the rules.[112]

Were these fair assessments of NCC's enforcement approach? The answer is a matter of judgment. On the one hand, NCC made strong attempts to cast its recommendations for penalties, where it made them, in procedural terms, usually by focusing on the fact that a government had failed to follow the pro-competitive recommendations of an independent review. On the other hand, NCC also objected to reviews on the basis of weak or unreasonable inferences between evidence and conclusions, a criterion that comes very close to substantive review,[113] in rather the same manner as a 'hard look' doctrine in judicial review comes very close to second-guessing.

Furthermore, NCC's willingness to take a 'hard look' was clearly much more in evidence where the possibility of enforcing pro-competitive reform existed. By comparison NCC did not seem to take equally energetic advantage of opportunities to ensure that factors militating *against* pro-competitive reform were duly considered. Indeed, NCC in effect had a different standard of proof depending on whether planned reform increases or decreases market competition. The NCC's view was that when governments make decisions to retain restrictions on competition, they may only do so after full independent public review, and can only diverge from the review recommendations if they "provide a rigorous case for [their] approach including demonstrating any flaws in the review's analysis and reasoning".[114]

By contrast, when a government chooses to *remove* restrictions on competition (i.e. to maximise market competition), NCC states that "the threshold CPA requirement does not mean that jurisdictions must always have conducted a full public review prior to removing restrictions in legislation".[115] Even more strongly, "governments may choose to disregard a review recommendation supporting a restriction".[116]

Overall, even if NCC does not directly substitute its judgement for that of political representatives, its routines and procedures allow for an *assumption* of overall community benefit only when competition is maximised. The die is thus cast more heavily against a subset of outcomes, even if no particular outcome is ever dictated by NCC.

The conflict over the legitimacy of NCC oversight is embedded in the issue of who has the legitimate 'last word' on the balancing: the technical assessment performed in the review itself or politicians making a strategic electoral calculus? Under meta-regulation and NCC oversight, it did remain open to politicians to make a choice not to implement pro-competitive reform. But it became a decision that had to be taken far more publicly and transparently than in the absence of meta-regulation. Further, it is true that the use of financial penalties effectively attached sanctions to such transparent political decisions, which could not but help provide a substantive incentive in favour of economic rationality having the last word.

NCC's legitimacy was really under pressure from two angles. From the point of view of politicians, the due process and transparency aspects of meta-regulation bit hard, throwing decisions that benefited discrete groups into a public spotlight that increased the risk of being seen as serving 'special interests'. Several of the central agency officials commented on the extent to which 'due process' in the sphere of regulatory *policymaking* decisions was an alien culture for politicians. From the point of view of the broader political community, the apparent preference for in favour of market infrastructural reform at the expense of social citizenship made National Competition Policy a flashpoint for long-building community concerns over a wide set of changes. This had serious political consequences, which I allude to further at the very end of this chapter.

In the wake of this double hostility, both from political executives and from the broader political community, an important debate began over 'renegotiating' National Competition Policy. While some of the more populist-oriented aspects of this aspect will appear in the final chapter, it is appropriate to close this long chapter on the technical minutiae of meta-regulation's patterns with a brief exploration of a particular technical amendment to the intergovernmental agreements. The story of this amendment reinforces the incipient *legality* of meta-regulation.

The Legal-Political Ambiguities of the 'Threshold Requirement'

The political ramifications of backlash against the second NCC tranche assessment, of which the Queensland reaction was one example, dominated the November 2000 meeting of federal and state heads of government in the Council of Australian Governments (COAG), the body responsible for ultimate *political* oversight and control of National Competition Policy. The meeting was fraught with conflict over the reform package and serious consideration was given to withdrawing from the intergovernmental agreements. However, in the end it was decided that the long-term benefits in "sustaining the competitiveness and flexibility of the Australian economy and contributing to higher standards of living" were worth the political costs,[117] and all participating governments ultimately reaffirmed their ongoing commitment to National Competition Policy.

However, in respect of the National Competition Council, the COAG meeting also introduced "several measures to clarify and fine-tune implementation arrangements for NCP".[118] In some respects, mainly at the level of the general agenda of NCC, these measures involved shifting more control back to COAG Senior Officials from the NCC, and in this way lessening meta-regulation's institutional insulation from politics. However, for the more micro-level dynamics of enforcing compliance, these 'fine-tuning' measures had more ambiguous implications, ones that are arguably most effectively interpreted as casting the role of the National Competition Council in enforcing compliance more firmly within a mode of incipient legality.

To illustrate this, consider the core amendment made to the 'guiding principle' of Clause 5(1) of the Competition Principles Agreement. That principle, as has been repeatedly stated in previous chapters, required that all regulatory policy choices surmount a 'threshold requirement' that they achieve a net benefit for the community as a whole in a manner as least restrictive of competition as possible. In the wake of the November 2000 COAG meetings, the intergovernmental agreements were in effect amended (by way of letter appendices rather than resigning) by adding the following clause:

> In assessing whether the threshold requirement of Clause 5 has been achieved, the NCC should consider whether the conclusion reached in the report is within a range of outcomes that could reasonably be reached based on the information available to a properly constituted review process. Within the range of outcomes that could reasonably be reached, it is a matter for Government to determine what policy is in the public interest.[119]

There is an interesting ambiguity in the effect of this clause, reflecting the political compromise secured by the meeting. On the one hand, the notion of a "range of outcomes that could reasonably be reached" eases the 'bite' of the meta-regulatory regime, loosening somewhat the weight of the assumed onus in favour of competition. Under the amended standard of assessment, even if there is a less restrictive policy alternative available to a department or government, the last word on whether that choice is overall in the public interest is explicitly given back to the government, rather than the NCC. There is, in other words, no 'right answer' divinable by the NCC but a range of possible answers, all of which are justifiable under meta-regulation. This would lessen the constraint imposed on regulatory policymaking by meta-regulation.

However while there might well be less constraint on specific *outcomes* under the amended approach, there is potential for a tightening of constraints on *process*. For the wider feasibility in permissible outcomes is conditioned on the existence of "information available to a properly constituted review process". And it was clear both from interviews with central agency officials and recent NCC documentation, that the notion of 'proper constitution' of review processes was intended to bear heavy interpretive weight.

The NCC's guidelines for the June 2001 'third tranche assessment' of competition payments stressed three consequences of the requirement for proper constitution: transparency, independence and "analytical rigour".[120] Central agency officials interpreted this as requiring that the search for the 'least restrictive' solution in regulatory policy choice involve publicly available reasoning undertaken by persons without a direct material interest in the outcomes.[121] Though consultation with such 'stakeholder' groups was to be encouraged, they should not, for true 'independence' to obtain, have significant control over the review process. Further the publicly available reasoning would have to show "analytical rigour", in the sense that there must be 'logical connections' between the evidence presented by the review and the outcome recommended. While quantitatively based proof of net benefit was *not* necessarily required, a chain of transparent justification had to be visible, at least if restrictions on competition were retained.[122] This interpretation veers so close to consideration of the substantive policy choice at stake that it is difficult to categorise as purely procedural.

The NCC therefore interpreted the amendment as continuing to give it the last word on independence, transparency and logical rigour in regulatory review. If any of independence, transparency or logical rigour was lacking, the resulting 'hard look' at process may in practice come close to 'second-guessing' any recommendation to retain restrictions on competition. This is effectively what happened in relation to the Queensland decisions to proceed with key water projects in the face of what the NCC considered inadequately rigorous exploration of the ecological and economic benefits.

Further, if a "properly constituted" review recommended *pro-competitive* reform, the NCC was willing to put its enforcement muscle behind that recommendation, which would come close to second-guessing a government decision to differ from the review. This is what happened when the NCC recommended financial penalties in response to the continuing non-compliance of the New South Wales government in relation to reform of the rice industry.

There is then, in this 'refinement' of the Competition Principles Agreement, an uneasy tension between the apparently increased scope for a range of outcomes in regulatory policy choice, and tougher constraints on review criteria both procedural and substantive. While this uneasy tension was almost certainly the result of political compromises necessary to secure ongoing commitment to the reforms, the particulars of its resolution are fascinatingly analogous to the way in which judicial review constrains public decision-making. Indeed, the precise phrasing of the amendment was, according to some officials, inspired by the logic of judicial review.[123] Like a court, the NCC insists that it does not set policy, but merely interprets the tasks it is given.[124] Like a court, public justification in terms of a neutral rationality does *constrain* political choice, though it does not direct it to specific ends. It leaves instead a zone of flexibility, within which a range of justifiable regulatory policy choices is feasible. But like a court, the detailed practices of imposing constraint at the margins can leak into substantive oversight where considerations of the rigour and logic of evidence come into play.

Of course, unlike courts, a fairly extensive and much less public dialogical process of political negotiation over penalties also takes place between participating governments and the NCC. But the somewhat porous boundary between politics and technocratic rationality reflects the *incipient* nature of the legality embodied in these institutional arrangements. And that too is shifting in a direction analogous to legality, at least insofar as transparent deliberation is concerned. The NCC now has the authority to request participating governments to make transparent their review documentation, as well as their "public interest reasons" supporting their final decisions, and the NCC itself is required to give a public statement of its reasons when recommending financial penalties.[125]

In effect, the early substantive political conflict over the relative breadth of the 'public interest' test[126] – whether it should include only 'economic' factors such as efficiency, productivity and competitiveness or also a broader array of social protection and equity values – was ultimately finessed into a compromise centred around procedure. The NCC could continue to stress the onus in favour of market competition and participating governments could continue to favour competing social values, provided each of them demonstrates publicly, with the assistance of neutral expert advice, the premises of their decision.

Because of the limits of neutrality and expertise in what are essentially social value judgements, however, a 'reasonably justifiable' outcome in terms of NCC's economic rationality may well differ from the politically defined 'reasonably justifiable' outcome that a state government may reach. At this point, the ultimate determinant will, as with many accounts of the impact of the rule of law, tend to be the participant with more raw power. Since the NCC in this configuration has the powerful back-up incentive/punishment of substantial financial incentives, its continuing preference for maximising market competition is likely to dominate the overall weight of the reform package's impact.

Conclusion

As this chapter has demonstrated, there is some considerable malleability within the application of meta-regulation. The 'translation' of important aspects of social welfare into the language of market failures or market distortion is feasible and secures some strategic political successes. But the malleability has its limits, and those limits tend to respect the implicit division of labour implied by the public choice perspective on politics. That is to say, even the politically charged machinations over amending the intergovernmental agreements described above did not extend explicitly to the *distributive* impacts of pro-competitive reform. Rather, conflicts over substantive distributive issues were finessed into a superficially procedural amendment.

The conflicts were to have their effect nonetheless, however. Over time, the corrosive distributive impact of National Competition Policy became very real, particularly in rural parts of Australia where the sparse distribution and low numbers of inhabitants made market governance frequently unprofitable. In July of 1998, the familiar two-party contours of the Australian political landscape were badly shaken. Pauline Hanson's One Nation party, a newly emergent populist party with a predominantly rural base, gained nearly 23% of the total primary vote in the Queensland state elections, displacing not only the Labour party but also the National-Liberal conservative coalition. Hostility to National Competition Policy was one of One Nation's primary policy planks.

Although the fortunes of the party have fluctuated considerably since 1998, they made a sufficiently strong showing in by-elections occurring in 2001 to catalyse a reversal of federal government policy on opening business postal services to competition. The link between National Competition Policy and broader political dissatisfactions remains exploitable, however much changes in the circumstances of rural Australia may in fact be attributable to forces other than meta-regulation (such as falling world commodity prices, technological changes and other government policies). The importance of distributive concerns, while something of a 'blind spot' in the early years of the reform programme, has more latterly won political recognition, in ways that illuminate some of the more elusive questions regarding the broader implications of meta-regulation for citizenship conceived of as collective identity. It is to this that the concluding chapter turns, after first pulling together the threads of the preceding chapters in summary form.

Notes

1   National Competition Council (2001), *Framework for the Third Tranche Assessment of Government's Progress with Implementing National Competition Policy and Related Reforms*, Ausinfo, Canberra.

2   Other examples where hybrid concerns of market facilitation, protection from risk and redistribution all converge include long-term unemployment services and child care.

3   OECD (1996), *Regulatory Reform: A Country Study of Australia*, Public Management Service, Paris.

4   Gas differs from the other utilities here, since it has been supplied, distributed and administered historically by the private sector.

5   Johnson, Michael (1993), 'The Water Industry Overseas – Lessons for Australia', in Rix, J.A. (ed), *Water in Australia: Managing Economic, Environmental and Community Reform*, Pluto Press and Public Sector Research Centre, UNSW, Sydney.

6   Campbell, Colin and Halligan, John (1992), *Political Leadership in an Age of Constraint: the Australian Experience*, University of Pittsburgh Press, Pittsburgh.

7   Rix, Stephen (1993), 'The Political Context of Public Sector Reform Debate', in Johnson, R. (ed), *Water in Australia: Managing Economic, Environmental and Community Reform*, Pluto Press and Public Sector Research Centre, University of New South Wales, Sydney, p.174.

8   Goggin, Gerald (1995), 'The Framework for Consumer Protection in NSW Utilities', in Johnston, C. (ed), *Consumer Rights and Utilities: Issues and Options for NSW*, Public Interest Advocacy Centre, Sydney; Johnston, Craig (ed), (1995), *Consumer Rights and Utilities: Issues and Options for NSW*, Public Interest Advocacy Centre, Sydney; Public Interest Advocacy Centre, Consumer Law Centre of Victoria, et al. (1995), *Voices in the Market: Consumer Consultation and Advocacy in an Era of Competition*, Consumers' Telecommunications Network, Surry Hills, Sydney; Walker, Dinneke (1995), *Regulation of Victoria's Energy and Water Utilities: An Analysis of the Protection of Consumers and the Public Interest*, The Consumer Law Centre of Victoria Ltd., Melbourne.

9   Swan, Antony, Regulatory Policy Officer, Sydney Water Corporation (1997), *Interview*, Morgan, February 10 1997.

10   After a change of government in late 1999, Victoria moved more in the direction that New South Wales had taken under Labour (i.e. towards a network structure involving a separation of social and economic regulatory authority and institutions, and a greater degree of arms-length independence from government for the relevant regulatory institutions).

11   Goggin, Gerald (1995), 'The Framework for Consumer Protection in NSW Utilities', in Johnston, C. (ed), *Consumer Rights and Utilities: Issues and Options for NSW*, Public Interest Advocacy Centre, Sydney.

12   A national body, the Australian Competition and Consumer Commission will in the

long run possibly play an overriding and coordinating role, at least in the arena of access to monopoly infrastructure.

13   Walker, Dinneke (1995), Regulation of Victoria's Energy and Water Utilities: An Analysis of the Protection of Consumers and the Public Interest, The Consumer Law Centre of Victoria Ltd., Melbourne.

14   Mack, Jenni (1995), 'Utilities Reform: State by State', Conference on *Consumer Protection and Utilities Reform*, Canberra, p.25.

15   Walker, Dinneke (1995), *Regulation of Victoria's Energy and Water Utilities: An Analysis of the Protection of Consumers and the Public Interest*, The Consumer Law Centre of Victoria Ltd., Melbourne, p.50.

16   Recent developments since the initial period of research further support a link between left-wing governance and a more transparent, fragmented network structure. The Victorian Labour government, elected in late 1999, promised to create an independent agency, the Essential Services Commission, to replace the Office of the Regulator-General, and also to establish an Essential Services Ombudsman for individual complaints.

17   New South Wales Government (1994), *Social Program Policy for NSW Government Trading Enterprises*, Sydney.

18   Moore, Gary, Director of New South Wales Council on Social Services (NCOSS) (1997), *Interview*, Morgan, February 20 1997.

19   Walker, Dinneke (1995), *Regulating for Consumer Protection: The Victorian Experience*. Consumer Protection and Utilities Reform, Canberra, p.15.

20   Hahn, Barry (1995), 'Consumer Advocacy and Financial Counselling' Conference on *Consumer Protection and Utilities Reform*, Canberra.

21   Yarmirr v Australian Telecommunications Corporation [1990] 96 ALR 739.

22   Mahoney, W. (1995), 'Strategies for Enforcing the Rights of Disadvantaged Groups in Relation to Utility Reform', in Johnston and Craig (eds), *Consumer Rights and Utilities: Issues and Options for NSW*, Public Interest Advocacy Centre, Sydney.

23   Scott and Disabled Peoples International, Unreported, Human Rights and Equal Opportunities Commission, March 19 1995 (Human Rights and Equal Opportunities Commission); discussed in Mahoney, W. (1995), 'Strategies for Enforcing the Rights of Disadvantaged Groups in Relation to Utility Reform', in Johnston and Craig (eds), *Consumer Rights and Utilities: Issues and Options for NSW*, Public Interest Advocacy Centre, Sydney.

24   A Labour federal government may have been prepared to pass federal regulation imposing 'consumer protection obligations' on utility corporations, but a Coalition federal government, traditionally more sensitive to states' rights, would not. This necessitated a change in tactics and a shift in focus on the part of the social welfare and consumer lobby.

25   McHugh, Jeanette (1995), 'Opening Address', Conference on *Consumer Protection and Utilities Reform*, Canberra, p.11.

26   McHugh, Jeanette (1995), 'Opening Address', Conference on *Consumer Protection and Utilities Reform*, Canberra, p.11.

27   Substantive redistribution is not ignored, but is addressed in separate lobbying strategies mainly directed at the CSO process, which is a much more discretion-saturated political process.

28   Johnston, Craig (1996), 'New Initiatives for Consumer Protection: Examples from an Industry in Transition – Electricity Retail in New South Wales and Victoria' in *Commercialised Government*, Sydney, p.7.

29   In fact, public interest groups in Victoria pushed to develop similar strategies to those of New South Wales, but had little success until a Labour government was elected in 1999. Prior to that they had to rely on generating adversarial publicity in public hearings held (and controlled) by the executive Office of the Regulator-General described above. Usually by the time the hearings were held, the framework rules were already set in place; thus Victoria's strategy could not under a right-wing government shift to a systemic level where disadvantaged consumer groups get more of a 'seat at the rulemaking table' (Walker, Dinneke (1995), *Regulation of Victoria's Energy and Water Utilities: An Analysis of the Protection of Consumers and the Public Interest*, The Consumer Law Centre of Victoria Ltd., Melbourne). The change of government on the one hand did not slow pursuit of market infrastructural goals insofar as electricity moved to full privatisation. However, the proliferation of network institutions gave the public interest groups a greater seat at the table in negotiating some social citizenship protections, such as minimum service provision standards in the consumer contracts that would govern privatised service delivery.

30   Johnston, Craig (1996), 'New Initiatives for Consumer Protection: Examples from an Industry in Transition – Electricity Retail in New South Wales and Victoria' in *Commercialised Government*, Sydney, p.3.

31   Public Interest Advocacy Centre (1996), *Wear Away Rock with Water ... Utilities and Consumer Advocacy: A Feasibility Study into the Development of a Utility Consumer's Advocacy Network in New South Wales and Recommendations for Action*, Public Interest Advocacy Centre and E3 Group, Sydney, p.20.

32   Hogan, Michael, Director, NSW Public Interest Advocacy Centre (1996), *Interview*, Morgan. October 4 1996; Johnston, Craig (1996), 'New Initiatives for Consumer Protection: Examples from an Industry in Transition – Electricity Retail in New South Wales and Victoria' in *Commercialised Government*, Sydney.

33   Public Interest Advocacy Centre (1996), *Wear Away Rock with Water ... Utilities and Consumer Advocacy: A Feasibility Study into the Development of a Utility Consumer's Advocacy Network in New South Wales and Recommendations for Action*, Public Interest Advocacy Centre and E3 Group, Sydney, p.3.

34   Public Interest Advocacy Centre (1996), *Wear Away Rock with Water ... Utilities and Consumer Advocacy: A Feasibility Study into the Development of a Utility Consumer's Advocacy Network in New South Wales and Recommendations for Action*, Public Interest Advocacy Centre and E3 Group, Sydney, p.4.

35   Public Interest Advocacy Centre (1996), *Wear Away Rock with Water ... Utilities and Consumer Advocacy: A Feasibility Study into the Development of a Utility Consumer's Advocacy Network in New South Wales and Recommendations for Action*, Public Interest Advocacy Centre and E3 Group, Sydney, p.6.

36   Public Interest Advocacy Centre (1996), *Wear Away Rock with Water ... Utilities and Consumer Advocacy: A Feasibility Study into the Development of a Utility Consumer's Advocacy Network in New South Wales and Recommendations for Action*, Public Interest Advocacy Centre and E3 Group, Sydney, p.10.

37   Public Interest Roundtable (1997), *National Competition Policy – Legislation Review: The Reality of Hilmer and Implications for the Public Interest*, notes on speakers taken by the author who was present, p.28.

38   Shames, Michael (1995), 'Competition Among Equals', Conference on *Consumer Protection and Utilities Reform*, Canberra.

39   Griffiths, Communication via Co-op Net mailing list (davidg@fox.net.au) (1998), *Email Communication*, Morgan, 30 March 1998.

40 New South Wales Government (1995), *Review of the Legislation Establishing the NSW Rice Marketing Board: Final Report*, Sydney.

41 New South Wales Government (1995), *Review of the Legislation Establishing the NSW Rice Marketing Board: Final Report*, Sydney, p.17.

42 New South Wales Government (1995), *Review of the Legislation Establishing the NSW Rice Marketing Board: Final Report*, Sydney, p.17.

43 New South Wales Government (1995), *Review of the Legislation Establishing the NSW Rice Marketing Board: Final Report*, Sydney, p.49.

44 New South Wales Government (1995), *Review of the Legislation Establishing the NSW Rice Marketing Board: Final Report*, Sydney, p.iv.

45 New South Wales Government (1995), *Review of the Legislation Establishing the NSW Rice Marketing Board: Final Report*, Sydney, p.19.

46 New South Wales Government (1995), *Review of the Legislation Establishing the NSW Rice Marketing Board: Final Report*, Sydney, p.19.

47 New South Wales Government (1995), *Review of the Legislation Establishing the NSW Rice Marketing Board: Final Report*, Sydney, p.21.

48 New South Wales Government (1995), *Review of the Legislation Establishing the NSW Rice Marketing Board: Final Report*, Sydney, p.26.

49 New South Wales Government (1995), *Review of the Legislation Establishing the NSW Rice Marketing Board: Final Report*, Sydney, p.32.

50 New South Wales Government (1995), *Review of the Legislation Establishing the NSW Rice Marketing Board: Final Report*, Sydney, p.35.

51 New South Wales Government (1995), *Review of the Legislation Establishing the NSW Rice Marketing Board: Final Report*, Sydney, p.37.

52 New South Wales Government (1995), *Review of the Legislation Establishing the NSW Rice Marketing Board: Final Report*, Sydney, p.36.

53 New South Wales Government (1995), *Review of the Legislation Establishing the NSW Rice Marketing Board: Final Report*, Sydney, p.39.

54 New South Wales Government (1995), *Review of the Legislation Establishing the NSW Rice Marketing Board: Final Report*, Sydney, p.40.

55 New South Wales Government (1995), *Review of the Legislation Establishing the NSW Rice Marketing Board: Final Report*, Sydney, p.39.

56 Public Interest Roundtable (1997), National Competition Policy – Legislation Review: The Reality of Hilmer and Implications for the Public Interest, Notes on speakers taken by the author who was present, p.8.

57 Though in practice 95% of Australian rice is produced in NSW.

58 New South Wales Government (1995), *Review of the Legislation Establishing the NSW Rice Marketing Board: Final Report*, Sydney, p.43.

59 Downing, Terry, Senior Policy Officer, NSW Cabinet Office (1997), *Interview*, Morgan. February 7 1997.

60 National Competition Council (2001), *Framework for the Third Tranche Assessment of Government's Progress with Implementing National Competition Policy and Related Reforms*, Ausinfo, Canberra, para. 13.16.

61 Commonwealth Government (1996), *Review of the Migration Agents Registration Scheme: Exposure Draft*, Australian Government Publishing Service, Canberra.

62 Commonwealth Government (1996), *Review of the Migration Agents Registration Scheme: Exposure Draft*, Australian Government Publishing Service, Canberra, p.3.

63 Commonwealth Government (1996), *Review of the Migration Agents Registration Scheme: Exposure Draft*, Australian Government Publishing Service, Canberra, p.3.

[64]   Australian Legislative Assembly (1992), *Hansard*, House of Representatives, May 27 1992. p.2936.

[65]   Commonwealth Government (1996), *Review of the Migration Agents Registration Scheme: Exposure Draft*, Australian Government Publishing Service, Canberra, p.39.

[66]   Commonwealth Government (1996), *Review of the Migration Agents Registration Scheme: Exposure Draft*, Australian Government Publishing Service, Canberra, p.14.

[67]   Commonwealth Government (1996), *Review of the Migration Agents Registration Scheme: Exposure Draft*, Australian Government Publishing Service, Canberra, p.13.

[68]   Commonwealth Government (1996), *Review of the Migration Agents Registration Scheme: Exposure Draft*, Australian Government Publishing Service, Canberra, p.14.

[69]   Commonwealth Government (1996), *Review of the Migration Agents Registration Scheme: Exposure Draft*, Australian Government Publishing Service, Canberra, p.15.

[70]   Commonwealth Government (1996), *Review of the Migration Agents Registration Scheme: Exposure Draft*, Australian Government Publishing Service, Canberra, p.15.

[71]   Commonwealth Government (1996), *Review of the Migration Agents Registration Scheme: Exposure Draft*, Australian Government Publishing Service, Canberra, p.17.

[72]   Commonwealth Government (1996), *Review of the Migration Agents Registration Scheme: Exposure Draft*, Australian Government Publishing Service, Canberra, p.17.

[73]   Commonwealth Government (1996), *Review of the Migration Agents Registration Scheme: Exposure Draft*, Australian Government Publishing Service, Canberra, p.20.

[74]   Commonwealth Government (1996), *Review of the Migration Agents Registration Scheme: Exposure Draft*, Australian Government Publishing Service, Canberra, p.20.

[75]   Commonwealth Government (1996), *Review of the Migration Agents Registration Scheme: Exposure Draft*, Australian Government Publishing Service, Canberra, p.22.

[76]   Coghlan, Assistant Commissioner, Office of Regulation Review, Productivity Commission, Canberra (1997), *Interview*, Morgan. February 15 1997.

[77]   Commonwealth Government (1996), *Review of the Migration Agents Registration Scheme: Exposure Draft*, Australian Government Publishing Service, Canberra, p.35.

[78]   Commonwealth Government (1996), *Review of the Migration Agents Registration Scheme: Exposure Draft*, Australian Government Publishing Service, Canberra, p.26.

[79]   Department of Immigration and Multicultural Affairs (2001), *Fact Sheet 72*, Public Affairs Section, Revised on 22 May 2001.

[80]   Victorian Government (1997), *Audit Act 1994: Review Report*, Melbourne.

[81]   Victorian Government (1997), *Audit Act 1994: Review Report*, Melbourne, p.17.

[82]   Victorian Government (1997), *Audit Act 1994: Review Report*, Melbourne p.104.

[83]   Pinkney (1997) 'Probes Set to Anger Kennett', *The Herald Sun*, p.15.

[84]   Victorian Government (1997), *Audit Act 1994: Review Report*, Melbourne, p.20.

85   Richards (1996) 'An Outside Watchdog is the Best Security', *The Age*, 11 December, Melbourne.

86   (1996) 'Editorial', *The Sunday Age*, 25 November 1996, Melbourne, p.3.

87   Richards (1996) 'An Outside Watchdog is the Best Security', *The Age*, 11 December, Melbourne.

88   (1996)'Editorial', *The Age*, 12 December 1996, Melbourne.

89   (1996) 'Editorial', *The Age*, 12 December 1996, Melbourne.

90   Victorian Government (1997), *Audit Act 1994: Review Report*, Melbourne, p.8.

91   Victorian Government (1997), *Audit Act 1994: Review Report*, Melbourne, p.28.

92   Victorian Government (1997), *Audit Act 1994: Review Report*, Melbourne, p.21.

93   It is not the case that competition between regulators necessarily always dilutes effective oversight. For example, third party inspections of industry for compliance with the US Clean Air Act fostered greater efficiency, greater internalisation of the costs of regulation and accidents to firms, and more socially cost effective accident prevention (Jweeping, E.R. (1996), *A Third Party Approach to Environmental Regulation: Possible Roles for Insurance Companies*, Ph.D. Dissertation, University of Pennsylvania.). However this model of regulation required complex roles for insurers as well as for firms and government, thus creating many layers and fostering a network structure.

94   Victorian Government (1997), *Audit Act 1994: Review Report*, Melbourne, p.117.

95   In the rice review, a finely balanced situation with good arguments both ways, the (Labour) government came down against pro-competitive reform. In the migration review, the ORR's preference for a less restrictive regulatory model than departmental bureaucrats was only outweighed by direct empirical arguments.

96   Victorian Government (1997), *Audit Act 1994: Review Report*, Melbourne, p.121.

97   Victorian Government (1997), *Audit Act 1994: Review Report*, Melbourne, p.122.

98   Victorian Government (1997), *Audit Act 1994: Review Report*, Melbourne, p.120.

99   Victorian Government (1997), *Audit Act 1994: Review Report*, Melbourne, p.7.

100   Victorian Government (1997), *Audit Act 1994: Review Report*, Melbourne, p.28.

101   Victorian Government (1997), *Audit Act 1994: Review Report*, Melbourne, p.27.

102   Victorian Government (1997), *Audit Act 1994: Review Report*, Melbourne, p.26.

103   Victorian Government (1997), *Audit Act 1994: Review Report*, Melbourne, p.28.

104   Victorian Government (1997), *Audit Act 1994: Review Report*, Melbourne, p.116.

105   Victorian Government (1997), *Audit Act 1994: Review Report*, Melbourne, p.120.

106   Harris, A.C. (1999), 'Revisiting the Review of the Victorian Audit Act', *Australian Accounting Review*, pp.32-35.

107   The Auditor-General's independence is now enshrined in the state Constitution rather than the Audit Act, recognising the constitutional importance of the office. Selection is no longer by an executive government process, but rather by a parliamentary select committee. Relations with the Parliament are further strengthened through a process of information sharing (*Australian Chartered Professional Accountants' Newsletter*, November 2000).

108   National Competition Council (1997), *Assessment of State and Territory Progress with Implementing National Competition Policy and Related Reforms*, Melbourne, p.17.

109   National Competition Council (1997), *Assessment of State and Territory Progress with Implementing National Competition Policy and Related Reforms*, Melbourne, pp.17-18.

110   Senior Official F, National Competition Council (2001), *Interview*, Morgan, 3 April 2001, p.8.

111 Peter Beattie, Queensland Premier, in radio interview on 'The World Today', Friday July 2, 1999, 12:53.

112 http://www.onlineopinion.com.au/July99/Hamill.htm

113 National Competition Council (2001), *Framework for the Third Tranche Assessment of Government's Progress with Implementing National Competition Policy and Related Reforms*, Ausinfo, Melbourne, para. 5.7.

114 National Competition Council (2001), *Framework for the Third Tranche Assessment of Government's Progress with Implementing National Competition Policy and Related Reforms*, Ausinfo, Melbourne, para. 5.8.

115 National Competition Council (2001), *Framework for the Third Tranche Assessment of Government's Progress with Implementing National Competition Policy and Related Reforms*, Ausinfo, Melbourne, para. 5.8.

116 National Competition Council (2001), *Framework for the Third Tranche Assessment of Government's Progress with Implementing National Competition Policy and Related Reforms*, Ausinfo, Melbourne, para. 5.9.

117 Coalition of Australian Governments (COAG) (2000), *Communiqué*, November 3 2000. p.4.

118 Coalition of Australian Governments (COAG) (2000), *Communiqué*, November 3 2000. p.4.

119 Coalition of Australian Governments (COAG) (2000), *Communiqué*, November 3 2000, Attachment.

120 National Competition Council (2001), *Framework for the Third Tranche Assessment of Government's Progress with Implementing National Competition Policy and Related Reforms*, Ausinfo, Melbourne, para. 5.2.

121 Senior Official F, National Competition Council (2001), *Interview*, Morgan, 3 April 2001, pp.7-8; Coghlan, Paul, Assistant Commissioner, Office of Regulation Review, Productivity Commission, Canberra (1997), *Interview*, Morgan. February 15 1997. p.8.

122 Senior Official F, National Competition Council (2001), *Interview*, Morgan, 3 April 2001, p.8.

123 Senior Official D and Senior Official E, New South Wales Department of the Premier and Cabinet (2001), *Interview*, Morgan, 9 March 2001, p.6.

124 Senior Official F, National Competition Council (2001), *Interview*, Morgan, 3 April 2001, p.4.

125 Coalition of Australian Governments (COAG) (2000), *Communiqué*, November 3 2000, Attachment.

126 As soon as the intergovernmental agreements were in place, the Productivity Commission and certain business groups secretly (and unsuccessfully) lobbied the National Competition Council to formally exclude matters other than 'economic' ones of efficiency, productivity and competitiveness from the public interest test (Moore, Gary, Director of New South Wales Council on Social Services (NCOSS) (1997), *Interview*, Morgan, February 20 1997).

6 Technocratic Citizenship

The primary question of this book has been this: does meta-regulation attenuate social citizenship? More expansively put, how do reflexively institutionalised procedures of regulatory reform that rely significantly on economic rationality impact upon the design, structure and outcomes of social policies underpinning the post-war welfare state? The broad answer to this question is that meta-regulation does not destroy social citizenship, but that it can and does alter its forms, instruments and discourses. It does so in ways that this chapter will argue amount to an endorsement of *technocratic citizenship*. From the perspective of those groups in society most exposed to the potential erosion of social citizenship under the influence of meta-regulation, technocratic citizenship is Janus-faced. On the one hand, the continuing opportunities for participation in regulatory policymaking on the part of vulnerable groups should not be underestimated. On the other hand, the resulting centrality of apolitical images of consumer sovereignty depoliticises social citizenship, masking the power relations encoded in policy conflicts, in ways familiar from studies of the rule of law. The difficulty of incorporating redistributive goals, and more broadly a sense of community, into the justificatory structure of meta-regulation is a key facet of the limitations of technocratic citizenship.

Before discussing in more depth the notion of technocratic citizenship, a more detailed summary of the argument to date, incorporating summary evidence from the preceding chapters, first follows.

The most successful response to meta-regulation on the part of vulnerable groups was a combination of strategic translation of their aspirations into the language of economic analysis, together with the use of 'network' structures that politically insulate future negotiations. Chapters Three, Four and Five sought to delineate an interpretive conversation which debated the limits of justifiable regulation in terms shaped powerfully by the assumptions of economic analysis. In this conversation, a dominant feature was the translation of social citizenship values into the language of economic analysis. Also present were patterns of silencing social citizenship values on the one hand, and on the other hand reiteration of those values in alternative discourses. The extent to which translation, silencing or reiteration occurred was influenced by the type of regulation at stake and the interest groups active in that sector, as well as, at a more macro level, political partisanship and institutional design.

Very broadly speaking, redistributive values were more at risk of being silenced than protective categories of regulation (environmental regulation, professional standards). Thus in the rice review, cost-pooling arrangements were excluded by the economic analysis, as was the free immigration advice provided to economically vulnerable citizens in the immigration review (Chapter Five). By contrast, in the latter review, the need for professional standards was cast as a response to the market failure of informational asymmetry between advisor and client, and in the utilities sector, environmental externalities were built into the pricing decisions of an independent pricing tribunal, at least where energetic interest groups with the relevant economic expertise were able to make such an argument in practical terms.

An important caveat to the differing fates of redistributive and protective categories of social citizenship regulation was the role of the relevant interest groups. The importance of conceptual categories within economic discourse meant that much strategic success depended on technocratic modes of participation, but this was not exhaustively the case. The raw political strength of interest groups can overcome the conceptual vulnerability of redistributive regulation. In this way the silencing effected by the economic analysis framework can sometimes be *reversed* by the influence of interest groups.

Three examples of this follow. First, pre-emptive strategies by organised interest groups may accommodate equity and redistributive regulation, as for example with the Utilities Consumer Advocacy Network secured by the Public Interest Advocacy Centre and associated groups of disadvantaged consumers in the NSW utility industry (Chapter Five). In a second example, a strong professional sector can defend social citizenship values even where meta-regulation marked them out as vulnerable, as occurred with lawyers in the migration review and the fate of subsidies for community immigration legal advice centres under the registration scheme. The final example is one where the vulnerability of a groups affected by the regulatory scheme is politically sensitive, as it was in relation to rural farmers in the rice review. In this instance, social citizenship values prevailed for some five years, although the fact that they were ultimately outweighed by the institutional muscle of the NCC's view in favour of deregulation suggests the political *risk* inherent in modes of participation that do not subscribe to technocratic imperatives.

This last example makes the important point that direct parliamentary support does not necessarily fare equally in contest with the stronger institutional support for the technocratic mode of reasoning represented by the NCC: an independent agency with reasonably significant resources, escalating tiers of fiscal penalties and considerable central political support. Further evidence for the technocratic nature of the participation encouraged under meta-regulation was the fate of the community morality (CM) perspective in the general community debate over the impact of National Competition Policy (Chapter Three).

The CM perspective emerged as the version of compromise most loyal to resisting the reframing effects of the meta-regulatory regime. Albeit inchoately, groups supporting it (mostly producer groups rather than consumer groups) struggled to retain the moral, distributive and collective dimensions of the public interest that its advocates felt were lost in translation into the language of economic analysis. Yet the CM perspective had virtually no success in the interstices of day-to-day bureaucratic routines implementing meta-regulation. For example, take the public interest interpretation clause secured by many of the groups sympathetic to the CM perspective (Chapter Two), which listed several community morality-type factors that must be taken into consideration in meta-regulatory review. In actual reviews, no formal reference was made to that clause, at least in any of the case studies undertaken here. The kinds of social citizenship values enumerated by the clause *were* in fact considered under the review processes, but only in the terms of, and always with primary reference to, the dominant aim of maximising market competition. Thus strategic translation (even where a Labour government oversaw the reviews), was the *sine qua non* for preserving social citizenship values under the meta-regulatory regime.

Necessary, but not sufficient, as the passing reference to Labour and to political partisanship reminds us. For at the most macro level of all, the political leanings of the relevant administration did impact on social citizenship. Broadly, social citizenship values were more likely to be put at risk when strong right-wing majorities were in power. For example, the Victorian agenda-setting process encompassed a greater portion of social, cultural and law-and-order legislation than either the federal or NSW governments' agendas (Chapter Four). Similarly, enhanced risk for social citizenship occurred in the audit review and the structure of utility reform in Victoria, as compared to the rice and migration reviews or the NSW utility sector (Chapter Five).

Even where 'politics matters', however, the salience of technocratic modes of participation continued to be significant. While left-wing governments might have made fewer inroads on social citizenship, these were outcomes achieved by erecting 'network structures' at an institutional level: independent bodies situated at arms-length from hierarchical chains of political command and partially insulated from political control. Compare for example, the links between IPART, EPA and the License-Regulator in the NSW utility industry as compared to the Victorian decision to give analogous functions to the hierarchically controlled Office of the Regulator-General. Further, in NSW, where consumer groups fought for and won the Utility Consumer Advocacy Network, preserving at least process rights for disadvantaged consumers, the independence and technical expertise of the network of semi-autonomous institutions in which those consumers would participate was also emphasised strongly.

Thus the preservation, up to a point, of social citizenship goals under meta-regulation, is feasible, whether by strategic translation, interest group lobbying, institutional design or traditional partisan leadership. The limits of that preservation relate to redistributive goals. But whether social citizenship values are preserved or whether they are narrowed or put at risk, there is a common thread. That common thread is an emphasis on apoliticism. Translation of social citizenship values into the language of economic analysis involves discursive autonomy from politics, emphasising neutral, technical expertise over value judgments. The development of network structures is an expression of institutional autonomy from politics, emphasising 'independent' bodies protected from having their agendas set by politicians. While the detail of implementation at the micro-level charted in previous chapters has often shown to what extent both conceptual and institutional aspects of meta-regulation are fluid, contingent and politicised, nevertheless the structure of justification is still significantly apolitical, as befits an incipient mode of legality.

The question then arises: what are the broader implications of this essentially apolitical mode of participation fostered under meta-regulation? Citizenship is importantly defined by the available modes of participation in collective decision-making. There has been extensive criticism directed to the 'economisation' of citizenship, excoriating the replacement of the citizen by the consumer as the prototypical 'figure' of political discourse.[1] Much of this criticism has a neo-republican inflection, assuming that what I am calling technocratic citizenship has the effect of marginalising the active creation of community. Active political citizens are, it is feared, replaced by apolitical passive consumers. But the micro-dynamics of implementing meta-regulation that this book has explored could give pause to this judgement. Is it not plausible that potentially *greater* possibilities for citizen-like deliberation lie in the new structures emerging from meta-regulation?

One interpretation of the evidence of this study in support of such a position might run as follows. Meta-regulation results in mandatory transparent justification of regulatory policy choice, in a forum of public debate, together with network structures that give the figure of the consumer practical avenues for voicing his or her concerns. Such a setting creates more opportunity for constructive engagement and dialogue over policy than the hierarchically controlled welfare state structures they replace. Hierarchical, informal institutional structures create high risks for regulatory actors: policy change is easy to secure but hard to hold on to and promises lavishly made can be reversed overnight. Symbolic politics, loquacious about its aspirations (whether to promote social citizenship or market infrastructures) all too easily becomes little more than propagandistic rhetoric. By contrast, in formalised network institutional structures, policy change is hard to secure but easy to hold onto once secured, because of the overlapping veto points and hurdles required to reverse change. Regulatory politics occurs less visibly in complex, technical arenas; it is arduous but not so high-risk. Genuine deliberation is arguably facilitated rather than narrowed, albeit that it takes place in technocratic terms.

I would suggest that there are indeed grounds for making such an argument on the basis of the material explored in this book. This is the reason for using the title 'technocratic citizenship' for the chapter: it captures the tension between the exclusivity implied by the possession of expert technical knowledge and the inclusivity promised by citizenship. Politics today may be conducted in technocratic terms, but it is no less political for that. But this does not mean that technocratic citizenship does not give cause for pause. For the difficulty of incorporating redistributive goals into the argumentative constraints of this incipient mode of legality is key here. It reminds us that a critical subset of particular outcomes are *not* fostered by the participatory structures of meta-regulation. In the remaining pages of the book, I want to explore that lacuna in technocratic citizenship, and try to illuminate a dimension of it that goes beyond material resources and touches on more elusive aspects of communal membership. I will ground these thoughts in part upon certain aspects of the political backlash in Australia against meta-regulation to which I alluded at the end of Chapter Five. But the implications are not context-specific.

It is clear by now that the dynamics of implementation in specific case studies show that meta-regulation failed to address redistributive values systematically. The shape of what was to come began to emerge in its early stages in the parliamentary inquiry explored in Chapter Three. That inquiry, known as the Hawker inquiry, was the first of three substantially similar public debates about the social effects of National Competition Policy. As Chapters Three and Five showed, a 'differentiated consumer sovereignty' perspective could secure limited social citizenship outcomes by strategic use of economic discourse, particularly the notion of market failure. By contrast, the 'community morality' perspective that sought to articulate an alternative vision less dependent on economic rationality did not generate concrete technical strategies in the bureaucratic fora of Chapters Four and Five. In material terms, this limit on meta-regulation's malleability had negative implications for the redistributive facets of regulatory structures.

Yet more was at stake than 'mere' redistribution. Often demands for redistribution of material resources were the residue of attempts to articulate broader resistance to economic rationality, invoking, for example, shared vulnerability, ethical communities, multi-faceted need. Applied in specific policy contexts with a burden of proof in favour of maximising market competition, these attempts were typically characterised as 'market distortions' that should appropriately be resolved, if at all, by political responses. Due to the heightened risk or inefficacy, for vulnerable politically weak groups, of such an avenue, over time the political cost of meta-regulation's 'blind spot' became more and more insistent. In the wake of the Hawker inquiry, a Productivity Commission Inquiry into the Impact of NCP on Rural and Regional Australia in 1999 was later itself followed by a Senate Select Committee Inquiry into the Socio-Economic Impact of NCP in 2000.

The principal effect of all these debates and inquiries, in tandem with the alarming political implications of the emergence of the reactionary populist political party One Nation, was to bring to the foreground the topic of 'adjustment assistance' as a necessary concomitant to meta-regulation. The National Competition Council itself became gradually more and more forthright about casting the absence of attention to this in the original design of the reform package as a weakness. In a speech highly representative of the debate and documentation surrounding National Competition Policy time at the time, the President of the National Competition Council stated:

> At times, notwithstanding there may be sound community benefit reasons for pursuing a reform, there will be substantial equity costs. That is, particular groups may suffer disproportionately ... The lack of a clearly articulated policy on adjustment assistance within the NCP agreements is, arguably, a major oversight. Such a clear articulation of policy would both signal a commitment to assisting the losers from reform and provide the basis for a consistent and equitable approach. Social assistance to change must become an integral part of reform.[2]

The need for 'adjustment assistance' was closely bound up with the design of meta-regulation. It reflected the cumulative effect of the logic of incipient legality traced in the previous chapters, a logic which was corrosive of redistributive regulatory policy. Yet perhaps ironically, discussion of adjustment assistance in the public sphere in Australia remained consistent with the general tenor of meta-regulation's concern to keep distributive issues clearly distinct from the 'technical' aspects of regulatory policy choice.

This can be seen by contrasting the discussion at the end of Chapter Five about the amendment to the intergovernmental agreements with the tenor of public debate over adjustment assistance. The amendment to the intergovernmental agreements was cast as a highly technical issue, despite its important political implications for recalibrating the balance between NCC and state government decision-making power. By contrast, distributive equity in the politics of adjustment assistance was explicitly given prominence as a *political decision*, rather than as a technical governance strategy. As such, it was cast as a *transitional* response to cushion the inevitability of pro-competitive change, rather than as a principled tempering of the distributive inequalities fostered by unmediated market competition.

In the same speech quoted above, the NCC President argued:

> Adjustment assistance should be about helping individuals and communities adapt to change in ways that will make them self-sufficient in the future ... The fundamental message we need to ensure is delivered is that we have little alternative to pursuing the kinds of changes NCP and related reforms are prompting. Talk of globalisation and its impacts is a commonplace now, but it is the fundamental context in which we have to see the questions of reform. Australia's economy is undergoing rapid change driven by innovations in communications, financial and information-based technologies. Our companies now compete globally in an environment in which technological advances are driving down costs and enabling entry to markets that were previously sheltered by barriers of information and distance. With the integration of markets, world's best practice is the new benchmark and survival depends on achieving it.[3]

Addressing equity via an explicitly temporary political response, as opposed to embedding equity values into the more enduring frameworks of institutional change mandated by meta-regulation, mirrors the impact of the reform package at more policy-specific levels, as described in Chapter Five. The vulnerability this implies for the stability of social citizenship values applies even more strongly at this macro-level. Essentially it could be seen as 'paying off the losers' in order to cement the extent to which the shadow of market competition can shape regulatory policy choice.

Material support for 'losers' in regulatory reform is by no means unimportant. But as we have seen, more is at stake than material redistribution. The less technocratic facet of citizenship, a sometimes elusive conception of collective identity or mutual ethical obligation, is also at stake. For many in Australia, the political backlash against National Competition Policy was grounded at its core not just on distributive impacts on key social groups, particularly those in rural areas, but also on the implications of the overall approach of the reform package for community identity. As the Queensland Premier, Peter Beattie, said in a radio interview shortly after the NCC had penalised Queensland in the second tranche assessment, "Are they about Australia or are they, which is what our view is, are they simply obsessed with some ideology?".[4]

If 'paying off the losers' is primarily a strategy to stabilise the larger project of entrenching the values of market competition that make the vulnerable portions of society feel excluded in the first place, then it is not a response that solidifies citizenship. There was, however, another dimension to the politics of adjustment assistance which is in tension with the rather bleaker aspects outlined above. The NCC's perspective also contained threads that *distinguished* the importance of equity values from 'paying off the losers', and linked them instead to notions of agency and power, autonomy and community. These notions were at the core of the 'community morality' perspective on meta-regulation (Chapter Three) that was so decisively silenced in specific bureaucratic trajectories of implementation (Chapters Four and Five).

The NCC speech already quoted provides a useful illustration of this chain of reasoning that typifies this linkage, In moving *away* from equity as 'paying off the losers' and towards autonomy, agency and community, we find first an effort to distinguish 'compensation' from 'adjustment costs':

> We need to draw a clear distinction between adjustment assistance and the calls for 'compensation' routinely made by any interest group faced with a government intent on removing its long-held privileges. The reality is that investments that are based largely or solely on regulatory restrictions are inherently risky, and those who take on these investments do so in the knowledge that government policies can and do change. [5]

The shift from retrospective equity to prospective equity is then fleshed out by emphasising the acquisition of skills, services and even modes of self-perception that will 'fit' a more highly competitive context better:

[A]djustment 'assistance' is about much more than money alone. A big cheque is an inadequate response if those affected by change don't know how to apply the proceeds to assist them to adjust. Sometimes, money may not be appropriate at all. Managing change involves advice and assistance (personal, business and financial), retraining, reskilling, and access to services, specifically by replacement of lost services with alternatives such as enhanced communications infrastructure.[6]

Finally the improved 'fit' between the individual characteristics and social contexts of those who are vulnerable to the distributive effects of maximising market competition is linked explicitly to a sense of community:

Taking action on these issues is imperative, not just on moral and equity grounds, but to help people feel more optimistic about their ability to adapt in a world where ongoing change is a part of life, and perhaps most important of all, to ensure that people don't feel that they have been forgotten or discarded by the rest of the community ... No-one should be regarded as an expendable cost of achieving the benefits of reform.[7]

This political development in the trajectory of National Competition Policy aims, in effect, to reconfigure community around collective values linked to the capacity to participate in a context of intensified market competition. This 'return of community' into the politics of meta-regulation reflects a crucially important facet of those politics. The linkage between community and advice, assistance, retraining and reskilling communicates that what is at stake is *structural power*: the collective power to define the basic structural architecture of our lives.

The framing of adjustment assistance in terms of providing support to those most impacted by the distributive blindness of competitive markets is an attempt to foster structural power at the level of individuals. But it is perhaps ironic, then, that the rhetorical context of meta-regulation so often emphasises a *lack* of such structural power at the level of the national community. Recall the NCC's "fundamental message": "we have little alternative to pursuing the kinds of changes NCP and related reforms are prompting".[8] Recall too that this is not only rhetoric, but justifies concrete and important technical aspects of the way meta-regulation is designed, such as the Australian regime's embedded onus of proof in favour of maximising market competition.

Here is an elision that is key to the bureaucratic politics of regulatory justification, and to the ways in which unfolding instances of such politics in the future may or may not respond to broader community concerns. That elision is, when brought to the fore, a contradiction between the possibilities and opportunities for structural power open to individuals or discrete groups under the discipline of meta-regulation, and those available to regional or national communities. Structural power is only possible for the former, for disaggregated units within a larger community that takes as given a world of regulatory policy choice committed to governance through market liberalism. In this context, there are indeed opportunities for articulating and developing choice, autonomy and influence. Those opportunities are more readily available to groups or individuals possessing technical expertise in the language and strategies of economic rationality, but they exist.

But technocratic citizenship under the aegis of economic rationality is not conducive to a policy environment that generates structural power at the broader community level. It provides an arena for active deliberation and participation only at a devolved and disaggregated level, at the level where sector-specific actors with highly technical sector-specific knowledge can shape the intricacy and details only of the particular policy sector under review. Social citizenship, however, necessitates decisions about *the overall trade-offs* between the costs and benefits of multiple policy sectors. Where markets fail, there are by definition no price signals coming from specific groups to channel resources: rather, a decision to give overriding value to non-market values or vulnerable sectors must be collectively reached in a political arena. But in the face of increasing energy, resources and institutional support for modes of incipient legality such as meta-regulation, such collective deliberation, if it occurs at all, is increasingly less able to shape regulatory decision-making.

In effect, to the extent that technocratic citizenship does provide increased opportunities for participation that shapes the terms of collective lives, it does so on in a way that brackets out the 'terms of production' of political life, embedding a presumption that market capitalism is the background constraint against which the battles of regulatory policy choice take place. In consequence, the choice or autonomy fostered by meta-regulation is akin to a choice between items on a pre-ordained menu rather than a capacity to design an altogether different menu.

The absence of structural power at the level of significantly sized communities, rather than sectoral interest groups, is arguably one important determinant of the growing political unrest at an international level related to the effects of international trade regimes on domestic regulatory politics. If, as Chapter One intimated, meta-regulation in Australia might be a foretaste of institutional changes in the making at the international level, it will be crucially important to foster a space for alternative stories to flourish: stories that link communities in ways other than the promise of economic growth through intensified market competition. For that story, as shown in this book, has important limits in its capacity to link competition and social citizenship. And so long as a disjunct between competition and social citizenship remains, we run the continuing risk that silenced stories will morph into stones and the politics of protest will escalate.

Notes

[1]   Oliver, D. (1997), 'The Underlying Values of Public and Private Law', *The Province of Administrative Law*, in Taggart, M. (ed), Hart Publishing, Oxford; Prosser, Tony (1997), *Law and Regulators*, Clarendon Press, Oxford; Freedland, M. and Sciarra, S. (1998), *Public Services and Citizenship in European Law*, Clarendon Press, Oxford; Taggart, M. (1999), 'Reinvented Government, Traffic Lights and the Convergence of Public and Private Law', *Public Law*, pp. 124 ff.

[2]   Samuels, Graeme (2001), Speech at *Conference on Regulatory Reform Management,* 9-13 July 2001, Sydney, p.12.

[3]   Samuels, Graeme (2001), Speech at *Conference on Regulatory Reform Management,* 9-13 July 2001, Sydney, p.16.

[4]   Beattie, Peter, Queensland Premier, in radio interview on The World Today - Friday, July 2, 1999 12.53pm.

[5]   Samuels, Graeme (2001), Speech at *Conference on Regulatory Reform Management,* 9-13 July 2001, Sydney, p.13.

[6]   Samuels, Graeme (2001), Speech at *Conference on Regulatory Reform Management,* 9-13 July 2001, Sydney, p.13.

[7]   Samuels, Graeme (2001), Speech at *Conference on Regulatory Reform Management,* 9-13 July 2001, Sydney, p.13.

[8]   Samuels, Graeme (2001), Speech at *Conference on Regulatory Reform Management,* 9-13 July 2001, Sydney, p.16.

Appendices

1   Competition Principles Agreement

11 April 1995

WHEREAS the Council of Australian Governments at its meeting in Hobart on 25 February 1994 agreed to the principles of competition policy articulated in the report of the *National Competition Policy Review*;

AND WHEREAS the Parties intend to achieve and maintain constant and complementary competition laws and policies which will apply to all businesses in Australia regardless of ownership;

THE COMMONWEALTH OF AUSTRALIA
THE STATE OF NEW SOUTH WALES
THE STATE OF VICTORIA
THE STATE OF QUEENSLAND
THE STATE OF WESTERN AUSTRALIA
THE STATE OF SOUTH AUSTRALIA
THE STATE OF TASMANIA
THE AUSTRALIAN CAPITAL TERRITORY, AND
THE NORTHERN TERRITORY OF AUSTRALIA agree as follows:

Interpretation

1.(1) In this Agreement, unless the context indicates otherwise:

"Commission" means the Australian Competition and Consumer Commission established by the Trade Practices Act;

"Commonwealth Minister" means the Commonwealth Minister responsible for competition policy;

"constitutional trade or commerce" means:
  (a) trade or commerce among the States;
  (b) trade or commerce between a State and a Territory or between two Territories; or
  (c) trade or commerce between Australia and a place outside Australia;

"Council" means the National Competition Council established by the Trade Practices Act;

"jurisdiction" means the Commonwealth, a State, the Australian Capital Territory or the Northern Territory of Australia;

"Party" means a jurisdiction that has executed, and has not withdrawn from, this Agreement;

"Trade Practices Act" means the *Trade Practices Act 1974.*

(2) Where this Agreement refers to a provision in legislation which has not been enacted at the date of commencement of this Agreement, or to an entity which has not been established at the date of commencement of this Agreement, this Agreement will apply in respect of the provision or entity from the date when the provision or entity commences operation.

(3) Without limiting the matters that may be taken into account, where this Agreement calls:

  (a)   for the benefits of a particular policy or course of action to be balanced against the costs of the policy or course of action; or
  (b)   for the merits or appropriateness of a particular policy or course of action to be determined; or

(c)   for an assessment of the most effective means of achieving a policy objective;

the following matters shall, where relevant, be taken into account:

(d)   government legislation and policies relating to ecologically sustainable development;

(e)   social welfare and equity considerations, including community service obligations;

(f)   government legislation and policies relating to matters such as occupational health and safety, industrial relations and access and equity;

(g)   economic and regional development, including employment and investment growth;

(h)   the interests of consumers generally or of a class of consumers;

(i)   the competitiveness of Australian businesses; and

(j)   the efficient allocation of resources.

(4) It is not intended that the matters set out in subclause (3) should affect the interpretation of "public benefit" for the purposes of authorisations under the Trade Practices Act.

(5) This Agreement is neutral with respect to the nature and form of ownership of business enterprises. It is not intended to promote public or private ownership.

Prices Oversight of Government Business Enterprises

2.(1) Prices oversight of State and Territory government business enterprises is primarily the responsibility of the State or Territory that owns the enterprise.

(2) The Parties will work cooperatively to examine issues associated with prices oversight of government business enterprises and may seek assistance in this regard from the Council. The Council may provide such assistance in accordance with the Council's work program.

(3) In accordance with these principles, State and Territory Parties will consider establishing independent sources of price oversight where these do not exist.

(4) An independent source of price oversight advice should have the following characteristics:

(a)   it should be independent from the government business enterprise whose prices are being assessed;

(b)   its prime objective should be one of efficient resource allocation, but with regard to any explicitly identified and defined community service obligations imposed on a business enterprise by the government or legislature of the jurisdiction that owns the enterprise;

(c)   it should apply to all significant government business enterprises that are monopoly, or near monopoly, suppliers of goods or services (or both);

(d)   it should permit submissions by interested persons; and

(e)   its pricing recommendations, and the reasons for them, should be published.

(5)   A Party may generally or on a case-by-case basis:

(a)   with the agreement of the Commonwealth, subject its government business enterprises to a prices oversight mechanism administered by the Commission; or

(b)   with the agreement of another jurisdiction, subject its government business enterprises to the pricing oversight process of that jurisdiction.

(6) In the absence of the consent of the Party that owns the enterprise, a State or Territory government business enterprise will only be subject to a prices oversight mechanism administered by the Commission if:

(a) the enterprise is not already subject to a source of price oversight advice which is independent in terms of the principles set out in subclause (4);

(b) a jurisdiction which considers that it is adversely affected by the lack of price oversight (an "affected jurisdiction") has consulted the Party that owns the enterprise, and the matter is not resolved to the satisfaction of the affected jurisdiction;

(c) the affected jurisdiction has then brought the matter to the attention of the Council and the Council has decided:
   i.   that the condition in paragraph (a) exists; and
   ii. that the pricing of the enterprise has a significant direct or indirect impact on constitutional trade or commerce;

(d) the Council has recommended that the Commonwealth Minister declare the enterprise for price surveillance by the Commission; and

(e) the Commonwealth Minister has consulted the Party that owns the enterprise.

Competitive Neutrality Policy and Principles

3.(1) The objective of competitive neutrality policy is the elimination of resource allocation distortions arising out of the public ownership of entities engaged in significant business activities: Government businesses should not enjoy any net competitive advantage simply as a result of their public sector ownership. These principles only apply to the business activities of publicly owned entities, not to the non-business, non-profit activities of these entities.

(2) Each Party is free to determine its own agenda for the implementation of competitive neutrality principles.

(3) A Party may seek assistance with the implementation of competitive neutrality principles from the Council. The Council may provide such assistance in accordance with the Council's work program.

(4) Subject to subclause (6), for significant government business enterprises which are classified as "Public Trading Enterprises" and "Public Financial Enterprises" under the Government Financial Statistics Classification:

(a) the Parties will, where appropriate, adopt a corporatisation model for these government business enterprises (noting that a possible approach to corporatisation is the model developed by the inter-governmental committee responsible for GTE National Performance Monitoring; and

(b) the Parties will impose on the Government business enterprise:

   i. full Commonwealth, State and Territory taxes or tax equivalent systems;
   ii. debt guarantee fees directed towards offsetting the competitive advantages provided by government guarantees; and
   iii. those regulations to which private sector businesses are normally subject, such as those relating to the protection of the environment, and planning and approval processes, on an equivalent basis to private sector competitors.

(5) Subject to subclause (6), where an agency (other than an agency covered by subclause (4)) undertakes significant business activities as part of a broader range of functions, the Parties will, in respect of the business activities:

(a) where appropriate, implement the principles outlined in subclause (4);or

(b) ensure that the prices charged for goods and services will take account, where appropriate, of the items listed in paragraph 4(b), and reflect full cost attribution for these activities.

(6) Subclauses (4) and (5) only require the Parties to implement the principles specified in those subclauses to the extent that the benefits to be realised from implementation outweigh the costs.

(7) Subparagraph (4)(b)(iii) shall not be interpreted to require the removal of regulation which applies to a Government business enterprise or agency (but which does not apply to the private sector) where the Party responsible for the regulation considers the regulation to be appropriate.

(8) Each Party will publish a policy statement on competitive neutrality by June 1996. The policy statement will include an implementation timetable and a complaints mechanism.

(9) Where a State or Territory becomes a Party at a date later than December 1995, that Party will publish its policy statement within six months of becoming a Party.

(10) Each Party will publish an annual report on the implementation of the principles set out in subclauses (1), (4) and (5), including allegations of non-compliance.

Structural Reform of Public Monopolies

4.(1) Each Party is free to determine its own agenda for the reform of public monopolies.

(2) Before a Party introduces competition to a sector traditionally supplied by a public monopoly, it will remove from the public monopoly any responsibilities for industry regulation. The Party will re-locate industry regulation functions so as to prevent the former monopolist enjoying a regulatory advantage over its (existing and potential) rivals.

(3) Before a Party introduces competition to a market traditionally supplied by a public monopoly, and before a Party privatises a public monopoly, it will undertake a review into:

    (a)   the appropriate commercial objectives for the public monopoly;

    (b)   the merits of separating any natural monopoly elements from potentially competitive elements of the public monopoly;

(c)   the merits of separating potentially competitive elements of the public monopoly;

(d)   the most effective means of separating regulatory functions from commercial functions of the public monopoly;

(e)   the most effective means of implementing the competitive neutrality principles set out in this Agreement;

(f)   the merits of any community service obligations undertaken by the public monopoly and the best means of funding and delivering any mandated community service obligations;

(g)   the price and service regulations to be applied to the industry; and

(h)   the appropriate financial relationships between the owner of the public monopoly and the public monopoly, including the rate of return targets, dividends and capital structure.

(4) A Party may seek assistance with such a review from the Council. The Council may provide such assistance in accordance with the Council's work program.

Legislation Review

5.(1) The guiding principle is that legislation (including Acts, enactments, Ordinances or regulations) should not restrict competition unless it can be demonstrated that:

(a)   the benefits of the restriction to the community as a whole outweigh the costs; and

(b)   the objectives of the legislation can only be achieved by restricting competition.

(2) Subject to subclause (3), each Party is free to determine its own agenda for the reform of legislation that restricts competition.

(3) Subject to subclause (4) each Party will develop a timetable by June 1996 for the review, and where appropriate, reform of all existing legislation that restricts competition by the year 2000.

(4) Where a State or Territory becomes a Party at a date later than December 1995, that Party will develop its timetable within six months of becoming a Party.

(5) Each Party will require proposals for new legislation that restricts competition to be accompanied by evidence that the legislation is consistent with the principle set out in subclause (1).

(6) Once a Party has reviewed legislation that restricts competition under the principles set out in subclauses (3) and (5), the Party will systematically review the legislation at least once every ten years.

(7) Where a review issue has a national dimension or effect on competition (or both), the Party responsible for the review will consider whether the review should be a national review. If the Party determines a national review is appropriate, before determining the terms of reference for, and the appropriate body to conduct the national review, it will consult Parties that may have an interest in those matters.

(8) Where a Party determines a review should be a national review, the Party may request the Council to undertake the review. The Council may undertake the review in accordance with the Council's work program.

(9) Without limiting the terms of reference of a review, a review should:

    (a) clarify the objectives of the legislation;

    (b) identify the nature of the restriction on competition;

    (c) analyse the likely effect of the restriction on competition and on the economy generally;

    (d) assess and balance the costs and benefits of the restriction; and

    (e) consider alternative means for achieving the same result including nonlegislative approaches.

(10) Each Party will publish an annual report on its progress towards achieving the objective set out in subclause (3). The Council will publish an annual report consolidating the reports of each Party.

Access to Services Provided by Means of Significant Infrastructure Facilities

6.(1) Subject to subclause (2), the Commonwealth will put forward legislation to establish a regime for third party access to services provided by means of significant infrastructure facilities where:

(a)   it would not be economically feasible to duplicate the facility;

(b)   access to the service is necessary in order to permit effective competition in a downstream or upstream market;

(c)   the facility is of national significance having regard to the size of the facility, its importance to constitutional trade or commerce or its importance to the national economy; and

(d)   the safe use of the facility by the person seeking access can be ensured at an economically feasible cost and, if there is a safety requirement, appropriate regulatory arrangements exist.

(2) The regime to be established by Commonwealth legislation is not intended to cover a service provided by means of a facility where the State or Territory Party in whose jurisdiction the facility is situated has in place an access regime which covers the facility and conforms to the principles set out in this clause unless:

(a)   the Council determines that the regime is ineffective having regard to the influence of the facility beyond the jurisdictional boundary of the State or Territory; or

(b)   substantial difficulties arise from the facility being situated in more than one jurisdiction.

(3) For a State or Territory access regime to conform to the principles set out in this clause, it should:

(a)   apply to services provided by means of significant infrastructure facilities where:

    i.   it would not be economically feasible to duplicate the facility;

    ii. access to the service is necessary in order to permit effective competition in a downstream or upstream market; and

    iii. the safe use of the facility by the person seeking access can be ensured at an economically feasible cost and, if there is a safety requirement, appropriate regulatory arrangements exist; and

(b) incorporate the principles referred to in subclause (4).

(4) A State of Territory access regime should incorporate the following principles:

(a) Wherever possible third party access to a service provided by means of a facility should be on the basis of terms and conditions agreed between the owner of the facility and the person seeking access.

(b) Where such agreement cannot be reached, Governments should establish a right for persons to negotiate access to a service provided by means of a facility.

(c) Any right to negotiate access should provide for an enforcement process.

(d) Any right to negotiate access should include a date after which the right would lapse unless reviewed and subsequently extended; however, existing contractual rights and obligations should not be automatically revoked.

(e) The owner of a facility that is used to provide a service should use all reasonable endeavours to accommodate the requirements of persons seeking access.

(f) Access to a service for persons seeking access need not be on exactly the same terms and conditions.

(g) Where the owner and a person seeking access cannot agree on terms and conditions for access to the service, they should be required to appoint and fund an independent body to resolve the dispute, if they have not already done so.

(h)   The decisions of the dispute resolution body should bind the parties; however, rights of appeal under existing legislative provisions should be preserved.

(i)   In deciding on the terms and conditions for access, the dispute resolution body should take into account:
i.   the owner's legitimate business interests and investment in the facility;
ii.   the costs to the owner of providing access, including any costs of extending the facility but not costs associated with losses arising from increased competition in upstream or downstream markets;
iii.   the economic value to the owner of any additional investment that the person seeking access or the owner has agreed to undertake;
iv.   the interests of all persons holding contracts for use of the facility;
v.   firm and binding contractual obligations of the owner or other persons (or both) already using the facility;
vi.   the operational and technical requirements necessary for the safe and reliable operation of the facility;
vii.   the economically efficient operation of the facility; and
viii.the benefit to the public from having competitive markets.

(j)   The owner may be required to extend, or to permit extension of, the facility that is used to provide a service if necessary but this would be subject to:

i.   such extension being technically and economically feasible and consistent with the safe and reliable operation of the facility;
ii.   the owner's legitimate business interests in the facility being protected; and
iii.   the terms of access for the third party taking into account the costs borne by the parties for the extension and the economic benefits to the parties resulting from the extension.

(k)   If there has been a material change in circumstances, the parties should be able to apply for a revocation or modification of the access arrangement which was made at the conclusion of the dispute resolution process.

(l)   The dispute resolution body should only impede the existing right of a person to use a facility where the dispute resolution body has considered whether there is a case for compensation of that person and, if appropriate, determined such compensation.

(m)   The owner or user of a service shall not engage in conduct for the purpose of hindering access to that service by another person.

(n)   Separate accounting arrangements should be required for the elements of a business which are covered by the access regime.

(o)   The dispute resolution body, or relevant authority where provided for under specific legislation, should have access to financial statements and other accounting information pertaining to a service.

(p)   Where more than one State or Territory regime applies to a service those regimes should be consistent and, by means of vested jurisdiction or other cooperative legislative scheme, provide for a single process for persons to seek access to the service, a single body to resolve disputes about any aspect of access and a single forum for enforcement of access arrangements.

Application of the Principles to Local Government

7.(1) The principles set out in this Agreement will apply to local government, even though local governments are not Parties to this Agreement. Each State and Territory Party is responsible for applying those principles to local government.

(2) Subject to subclause (3), where clauses 3, 4 and 5 permit each Party to determine its own agenda for the implementation of the principles set out in those clauses, each State and Territory Party will publish a statement by June 1996:

(a)   which is prepared in consultation with local government; and

    (b)   which specifies the application of the principles to particular local government activities and functions.

(3) Where a State or Territory becomes a Party at a date later than December 1995, that Party will publish its statement within six months of becoming a Party.

Funding of the Council

8. The Commonwealth will be responsible for funding the Council.

Appointments to the Council

9.(1) When the Commonwealth proposes that a vacancy in the office of Council President or Councillor of the Council be filled, it will send written notice to the States and Territories that are Parties inviting suggestions as to suitable persons to fill the vacancy. The Commonwealth will allow those Parties a period of thirty five days from the date on which the notice was sent to make suggestions before sending a notice of the type referred to in subclause (2).

(2) The Commonwealth will send to the States and Territories that are Parties written notice of persons whom it desires to put forward to the Governor- General for appointment as Council President or Councillor of the Council.

(3) Within thirty five days from the date on which the Commonwealth sends a notice of the type referred to in subclause (2), the Party to whom the Commonwealth sends a notice will notify the Commonwealth Minister in writing as to whether the Party supports the proposed appointment. If the Party does not notify the Commonwealth Minister in writing within that period, the Party will be taken to support the proposed appointment.

(4) The Commonwealth will not put forward to the Governor-General a person for appointment as a Council President or Councillor of the Council unless a majority of the States and Territories that are Parties support, or pursuant to this clause are taken to support, the appointment.

Work Program of the Council, and Referral of Matters to the Council

10.(1)The work of the Council (other than work relating to a function under Part IIIA of the Trade Practices Act or under the *Prices Surveillance Act 1983)* will be the subject of a work program which is determined by the Parties.

(2) Each Party will refer proposals for the Council to undertake work (other than work relating to a function under Part IIIA of the *Trade Practices Act* or under the *Prices Surveillance Act 1983)* to the Parties for possible inclusion in the work program.

(3) A Party will not put forward legislation conferring additional functions on the Council unless the Parties have determined that the Council should undertake those functions as part of its work program.

(4) Questions as to whether a matter should be included in the work program will be determined by the agreement of a majority of the Parties. In the event that the Parties are evenly divided on a question of agreeing to the inclusion of a matter in the work program, the Commonwealth shall determine the outcome.

(5) The Commonwealth Minister will only refer matters to the Council pursuant to subsection 29B(1) of the Trade Practices Act in accordance with the work program.

(6) The work program of the Council shall be taken to include a request by the Commonwealth for the Council to examine and report on the matters specified in subclause 2(2) of the Conduct Code Agreement.

Review of the Council

11. The Parties will review the need for, and the operation of, the Council after it has been in existence for five years.

Consultation

12. Where this Agreement requires consultation between the Parties or some of them, the Party initiating the consultation will:

(a)   send to the Parties that must be consulted a written notice setting out the matters on which consultation is to occur;

(b)   allow those Parties a period of three months from the date on which the notice was sent to respond to the matters set out in the notice; and

(c)   where requested by one or more of those Parties, convene a meeting between it and those Parties to discuss the matters set out in the notice and the responses, if any, of those Parties.

New Parties and Withdrawal of Parties

13.(1)A jurisdiction that is not a Party at the date of this Agreement commences operation may become a Party by sending written notice to all the Parties.

(2) A Party may withdraw from this Agreement by sending written notice to all other Parties. The withdrawal will become effective six months after the notice was sent.

(3) If a Party withdraws from this Agreement, this Agreement will continue in force with respect to the remaining Parties.

Sending of Notices

14. A notice is sent to a Party by sending it to the Minister responsible for the competition legislation of that Party.

Review of this Agreement

15. Once this Agreement has operated for five years, the Parties will review its operation and terms.

Commencement of this Agreement

16. This Agreement commences once the Commonwealth and at least three other jurisdictions have executed it.

2 Conduct Code Agreement

11 April 1995

WHEREAS the Council of Australian Governments at its meeting in Hobart on 25 February 1994 agreed to the principles of competition policy articulated in the report of the National Competition Policy Review;

AND WHEREAS the Parties intend to achieve and maintain constant and complementary competition laws and policies which will apply to all businesses in Australia regardless of ownership;

THE COMMONWEALTH OF AUSTRALIA
THE STATE OF NEW SOUTH WALES
THE STATE OF VICTORIA
THE STATE OF QUEENSLAND
THE STATE OF WESTERN AUSTRALIA
THE STATE OF SOUTH AUSTRALIA
THE STATE OF TASMANIA
THE AUSTRALIAN CAPITAL TERRITORY, AND
THE NORTHERN TERRITORY OF AUSTRALIA agree as follows:

Interpretation

1.(1) In this Agreement, unless the context indicates otherwise:

"Commission" means the Australian Competition and Consumer Commission established by the Trade Practices Act;

"Commonwealth Minister" means the Commonwealth Minister responsible for competition policy;

"Competition Code" means the text in:

(a)   the Schedule version of Part IV of the Trade Practices Act;
(b)   the remaining provision of that Act (except sections 2A, 5, 6 and 172), so far as they would relate to the Schedule version if the Schedule version were substituted for Part IV; and

(c)   the regulations under that Act, so far as they relate to any provision covered by paragraph (a) or (b) applying as a law of a participating jurisdiction;

"Competition Laws" means:

(a)   Part IV of the Trade Practices Act and the remaining provisions of that Act, so far as they relate to that Part; and

(b)   the Competition Code of the participating jurisdictions;

"Council" means the National Competition Council established by the Trade Practices Act;

"fully-participating jurisdiction" means:

(a)   until the end of twelve months after the day on which the *Competition Policy Reform Act 1995* receives the Royal Assent ó a State or Territory that is a party to this Agreement; and

(b)   after that date – has the meaning given by section 4 of the Trade Practices Act;

"jurisdiction" means the Commonwealth, a State, the Australian Capital Territory or the Northern Territory of Australia;

"legislation" includes Acts, enactments, Ordinances and regulations;

"modifications" has the meaning given by section 150A of the Trade Practices Act;

"participating jurisdiction" has the meaning given by section 150A of the Trade Practices Act;

"Party" means a jurisdiction that has executed, and has not withdrawn from, this Agreement;

"Trade Practices Act" means the *Trade Practices Act 1974*.

(2) Where this Agreement refers to a provision in legislation which has not been enacted at the date of commencement of this Agreement, or to an entity which has not been established at the date of commencement of this Agreement, this Agreement will apply in respect of the provision or entity from the date when the provision or entity commences operation.

Exceptions from the Competition Laws

2.(1) Where legislation, or a provision in legislation, is enacted or made in reliance upon section 51 of the Competition Laws, the Party responsible for the legislation will send written notice of the legislation to the Commission within 30 days of the legislation being enacted or made.

(2) After four months from when a Party sends written notice to the Commission pursuant to subclause (1), the Commonwealth Minister will not table in the Commonwealth Parliament regulations made for the purposes of paragraph 51(1C)(f) of the Trade Practices Act in respect of the legislation referred to in the notice, unless the Commonwealth Minister tables in the Parliament at the same time a report by the Council on:

(a)　whether the benefits to the community from the legislation referred to in the notice, including the benefits from transitional arrangements, outweigh the costs;

(b)　whether the objectives achieved by restricting competition by means of the legislation referred to in the notice can only be achieved by restricting competition; and

(c)　whether the Commonwealth should make regulations for the purposes of paragraph 51(1C)(f) of the Trade Practices Act.

(3) Each Party will, within three years of the date on which the *Competition Policy Reform Act 1995* receives the Royal Assent, send written notice to the Commission of legislation for which that Party is responsible, which;

(a)　existed at the date of commencement of this Agreement;

(b)　was enacted or made in reliance upon section 51 of the Trade Practices Act (as in force at the date of commencement of this Agreement); and

(c)　will continue to except conduct pursuant to section 51 of the Trade Practices Act after three years from the date on which the *Competition Policy Reform Act 1995* receives the Royal Assent.

Funding of the Commission

3. The Commonwealth will be responsible for funding the Commission.

Appointments to the Commission

4.(1) When the Commonwealth proposes that a vacancy in the office of Chairperson, Deputy Chairperson, member or associate member of the Commission be filled, it will send written notice to the Parties that are fully-participating jurisdictions inviting suggestions as to suitable persons to fill the vacancy. The Commonwealth will allow those Parties a period of thirty five days from the date on which the notice was sent to make suggestions before sending a notice of the type referred to in subclause (2) or (3).

(2) The Commonwealth will send to the Parties that are fully participating jurisdictions written notice of persons whom it desires to put forward to the Governor-General for appointment as Chairperson, Deputy Chairperson or member of the Commission.

(3) The Commonwealth will send to the parties that are fully-participating jurisdictions written notice of person whom it desires to put forward to the Commonwealth Minister for appointment as associate members of the Commission.

(4) Within thirty five days from the date on which the Commonwealth sends a notice of the type referred to in subclause (2) or (3), the Party to whom the Commonwealth sends a notice will notify the Commonwealth Minister in writing as to whether the Party supports the proposed appointment. If the Party does not notify the Commonwealth Minister in writing within that period, the Party will be taken to support the proposed appointment.

(5) The Commonwealth will not put forward to the Governor-General a person for appointment as a Chairperson, Deputy Chairperson or member of the Commission unless a majority of the fully-participating jurisdictions support, or pursuant to this clause, are taken to support the appointment.

(6) The Commonwealth will not put forward to the Commonwealth Minister a person for appointment as an associate member of the

commission unless a majority of the fully-participating jurisdictions support, or pursuant to this clause are taken to support, the appointment.

The Competition Code

5.(1) The Parties agree that the Competition Code text should apply by way of application legislation to all persons within the legislative competence of each State and Territory.

(2) Each State and Territory that is a Party will put forward for the consideration by their legislatures legislation which implements the principle set out in subclause (1).

(3) If the Commonwealth Minister is satisfied that the laws of a participating jurisdiction have made significant modifications to the Competition Code text in its application to persons within the legislative competence of the participating jurisdiction, the Commonwealth Minister may publish a notice in the Commonwealth of Australia Gazette stating that the Commonwealth Minister is so satisfied. Any such notice is to be published before the expiry of two months from the date on which the Commonwealth received written notice pursuant to subclause 6(8).

(4) If the Commonwealth Minister has published a notice of the type specified in subclause (3), the Commonwealth Minister may revoke that notice by publishing a further notice in the Commonwealth of Australia Gazette.

Modifications to the Competition Laws

6.(1) It is the intention of the Parties that where modifications are made to provisions of either Part IV of the Trade Practices Act or of the Schedule version of Part IV of that Act, similar modifications will be made to corresponding provisions of the other.

(2) The Commonwealth will consult with fully-participating jurisdictions before it puts forward for parliamentary consideration any modification to Part IV of the Trade Practices Act of to the Competition Code text.

(3) At the conclusion of the Commonwealth's consultation with the fully participating jurisdictions in relation to proposed amendments to the

Competition Code text, the Commonwealth will call a vote on the proposed amendments by sending written notice to each fully-participating jurisdiction.

(4) For the purposes of voting:

    (a)   the Commonwealth will have 2 votes;

    (b)   each fully-participating jurisdiction will have 1 vote; and

    (c)   the Commonwealth will have a casting vote.

(5) If a fully-participating jurisdiction does not vote in respect of a proposed amendment within thirty five days of the Commonwealth sending notice under subclause 6(3), that jurisdiction will be taken to have voted in favour of the amendment.

(6) The Commonwealth will not put forward for parliamentary consideration an amendment to the Competition Code text unless a majority of the votes of the Commonwealth and the fully-participating jurisdictions support the amendment.

(7) The Commonwealth will not be obliged to put forward for parliamentary consideration any amendment with which it does not concur.

(8) Each Party will send written notice to all other Parties setting out modifications to the Competition Laws that have been made by the legislature of that Party, or by any person.

Consultation

7. Where clause 6 requires consultation between the Parties or some of them, the Party initiating the consultation will:

    (a)   send to the Parties that must be consulted a written notice setting out the matters on which consultation is to occur;

    (b)   allow those Parties a period of three months from the date on which the notice was sent to respond to the matters set out in the notice; and

(c)   where requested by one or more of those Parties, convene a meeting between it and those Parties to discuss the matters set out in the notice and the responses, if any, of those Parties.

New Parties and Withdrawal of Parties

8. (1) A jurisdiction that is not a Party at the date of this Agreement commences operation may become a Party by sending written notice to all the Parties.

(2) A Party may withdraw from this Agreement by sending written notice to all other Parties. The withdrawal will become effective six months after the notice was sent.

(3) If a Party withdraws from this Agreement, this Agreement will continue in force with respect to the remaining Parties.

Sending of Notices

9. A notice is sent to a Party by sending it to the Minister responsible for the competition legislation of that Party.

Review of this Agreement

10. Once this Agreement has operated for five years, the Parties will review its operation and terms.

Commencement of this Agreement

11. This Agreement commences once the Commonwealth and at least three other jurisdictions have executed it.

3 Agreement to Implement the National Competition Policy and Related Reforms

11 April 1995

WHEREAS the Council of Australian Governments at its meeting in Canberra on 11 April 1995 agreed to a program for the implementation of the National Competition Policy and related reforms;

AND WHEREAS the Commonwealth and the States have agreed to financial arrangements in relation to the implementation of the National Competition Policy (NCP) and related reforms;

THE COMMONWEALTH OF AUSTRALIA
THE STATE OF NEW SOUTH WALES
THE STATE OF VICTORIA
THE STATE OF QUEENSLAND
THE STATE OF WESTERN AUSTRALIA
THE STATE OF SOUTH AUSTRALIA
THE STATE OF TASMANIA
THE AUSTRALIAN CAPITAL TERRITORY, AND
THE NORTHERN TERRITORY OF AUSTRALIA agree as follows:

The provision of financial assistance by the Commonwealth is conditional on the States making satisfactory progress with the implementation of NCP and related reforms (as set out below).

The Commonwealth's commitment is on the basis that the financial arrangements will need to be reviewed if Australia experiences a major deterioration in its economic circumstances.

The Commonwealth will maintain the real per capita guarantee of the FAGs pool on a rolling three year basis.

This will involve the Commonwealth extending the guarantee to 1997-98 now.

- The per capita element will have an estimated annual cost to the Commonwealth of $2.4 billion by 2005-06.

- Local government will benefit from the link between the State and Local government FAGs pools.

There will also be three tranches of general purpose payments in the form of a series of Competition Payments.

- The first tranche of Competition Payments will commence in July 1997 and will be made quarterly thereafter.

- The annual payment from 1997-98 under the first tranche will be $200 million in 1994-95 prices.

- It will be indexed annually to maintain its real value over time.

- Commencement of the first tranche of the Competition Payments and the per capita guarantee is subject to the States meeting the conditions set out below.

- The second and third tranches of the Competition Payments will commence in 1999-2000 and 2001-02. The annual Competition Payments will be $400 million, in 1994-95 prices, from 1999-2000 and $600 million, in 1994-95 prices, from 2001-2002. These payments will be indexed in real terms.

The Competition Payments to be made to the States in relation to the implementation of National Competition Policy (NCP) and related reforms will form a pool separate from the FAGs pool and be distributed to the States on a per capita basis. These Competition Payments will be quarantined from assessments by the Commonwealth Grants Commission.

- If a State has not undertaken the required action within the specified time, its share of the per capita component of the FAGs pool and of the Competition Payments pool will be retained by the Commonwealth.

Prior to 1 July 1997, 1 July 1999, and 1 July 2001 the National Competition Council will assess whether the conditions for payments to the States to commence on those dates have been met.

Conditions for Payments to States

The first payments will be made in 1997-98 to each participating State as at the date of the payment and depending upon:

(i) that State giving effect to the Competition Policy Intergovernmental Agreements and, in particular, meeting the deadlines prescribed therein, in relation to the review of regulations and competitive neutrality;

(ii) effective implementation of all COAG agreements on:

- electricity arrangements through the National Grid Management Council,
- the national framework for free and fair trade in gas, and

(iii) effective observance of road transport reforms.

Payments under the second tranche of the Competition Payments will commence in 1999-2000 and be made to each participating State as at the date of the payment and depending upon:

(i) that State continuing to give effect to the Competition Policy Intergovernmental Agreements including meeting all deadlines;

(ii) effective implementation of all COAG agreements on:

- the establishment of a competitive national electricity market,
- the national framework for free and fair trade in gas, and
- the strategic framework for the efficient and sustainable reform of the Australian water industry; and

(iii) effective observance of road transport reforms.

Payments under the third tranche will commence in 2001ñ02 and be made to each participating State as at the date of the payment and depending on the State:

- having given full effect to, and continues to observe fully, the Competition Policy Intergovernmental Agreements; and
- having fully implemented, and continues to observe fully, all COAG agreements with regard to electricity, gas, water and road transport.
-

Full details of the conditions are available as set out in [this] attachment:

ATTACHMENT

Conditions of Payments to the States

(a) Per capita Guarantee and First Tranche of the Competition Payments

Payment under the extension of the per capita guarantee and the first tranche will start in 1997-98 to each State and Territory that:

- has signed the Competition Principles Agreement and the Conduct Code Agreement at the COAG meeting in April 1995;

- in accordance with the Conduct Code Agreement, passed the required application legislation so that the Conduct Code applied within that State or Territory jurisdiction by 12 months after the Commonwealth's Competition Policy Reform Bill received the Royal Assent;

- is a fully participating jurisdiction under the Competition Policy Reform Bill and a party to the Competition Principles Agreement at the time at which the payment is made (States and Territories must apply the Conduct Code as a law of the State without making significant modifications to the Code in its application to persons within their legislative competence and must remain a party to both Competition Policy Intergovernmental Agreements);

- is meeting all its obligations under the Competition Principles Agreement, which include, but are not limited to:

  - when undertaking significant business activities or when corporatising their government business enterprises, having imposed on these activities or enterprises full government taxes or tax equivalent systems, debt guarantee fees directed towards offsetting the competitive advantages provided by government guarantees and those regulations to which private sector businesses are normally subject on an equivalent basis to the enterprises' private sector competitors,

- having published a policy statement on competitive neutrality by June 1996 and published the required annual reports on the implementation of the competitive neutrality principles,
- having developed a timetable by June 1996 for the review and, where appropriate, reform of all existing legislation which restricts competition by the year 2000,
- having published by June 1996 a statement specifying the application of the principles in the Competition Principles Agreement to local government activities and functions (this statement to be prepared in consultation with local government); and

- (for relevant jurisdictions) has taken all measures necessary to implement an interim competitive National Electricity Market, as agreed at the July 1991 special Premiers' Conference, and subsequent COAG agreements, from 1 July 1995 or on such other date as agreed by the parties, including signing any necessary Heads of Agreement and agreeing to subscribe to the National Electricity Management Company and National Electricity Code Administrator;

- (for relevant jurisdictions) has implemented any arrangements agreed between the parties as necessary to introduce free and fair trading in gas between and within the States by 1 July 1996 or such other date as agreed between the parties, in keeping with the February 1994 COAG agreement; and

- effective observance of the agreed package of road transport reforms.

(b) Second Tranche of the Competition Payments

Payments under the second tranche will commence in 1999-2000, and be made each year thereafter to the States and Territories that have undertaken the following specified reforms by July 1999 in so far as they apply to them:

- (for relevant jurisdictions) completion of the transition to a fully competitive National Electricity Market by 1 July 1999;

- (for relevant jurisdictions) full implementation of free and fair trading in gas between and within the States including the phasing out of transitional arrangements in accordance with the schedule to be agreed between the parties;

- implementation of the strategic framework for the efficient and sustainable reform of the Australian water industry and the future processes as endorsed at the February 1994 COAG meeting and embodied in the Report of the Expert Group on Asset Valuation Methods and Cost-Recovery Definitions, February 1995;

- continuing to be a fully participating jurisdiction under the Competition Policy Reform Bill and a party to the Competition Principles Agreement at the time at which the payment is made;

- continued effective observance of the agreed package of road transport reforms; and

- meeting all obligations under the Competition Policy Intergovernmental Agreements.

(c) Third Tranche of Competition Payments

Payment under the third tranche will commence in 2001-02 and be made each year thereafter to the States and Territories on the basis of each State's or Territory's progress on the implementation of the following reforms:

- the extent to which each State and Territory has actually complied with the competition policy principles in the Competition Principles Agreement, including the progress made in reviewing, and where appropriate, reforming legislation that restricts competition;

- whether the State and Territory has remained a fully participating jurisdiction as defined in the Competition Policy Reform Bill;

- the setting of national standards in accordance with the Principles and Guidelines for National Standard Setting and Regulatory

Action and advice from the Office of Regulation Review on compliance with these principles and guidelines; and

- continued effective observance of reforms in electricity, gas, water and road transport.

Bibliography

Abbott, Frederick (2000), 'Distributed Governance at the WTO-WIPO: An Evolving Model for Open-architecture Integrated Governance', *Journal of International Economic Law* Vol. 3, No. 1, pp.63-81.

Acton, H.B. (1993), *The Morals of Markets and Related Essays*, Liberty Fund, Indianapolis.

Adler, Matthew (1999), 'Rethinking Cost-Benefit Analysis', *Yale Law Journal*, pp.109 ff.

Administrative Review Council (1992), *Rule Making by Commonwealth Agencies*, Australian Government Publishing Service, Canberra.

Administrative Review Council (1995), *Government Business Enterprises and Commonwealth Administrative Law*, Australian Government Publishing Service, Canberra.

Administrative Review Council (1995), *Better Decisions: Review of Commonwealth Merits Review Tribunals*, Australian Government Publishing Service, Canberra.

Allars, Margaret (1991), 'Managerialism and Administrative Law' *Canberra Bulletin of Public Administration* Vol. 66, pp.50-62.

Allars, Margaret (1995), 'Private Law but Public Power: Removing Administrative Law Review from Government Business Enterprises', *Public Law Review* Vol. 6, No. 1.

Alvarez, S., Dagnino, E. and Escobar, A. (eds) (1998), *Cultures of Politics/Politics of Culture: Re-visioning Latin American Social Movements*, Westview Press, Boulder, Colorado.

Aman, Albert (1998), 'The Globalising State: A Future-oriented Perspective on the Public/Private Distinction, Federalism, and Democracy', *Vanderbilt Journal of Transnational Law* Vol. 31, pp.769-870.

Amin, Ash (ed) (1994), *Post-Fordism: A Reader*, Blackwell, Oxford, England.

Armstrong, Kenneth (2000), *Regulation, Deregulation, Re-regulation*, Kogan Page, London.

Ashworth, Andrew (2000), 'Is the Criminal Law a Lost Cause?' *Law Quarterly Review*, pp.225-256.

Australian Chamber of Commerce and Industry (1992), *Liberating Enterprise to Improve Competitiveness*, unpublished report obtained by author in interview with Booth, 1997.

Australian Chamber of Commerce and Industry (1996), *Changing the Onus for Regulation*, Submission to the Small Business Deregulation Taskforce.

Ayres, Ian and Braithwaite, John (1992), *Responsive Regulation: Transcending the Deregulation Debate*, Oxford University Press, Oxford.

Bakker, I. (2000), 'The Greening of Capitalism? Privatising Water in England and Wales', Working Paper on file with author.

Bakker, I. and Miller, R. (1996), 'Escape from Fordism: the Emergence of Alternative Forms of State Administration and Output', in Boyer, R and Drache, D. (eds), *States Against Markets: The Limits of Globalisation*, Routledge, London.

Baldwin, R. (1995), *Rules and Government*, Clarendon Press, Oxford.

Baldwin, R. and Cave (1999), Understanding Regulation: Theory, Strategy and Practice, Oxford University Press, Oxford.

Baldwin, R. and McCrudden, C. (1987), *Regulation and Public Law*, Weidenfeld and Nicolson, London.

Baldwin, R., Scott, C., and Hood, C. (eds) (1998), *A Reader on Regulation*, Oxford Readings in Socio-Legal Studies, Oxford University Press, Oxford.

Bandes, Susan (ed) (1999), *The Passions of Law*, New York University Press, New York.

Bardach, E. and Kagan, R. (1982), *Going by the Book*: The Problem of Regulatory Unreasonableness, Temple University Press, Philadelphia.

Bardach, E. and Pugliaresi, L. (1977), 'The Environmental Impact Statement vs. The Real World', *The Public Interest* Vol. 49, pp.22-38.

Barlow, Maude (2000), 'Commodification of Water: Wrong Prescription', Paper given on behalf of *The Blue Planet Project* at 10th Stockholm Water Symposium, Stockholm, Sweden.

Barron, Anne (2000), 'Feminism, Aestheticism and the Limits of Law', *Feminist Legal Studies* Vol. 8, pp.275-317.

Barth, J., Caprio, G. and Levine, R. (2001), 'Bank Regulation and Supervision: What Works Best?', SSRN Electronic Paper Collection, http://papers.ssrn.com/paper.taf?abstract_id=269488,

Beck, Ulrich (1998), *Democracy without Enemies*, Polity Press, Cambridge.

Bell, S. and Head, B. (1994), 'Australia's Political Economy: Critical Themes and Issues', in Head, B. (ed) *State, Economy and Public Policy in Australia*, Oxford University Press, Melbourne.

Bergkamp, Lucas (2001), 'Biotech Food and the Precautionary Principle under EU and WTO Law, SSRN Electronic Paper Collection, http://papers.ssrn.com/paper.taf?abstract_id=283081

Bergman, M. and Lane, J-E. (1990), 'Public Policy in a Principal-Agent Framework', *Journal of Theoretical Politics*, Vol. 2, pp.339-352.

Black, Julia (1995), 'Which Arrow? Rule Type and Regulatory Policy', *Public Law*, pp.94-118.

Black, Julia (1996), 'Constitutionalising Self-regulation', *Modern Law* Review, Vol. 59, pp.24 ff.

Black, Julia (1999), 'Talking about Regulation', *Public Law* Spring Vol., pp.77-105.

Blankenburg, Erhard (1984), 'The Poverty of Evolutionism: a Critique of Teubner's Case for 'Reflexive Law'', *Law and Society Review* Vol. 18, No. 2, pp.273-290.

Bloomfield, Maxwell (2000), *Peaceful Revolution: Constitutional Change and American Culture from Progressivism to the New Deal*, Harvard University Press, Cambridge.

Boden, R. and Froud, J. (1996), 'Obeying the Rules: Accounting for Regulatory Compliance Costs in the United Kingdom', *Accounting, Organisations and Society* Vol. 21, No. 6, pp.529-547.

Boerzel, Tanya (1998), 'Organising Babylon – On the Different Conceptions of Policy Networks', *Public Administration* Vol. 76, No. 2, pp.253-273.

Boerzel, Tanya (2000), 'Private Actors on the Rise? The Role of Non-State Actors' in *Compliance with International Institutions*, Max Planck Project Group in Common Goods, accessible in SSRN Electronic Paper Collection, http://papers.ssrn.com/paper.taf?abstract_id=267733.

Boston, Jonathan (1995), 'Lessons from the Antipodes', in O'Toole, B.A.J. (ed) *Next Steps: Improving Management in Government?*, Ashgate Ltd., Aldershot.

Boyer, R. and Drache, D. (eds), *States Against Markets: The Limits of Globalisation*, Routledge, London.

Braithwaite, J. and Drahos, P. (2000), *Global Business Regulation*, Cambridge University Press, Cambridge.

Braithwaite, J. and Grabowsky, P. (1986), *Of Manners Gentle: Enforcement Strategies of Australian Business Regulatory Agencies*, Oxford University Press, Melbourne.

Braithwaite, J., Walker, J. and Grabosky, P. (1987), 'An Enforcement Taxonomy of Regulatory Agencies', *Law and Policy* Vol. 9, No. 2, pp.323-351.

Breyer, Stephen (1982), *Regulation and its Reform*, Harvard University Press, Cambridge.

Briscoe, Salas and Pena (1998), *Managing Water as an Economic Resource: Reflections on the Chilean Experience*, Environmental Economics Series Paper No. 6, World Bank Environment Department, Washington D.C.

Buck, Stuart (2001), 'Replacing Spectrum Auctions with a Spectrum Commons', SSRN Electronic Paper Collection, http://papers.ssrn.com/paper.taf?abstract_id=268744

Bulmer, M. and Rees, A. (eds) (1996), *Citizenship Today: The Contemporary Relevance of T.H. Marshall*, UCL Press, London.

Campbell, Colin and Halligan, John (1992), *Political Leadership in an Age of Constraint: The Australian Experience*, University of Pittsburgh Press, Pittsburgh.

Campen, James (1986), *Benefit, Cost and Beyond: the Political Economy of Benefit-Cost Analysis*, Ballinger Pub Co., Cambridge, Massachusetts.

Capling, Ann and Galligan, Brian (1992), *Beyond the Protective State: the Political Economy of Australia's Manufacturing Industry Policy*, Cambridge University Press, New York.

Carlson, Steven (1999), 'Municipal Ownership of the Information Highway' *Rutgers Computer and Technology Law Journal* Vol. 25, pp.1-95.

Carroll, P. and Painter, M. (1995), 'The Federal Politics of Microeconomic Reform: An Overview and Introduction', in Painter, M. (ed) *Microeconomics Reform and Federalism*, Federalism Research Centre, ANU, Canberra.

Carter, President (1978), Executive Order 12,044 (1978), 24 March 1978.

Cass, R. and Haring, F. (1998), 'Domestic Regulation and International Trade: Where's the Race? – Lessons from Telecommunications and Export Control', SSRN Electronic Paper Collection, http://papers.ssrn.com/paper.taf?abstract_id=211668.

Castles, Stephen (1988), *Australian Public Policy and Economic Vulnerability: a Comparative and Historical Perspective*, Allen and Unwin, Sydney.

Castles, Stephen (ed) (1991), *Australia Compared: People, Policies and Politics*, Allen and Unwin, Sydney.

Centre for International Economics (1999), *Guidelines for National Competition Policy Legislation Reviews*, www.intecon.com.au and Centre for International Economics, Melbourne (also on file with author).

Cerny, Philip (1995), 'Globalisation and the Changing Logic of Collective Action', *International Organisation* Vol. 49, pp.595-625.

Charnowitz, Steve (2001), 'Rethinking WTO Trade Sanctions', *American Journal of International Law* Vol. 95, No. 4, pp.793-832.

Charny, David (2000), 'Regulatory Competition and the Global Coordination of Labour Standards', *Journal of International Economic Law* Vol. 3, No. 2, pp. 281-302.

Chayes, Abram (1976), 'The Role of the Judge in Public Law Litigation', *Harvard Law Review*, Vol. 89, pp.1281-1316.

Churchman, Susan (1996), 'National Competition Policy – Its Evolution and Implementation: A Study in Intergovernmental Relations', *Australian Journal of Public Administration*, Vol. 55, No. 2.

Clarke, J. and Newman, J. (1997), *The Managerial State: Power, Politics and Ideology in the Remaking of Social Welfare*, Sage Publications, London.

Coffee, John (1992), 'Paradigms Lost: the Blurring of the Civil and Criminal Law Models – And What Can Be Done About It', *Yale Law Journal* Vol. 101, No. 2, pp.1875-1893.

Collins, Hugh (1999), *Regulating Contracts*, Oxford University Press, Oxford.

Colong Foundation for Wilderness (1996), *The Colong Bulletin*, Sydney.

Comaroff, John (1997), 'The Discourse of Rights in Colonial South Africa: Subjectivity, Sovereignty, Modernity', in Sarat and Kearns, T. (eds), *Identities, Politics and Rights*, University of Michigan Press, Ann Arbor.

Commonwealth Government (1996), *Commonwealth Legislation Review Schedule*, Australian Government Publishing Service, Canberra.

Commonwealth Government (1996), *Review of the Migration Agents Registration Scheme: Exposure Draft*, Australian Government Publishing Service, Canberra.

Commonwealth Parliament of Australia (1971), *Administrative Review (Kerr) Committee Report*, Australian Government Publishing Service, Canberra.

Commonwealth Parliament of Australia (1973), *(Bland) Committee on Administrative Discretions: Final Report*, Australian Government Publishing Service, Canberra.

Commonwealth Parliament of Australia (1973), *(Ellicott) Committee on Review of Prerogative Procedure*, Australian Government Publishing Service, Canberra.

Commonwealth Parliament of Australia (1994), *Report on Legislative Instruments Bill 1994, Senate Standing Committee on Regulations and Ordinances*, Australian Government Publishing Service, Canberra.

Commonwealth Parliament of Australia (1995), *Report on the Legislative Instruments Bill 1994*, House of Representatives Standing Committee on Legal and Constitutional Affairs, Australian Government Publishing Service, Canberra.

Commonwealth Parliament of Australia (1995), *Submissions to Inquiry into Aspects of the National Competition Policy Reform Package, Volumes 1-8*, House of Representatives Standing Committee on Banking, Finance and Public Administration, Australian Government Publishing Service, Canberra.

Confederation of Australian Industry and Victorian Chamber of Manufacturers (1980), *Government Regulation in Australia*, Melbourne.

Confederation of Bushwalking Clubs (1995), *Bushwalker*, Newsletter of the Confederation of Bushwalking Clubs (NSW) Inc, Sydney.

Considine, Mark (1988), 'The Corporate Management Framework as Administrative Science: A Critique', *Australian Journal of Public Administration* Vol. 47, No. 1, pp.1-18.

Coombe, Rosemary (1998), *The Cultural Life of Intellectual Properties: Authorship, Appropriation and the Law*, Duke University Press, Durham.

Cooter, Robert (1984), 'Prices and Sanctions' *Columbia Law Review*, Vol. 84, No. 2, pp.1523-1560.

Council of Australian Governments (COAG) (2000), *Communiqué*, November 3 2000.

Council of Australian Governments (COAG) (1997), *Principles and Guidelines for National Standard Setting and Regulatory Action by Ministerial Councils and Standard-Setting Bodies*, on file with author, November 1997.

Couso, Javier (1999), 'The Birth of Judicial Politics in Chile: The Case of the Constitutional Protection against Administrative Expropriation', Paper presented at the Annual Meeting of the Law and Society Association, Chicago, USA, on file with author.

Couso, Javier (n.d.), 'The Economic Constitution of Chile: The Lochner Era Reborn?', unpublished paper on file with author.

Couso, Javier (n.d.), 'The Multilateral Agreement on Investment and Regulatory Takings: a Case Study of Changes in the Production of Law', unpublished paper on file with author.

Cranston, Ross (1979), *Regulating Business: Law and Consumer Agencies*, Oxford University Press, Oxford.

Craven, Greg (1989), 'Consultation and the Making of Subordinate Legislation – A Victorian Initiative', *Melbourne University Law Review* Vol. 15, pp.95 ff.

Crawford, Peter (1996), *The Serious Business of Governing: Reform in Government and Transformation in the Public Sector*, Hale & Iremonger and the Royal Institute of Public Administration, Sydney.

Croley, Steven (1998), 'Theories of Regulation: Incorporating the Administrative Process', *Columbia Law Review* pp.1-168.

Daintith, Terence (1994), 'The Techniques of Government', in Oliver, D. (ed), *The Changing Constitution*, Clarendon Press, Oxford.

Daintith, Terence (1998), 'Legal Measures and their Analysis', in Baldwin, R., Scott, C. and Hood C. (eds), *A Reader on Regulation*, Oxford University Press, Oxford.

Daintith, T. and Page, A. (1999), *The Executive in the Constitution*, Oxford University Press, Oxford.

Daniels, Tony (1996), Speech to Business Council of Australia, Copy obtained by author in interview.

de Cavalho, David (1996), *Competitive Care: Understanding the Implications of National Competition Policy and the COAG agenda for the Community Services Sector*, Australian Catholic Social Welfare Commission, Canberra.

De Maria, William (1992), 'The Administrative Appeal Tribunal in Review: On Remaining Seated During the Standing Ovation', in McMillan, J. (ed), *Administrative Law: Does the Public Benefit?*, Australian Institute of Administrative Law, Canberra.

Deakin (1997), 'Private Law, Economic Rationality and the Regulatory State', in Birks (ed), *The Classification of Obligations*, Clarendon Press, Oxford.

Deighton-Smith (1997), 'The Machinery of Regulatory Reform', The OECD Observer Vol. 206.

Department of Immigration and Multicultural Affairs (2001), *Fact Sheet 72*, Public Affairs Section, Australian Government Publishing Service, Canberra.

Department of Trade and Industry (1994), *Deregulation: Cutting Red Tape*, HMSO, London.

Derthick, Martha and Quirk, Paul (1985), *The Politics of Deregulation*, Brookings Institution, Washington D.C.

Dezalay, Yves (1995), 'Introduction' in Dezalay, Y. and Sugarman D. (eds), *Professional Competition and Professional Power*, Routledge, London.

Dezalay, Yves and Garth, Bryant (1996), *Dealing in Virtue*, University of Chicago Press, Chicago.

Diver, Colin (1998), 'The Optimal Precision of Administrative Rules', in Baldwin, R., Scott, C. and Hood, C. (eds), *A Reader on Regulation*, Oxford University Press, Oxford.

Dworkin, Ronald (1986), *Law's Empire*, Belknap Press, Cambridge, Mass.

Dyzenhaus, David (ed) (1999), *Recrafting the Rule of Law: the Limits of Legal Order*, Hart Publishing, Oxford.

Eagleton, Terry (2000), *The Idea of Culture,* Blackwell Publishing, Oxford.

Eggers, B. and MacKenzie (2000), 'The Cartagena Protocol on Biosafety', *Journal of International Economic Law*, Vol. 3, No. 3.

Epstein, Richard (1995), *Simple Rules for a Complex World*, Harvard University Press, Cambridge.

Esping-Anderson, Gospa (1990), *The Three Worlds of Welfare Capitalism*, Polity Press, Cambridge.

Evans, Gail E. (2000), *Lawmaking under the Trade Constitution: A Study in Legislating by the World Trade Organisation*, Kluwer Law International, The Hague.

Evans, Peter (1995), *Embedded Autonomy: States and Industrial Transformation*, Princeton University Press, Princeton.

Ewick, P. and Silbey, S. (1998), *The Common Place of Law: Stories from Everyday Life*, University of Chicago Press, Chicago.

Farber, D. and Frickey, P. (1987), 'The Jurisprudence of Public Choice', *Texas Law Review*, Vol. 65, No. 5, pp.873-928.

Farina, Cynthia (2001), 'Faith, Hope, and Rationality or Public Choice and the Perils of Occam's Razor', *Florida State University Law Review*, Vol. 28, pp. 109-135.

Fidler, David (1999), 'The Rule of Law in the Era of Globalisation (Symposium)' *Indiana Journal of Global Legal Studies*, Vol. 6.

Fisher, Elizabeth (2000), 'Drowning by Numbers: Standard Setting in Risk Regulation and the Pursuit of Accountable Public Administration', *Oxford Journal of Legal Studies*, Vol. 20, No. 1, pp.109-130.

Ford, President, (1974) Executive Order 11,821 27 November 1974.

Forster, Head, and Wanna (1991), 'The Effectiveness of the Business Regulation Review Unit', in McCoy, H.A. (ed), *Deregulation or Better Regulation*, Centre for Australian Public Sector Management, Brisbane.

Frankenfeld, P. (1992), 'Technological Citizenship: A Normative Framework for Risk Studies', *Science, Technology and Human Values,* Vol. 17, pp.459-484.

Freedland, M. and Sciarra, S. (1998), *Public Services and Citizenship in European Law*, Clarendon Press, Oxford.

Freeman, Jody (1997), 'Collaborative Governance in the Administrative State' *University of California Law Review*, Vol. 45, pp.1-228.

Freeman, Jody (1999), 'Private Parties, Public Functions and the Real Democracy Problem in the New Administrative Law?' in Dyzenhaus, D. (ed), *Recrafting the Rule of Law: the Limits of Legal Order*, Hart Publishing, Oxford.

Freeman, Jody (2000), 'The Private Role in Public Governance', *New York University Law Review*, Vol. 75, pp.543-675.

Freiberg, A. and O'Malley, P. (1984), 'State Intervention and the Civil Offence' *Law and Society Review*, Vol. 18, No. 3, pp.373-394.

Frieden, J. and Lake, D. (eds) (1991), *International Political Economy: Perspectives on Global Power and Wealth*, St. Martin's Press, New York.

Frug, Gerald (1984), 'The Ideology of Bureaucracy', *Harvard Law* Review, Vol. 97, pp.1276-1377.

Galanter, Marc (1974), 'Why the 'Haves' Come out Ahead: Speculations on the Limits of Legal Change', *Law and Society Review*, Vol. 9, pp.95-160.

Ganz, Gabriele (1977), *Government and Industry: The Provision of Financial Assistance to Industry and its Control*, Professional Books, London.

Garth, B., and Dezalay, Y. (1995), 'Merchants of Law as Moral Entrepreneurs – Constructing International Justice from the Competition of Transnational Business Disputes', *Law and Society Review*, Vol. 29, pp.27-64.

Geistfeld, Mark (2001), 'Reconciling Cost-Benefit Analysis with the Principle That Safety Matters More Than Money', *New York University Law Review*, Vol. 76, pp.114-189.

Gerritsen, Rolf (1994), 'Microeconomic Reform', in Head, B.A. (ed), *State, Economy and Public Policy in Australia*, Oxford University Press, Melbourne.

Giddens, Anthony (1999), *The Third Way: The Renewal of Social Democracy*, Polity Press, Malden, Massachusetts.

Gillman, Howard (1996), *The Constitution Besieged: the Rise and Demise of Lochner Era Police Powers Jurisprudence*, Duke University Press, Durham.

Goggin, Gerald (1995), 'The Framework for Consumer Protection in NSW Utilities', in Johnston, C. (ed), *Consumer Rights and Utilities: Issues and Options for NSW*, Public Interest Advocacy Centre, Sydney.

Goodin, Robert (1985), *Protecting the Vulnerable: A Reanalysis of Our Social Responsibilities*, Chicago University Press, Chicago.

Graham, Cosmo (1998), 'Is there a Crisis in Accountability?' in Baldwin, R., Scott, C. and Hood C. (eds), *A Reader on Regulation*, Oxford University Press, Oxford.

Graham, Cosmo (2000), *Regulating Public Utilities: A Constitutional Approach*, Hart Publishing, Portland, Oregon.

Griffiths, David (1998), 'Communication via Co-op Net mailing list (davidg@fox.net.au)', *Email Communication*, Morgan, San Francisco.

Gunningham, N., Grabosky, P. and Sinclair, D. (1998), *Smart Regulation: Designing Environmental Policy*, Clarendon Press, Oxford.

Gutmann, A. and Thompson, D. (1996), *Democracy and Disagreement*, Belknap Press of Harvard University Press, Cambridge, Massachusetts.

Hahn, Barry (1995), 'Consumer Advocacy and Financial Counselling' Conference on *Consumer Protection and Utilities Reform*, Canberra.

Hahn, Robert (1998), 'Government Analysis of the Benefits and Costs of Regulation', *Journal of Economic Perspectives*, Vol. 12, No. 4, pp.201-210.

Haines, Fiona (1997), *Corporate Regulation: Beyond Punish or Persuade*, Clarendon Press, New York.

Hall, Peter (ed) (1989), *The Political Power of Economic Ideas*, Princeton University Press, Princeton, New Jersey.

Hancher, L. and Moran, M. (1989), 'Organising Regulatory Space', in Hancher and Moran (eds), *Capitalism, Culture and Regulation*, Oxford University Press, Oxford.

Handler, Joel (1996), *Down from Bureaucracy: the Ambiguity of Privatisation and Empowerment*, Princeton University Press, Princeton, New Jersey.

Harlow, Carol (1998), 'Public Service, Market Ideology, and Citizenship', in Freedland, M. and Sciarra S. *Public Services and Citizenship in European Law*, Oxford University Press, New York.

Harper, Malcolm (2000), *Public Services through Private Enterprise: Micro-Privatisation for Improved Delivery*, Sage Publications, London.

Harris, A.C. (1999), 'Revisiting the Review of the Victorian Audit Act', *Australian Accounting Review*, pp.32-35.

Harris, R. and Milkis, S. (1989), *The Politics of Regulatory Change: A Tale of Two Agencies*, Oxford University Press, New York.

Hart, H.L.A. (1961), *The Concept of Law*, Clarendon Press, Oxford.

Hawkins, Keith (1984), 'Environment and Enforcement' in Baldwin, R., Scott, C. and Hood C. (eds), *A Reader on Regulation*, Oxford University Press, Oxford.

Hawkins, Keith (1989), 'Rule and discretion in Comparative Perspective: The Case of Social Regulation', *Ohio State Law Journal*, Vol. 50, pp.663-679.

Hawkins, Keith (1990), 'Reply to Pearce and Tombs', *British Journal of Criminology*, pp.444-466.

Hayek, Friedrich (1962), *The Road to Serfdom*, Routledge, London.

Hayek, Friedrich (1979), *Law, Legislation and Liberty*, Routledge, London.

Henderson, D. (1995), 'The Revival of Economic Liberalism: Australia in an International Prespective', *Australian Economic Review*, pp.1 ff.

Hendley, Kathryn (1996), *Trying to Make Law Matter*, University of Michigan Press, Ann Arbor.

Heritier, Adrienne (2001), *The Politics of Public Services in European Regulation*, SSRN Electronic Paper Collection, Max Planck Project Group in Common Goods, http://papers.ssrn.com/paper.taf?abstract_id=269314.

Hilmer, F. (1994), 'The Bases of Competition Policy', Paper given at a conference *Trade Practices: A New Regime in the Making*, Hotel Inter-Continental, Sydney.

Hilmer, Rayner and Taperell (1993), *National Competition Policy: Executive Overview*, Independent Committee of Inquiry into National Competition Policy, Canberra.

Hirschmann, Albert (1977), *The Passions and the Interests: Political Arguments for Capitalism Before its Triumph*, Princeton University Press, Princeton, New Jersey.

Hirst, Paul (1994), *Associative Democracy: New Forms of Economic and Social Governance*, University of Massachusetts Press, Amherst.

Hoggett, Paul (2000), 'Social Policy and the Emotions', in Lewis, Gewirtz and Clarke (eds), *Rethinking Social Policy*, Sage Publications, London.

Holt, Philip (1994), Business Perspectives on Hilmer. Paper given at Conference *Trade Practices: A New Regime in the Making*, Hotel Inter-Continental, Sydney.

Hood, Christopher (1983), *The Tools of Government*, MacMillan, London.

Hood, Christopher (2000), *The Art of the State*, Clarendon Press, Oxford.

Hood, C. and Scott, C. (1996), 'Bureaucratic Regulation and New Public Management in the United Kingdom: Mirror-image Developments?', *Journal of Law and Society*, Vol. 23, No. 3, pp.321-345.

Hood, C. and Scott, C. (2000), 'Regulation of Government: Has it Increased, is it Increasing, Should it be Diminished?', *Public Administration*, Vol. 78, No. 2, pp.283-304.

Hood, C., Scott, C. et al. (1999), *Regulation Inside Government: Waste-Watchers, Quality Police and Sleaze-Busters*, Oxford University Press, Oxford.

Hunt, Alan (1993), *Explorations in Law and Society: Towards a Constitutive Theory of Law*, Routledge, New York.

Hutter, Bridget (1997), *Compliance: Regulation and Environment*, Oxford University Press, Oxford.

Illich, Ivan (1973), *Tools of Conviviality*, Harper and Row, New York.

Inozemtsev, V.L. (1998), 'Exploitation: A Phenomenon of Consciousness and Social Conflict', *Sociological Research*, Vol. 37, No. 6, pp.67-86.

International Congress of Jurists (1959), *The Rule of Law in a Free Society: A Report on the International Congress of Jurists in Delhi*, Norman Marsh (ed), International Congress of Jurists, New Delhi, India.

Jacob, Herbert (1992), 'The Elusive Shadow of the Law', *Law and Society Review*, Vol. 26, pp.565-590.

Jacobs, Scott (1999), 'The Second Generation of Regulatory Reforms', Paper given at IMF Conference on Second Generation Reforms, on file with author.

Jessop, Bob (1993), 'Towards a Schumpeterian Workforce State? Preliminary Remarks on Post-Fordist Political Economy', *Studies in Political Economy*, Vol. 40, pp.7-39.

Joerges, Christian (2001), 'Law, Science and the Management of Risks to Health at the National, European and International Level – Stories on Baby Dummies, Mad Cows and Hormones in Beef', *Columbia Journal of European Law*, Vol. 7, pp. 1-19.

Johnson, Michael (1993), 'The Water Industry Overseas – Lessons for Australia', in Rix, J.A. (ed), *Water in Australia: Managing Economic, Environmental and Community Reform*, Pluto Press and Public Sector Research Centre, UNSW, Sydney.

Johnston, Craig (1995), *Privatisation of Utilities: How Are Consumers Affected?*, Australian Consumers' Council, Australian Government Publishing Service, Canberra.

Johnston, Craig (ed) (1995), *Consumer Rights and Utilities: Issues and Options for NSW*, Public Interest Advocacy Centre, Sydney.

Johnston, Craig (1995), 'Riding the Wild Surf: Participatory Implementation of Competition Policy in New South Wales', Paper presented at Conference *What Price Competition Policy?*, University of New South Wales, Sydney.

Johnston, Craig (1996), 'New Initiatives for Consumer Protection: Examples from an Industry in Transition – Electricity Retail in New South Wales and Victoria' in *Commercialised Government*, Sydney.

Jweeping, E. R. (1996), *A Third Party Approach to Environmental Regulation: Possible Roles for Insurance Companies*, Ph.D. Dissertation, University of Pennsylvania.

Kagan, Robert (1991), 'Adversarial Legalism and American Government', *Journal of Policy Analysis and Management*, Vol. 10, pp.369-406.

Kagan, R. and Scholz, J. (1984), 'The Criminology of the Corporation and Regulatory Enforcement Strategies', in Hawkins, K. (ed) (1984), *Enforcing Regulation*, Kluwer-Nijhoff, Boston.

Kahn, Paul (1999), *The Cultural Study of Law: Reconstructing Legal Scholarship*, University of Chicago Press, Chicago.

Kay, J. and Vickers, J. (1994), 'Regulatory Reform: an Appraisal', in Wheeler, S. (ed), *A Reader on the Law of the Business* Enterprise, Oxford University Press, Oxford.

Keck, M. and Sikkink, K. (1989), *Activists Beyond Borders: Transnational Advocacy Networks in International Politics*, Cornell University Press, Ithaca.

Kelman, Stephen (1981), 'Cost-Benefit Analysis - an Ethical Critique', *Regulation*, Jan/Feb.

Kendall and Stiles (1998), 'Civil Society Eempowerment and Multilateral Donors: International Institutions and New International Norms', *Global Governance*, Vol. 4, pp.199-216.

Kelsey, Jane (1995), *Economic Fundamentalism*, Pluto Press, Sydney.

Kim, Hwa-Jin, (2001), 'Taking International Soft Law Seriously: Its Implications for Global Convergence in Corporate Governance', *Journal of Korean Law*, Vol. 1, No. 1, pp.1-50.

King, Desmond (1987), *The New Right: Politics, Markets and Citizenship*, Macmillan Education, Basingstoke.

King, Desmond (1999), *In the Name of Liberalism: Illiberal Social Policy in the United States and Britain*, Oxford University Press, Oxford.

King, S. and Maddock, R. (1996), *Unlocking the Infrastructure: The Reform of Public Utilities in Australia*, Allen and Unwin, Sydney.

Klug, Heinz (2000), *Constituting Democracy: Law, Globalism and South Africa's Political Reconstruction*, Cambridge University Press, New York.

Kojeve, Alexandre (2000), *Outline of a Phenomenology of Right*, Rowan and Littlefield, Lanham.

Krygier, Martin (2002), 'Selznick's Subjects', in Kagan, R., Krygier, M. and Winston, K. (eds), *Legality and Community: on the Intellectual Legacy of Philip Selznick*, Berkeley Public Policy Press, Berkeley.

Lacey, Nicola (1994), 'Government as Manager, Citizen as Consumer: The Case of the Criminal Justice Act 1991', *Modern Law Review*, Vol. 57, pp.534-554.

Lange, Bettina (1998), 'Understanding Regulatory Law: Empirical versus Systems-Theoretical Approaches', *Oxford Journal of Legal Studies*, Vol. 18, pp. 499 ff.

Latour, Bruno (1986), 'The Powers of Association', in Law, J. (ed), *Power, Action and Belief: A New Sociology of Knowledge?*, Routledge and Kegan Paul, London.

Lipschutz, R. and Mayer, J. (1996), *Global Civil Society and Global Environmental Governance: The Politics Of Nature from Place to Planet*, State University of New York Press, Albany.

Luhmann, Niklas (1985), *A Sociological Theory of Law*, Routledge and Kegan Paul, London.

MacIntyre, Alastair (1981), *After Virtue: A Study in Moral Theory*, University of Notre Dame Press, Notre Dame.

Mack, Jenni (1995), 'Utilities Reform: State by State', Conference on *Consumer Protection and Utilities Reform*, Canberra.

Mahoney, W. (1995), 'Strategies for Enforcing the Rights of Disadvantaged Groups in Relation to Utility Reform', in Johnston and Craig (eds), *Consumer Rights and Utilities: Issues and Options for NSW*, Public Interest Advocacy Centre, Sydney.

Majone, Giandomenico (1989), *Evidence, Argument and Persuasion in the Policy Process*, Yale University Press, New Haven.

Majone, Giandomenico (1990), *Deregulation or Re-regulation?: Regulatory Reform in Europe and the United States,* Pinter Publishers, London.

Majone, Giandomenico (1993), 'The European Community between Social Policy and Social Regulation', *Journal of Common Market Studies*, Vol. 31, No. 2, pp. 153-170.

Majone, Giandomenico (1995), *The Development of Social Regulation in the European Community: Policy Externalities, Transaction Costs, Motivational Factors*, European University Institute, Florence.

Majone, Giandomenico (ed) (1996), *Regulating Europe*, European Public Policy Series, Routledge, London.

Majone, Giandomenico (1997), 'The New European Agencies: Regulation by Information', *Journal of European Public Policy*, Vol. 4, No. 2, pp.262-275.

Majone, Giandomenico (2000), 'The Credibility of Community Regulation', *Journal of Common Market Studies*, Vol. 38, pp.273-302.

Malanczuk, P. (2000), 'State-State and Investor-State Dispute Settlement in the OECD Draft Multilateral Investment Agreement', *Journal of International Economic Law*, Vol. 3, No. 3, pp.417-439.

Malecki, Edward (1997), *Technology and Economic Development: the Dynamics of Local, Regional, and National Competitiveness*, Longman, Essex.

Malloy, Robin, (2000), *Law and Market Economy*, Cambridge University Press, Cambridge.

Marcuse, Herbert (1964), *One-Dimensional Man: Studies in the Ideology of Advanced Industrial Society*, Beacon Press, Boston.

Marquand, David (1988), *The Unprincipled Society: New Demands and Old Politics*, Jonathan Cape Ltd, London.

Marshall, T.H. (1950), *Citizenship and Social Class and Other Essays*, Cambridge University Press, Cambridge.

Mascarenhas, R. (1988), 'Government-Public Enterprise Relations – A Comparative Perspective', *Australian Journal of Public Administration*, Vol. 47, No. 1, pp.35-48.

Mashaw, Jerry (1983), *Bureaucratic Justice*, Yale University Press, New Haven.

Mashaw, Jerry (1985), 'Prodelegation: Why Administrators Should Make Political Decisions', *Journal of Law, Economics and Organisation*, Vol. 1, No. 1, pp. 81-100.

Massey, Andrew (1993), *Managing the Public Sector: A Comparative Analysis of the United Kingdom and the United States*, Edward Elgar, Aldershot, UK; Brookfield, Vermont.

McBarnet, D. and Whelan C. (1991), 'The Elusive Spirit of the Law: Formalism and the Struggle for Legal Control' *Modern Law* Review, Vol. 54, pp.848 ff.

McCann, Michael (1994), *Rights at Work: Pay Equity Reform and the Politics of Legal Mobilisation*, University of Chicago Press, Chicago.

McCullough, David (1993), *Consultation and Regulatory Analysis in Agency Rulemaking in Australia*, LLM thesis, University of California at Berkeley.

McGarity, Thomas O. (1991), *Reinventing Rationality: the Role of Regulatory Analysis in the Federal Bureaucracy*, Cambridge University Press, Cambridge.

McGinnis, J. and Movsesian, M. (2000), 'The World Trade Constitution: Reinforcing Democracy through Trade', *Harvard Law Review*, Vol. 114, pp. 511-605.

McHugh, Jeanette (1995), 'Opening Address', Conference on *Consumer Protection and Utilities Reform*, Canberra.

Meidinger, Errol (1987), 'Regulatory Culture: A Theoretical Outline', *Law and Policy*, Vol. 9, No. 3, pp.355-386.

Melnick, Shep (1990), 'The Politics of Benefit-Cost Analysis', in *Valuing Health Risks, Costs, and Benefits for Environmental Decision Making: Report of a Conference*, Hammond and Coppock, National Academy Press, Washington D.C.

Mendez, J., O'Donnell, G. and Pinherio, P.S. (eds) (1999), *The (Un)Rule of Law and the Underprivileged in Latin America*, University of Notre Dame Press, Notre Dame.

Merry, Sally (1990), *Getting Justice and Getting Even*, Chicago University Press, Chicago.

Miller, J. and Yandle, J. (eds) (1979), *Benefit-Cost Analyses of Social Regulation: Case Studies from the Council on Wage and Price Stability*, American Enterprise Institute for Public Policy Research, Washington D.C.

Minow, Martha (1990), *Making All the Difference: Inclusion, Exclusion and American Law*, Cornell University Press, Ithaca.

Mnookin, R. and Kornhauser, L. (1979), 'Bargaining in the Shadow of the Law: the Case of Divorce', *Yale Law Journal* Vol. 88, pp.950-997.

Mueller (1993), 'Universal Service in Telephone History', *Telecommunications Policy*, Vol. 17, pp.352-336.

Muetzelfeldt, Michael (1992), 'Economic Rationalism in its Social Context', in Muetzelfeldt (ed), *Society, State and Politics in Australia*, Pluto Press Australia Ltd, Sydney.

Murphy, T. and Whitty, N. (2000), 'Crowning Glory: Public Law, Power and the Monarchy', *Social and Legal Studies*, Vol. 9, pp.7 ff.

National Competition Council (1996), *Considering the Public Interest under National Competition Policy*, Melbourne.

National Competition Council (1997), *Compendium of National Competition Policy Agreements*, Melbourne.

National Competition Council (1997), *Assessment of State and Territory Progress with Implementing National Competition Policy and Related Reforms*, Melbourne.

National Competition Council (2001), *Framework for the Third Tranche Assessment of Government's Progress with Implementing National Competition Policy and Related Reforms*, Ausinfo, Melbourne.

Needham, Douglas (1983), *The Economics and Politics of Regulation: A Behavioural Approach*, Littlebrown and Co, Toronto.

Neiman, Max (1980), 'The Virtues of Heavy-Handedness in Government', in Brigham, J. and Brown (eds), *Law and Policy (Special issue: Distinguishing Penalities and Incentives*, pp.11-34.

New South Wales Chamber of Manufacture (1994), *Competitive Industry Policy – The Way Forward*, Submission made to Commonwealth Government, New South Wales, Australia.

New South Wales Department of Community Services (1992), *Improving Services by Listening and Responding: Report of the Working Party on Appeals and Complaints Mechanisms for Community Services in NSW*, Working Party on Appeals and Complaints Mechanisms for Community Services in NSW, Sydney.

New South Wales Government (1994), *Social Program Policy for NSW Government Trading Enterprises*, Sydney.

New South Wales Government (1995), *Review of the Legislation Establishing the NSW Rice Marketing Board: Final Report*, Sydney.

New South Wales Government (1996), *Legislation Review Schedule*, Sydney.

New South Wales Parliament, (1989), *Legislation for the Staged Review of NSW Statutory Rules*, Regulation Review Committee, Sydney.

New South Wales Parliament (1993), *Report on Future Directions for Regulatory Review in New South Wales*, Regulation Review Committee, Sydney.

New South Wales Parliament (1994), *Report in Relation to the Committee's Inquiry into the Clean Waters Act 1970 Regulation (Relating to Standards for*

Waters and Testing Procedures) and as to the Compliance with the Requirements of the Subordinate Legislation Act (NSW) 1989 in the Making of that Legislation, Regulation Review Committee, Sydney.

New South Wales Parliament (1995), *Report Arising out of an Inquiry into the Sydney Water Corporation Limited (Catchment Management) Regulation 1995*, Regulation Review Committee, Sydney.

Niskanen, William (1998), *Bureaucracy: Servant or Master? – Lessons from America*, Institute of Economic Affairs, London.

Noah, Lars (2000), 'Interpreting Agency Enabling Acts: Misplaced Metaphors in Administrative Law', *William and Mary Law Review*, Vol. 41, No. 5, pp.1463-1530.

Noll, R. and Owen, B. (1983), *The Political Economy of Deregulation: Interest Groups in the Regulatory Process*, American Enterprise Institute for Public Policy Research, Washington D.C.

Nonet, P. and Selznick, P. (1978), *Law and Society in Transition: Toward Responsive Law*, Harper and Row, New York.

Norton, Andrew (1996), 'Nationality, Utility, Liberty: An Editorial Interview with Greg Melleuish and Chandran Kukathas, *Policy*, pp.31-36.

O'Connor, Deirde (1991), 'Future Directions for Australian Administrative Law' *Canberra Bulletin of Public Administration*, Vol. 66, pp.135-137.

OECD (1992), *Regulatory Reform, Privatisation and Competition Rules*, Paris.

OECD (1995), *Recommendation of the Council of the OECD on Improving the Quality of Government Regulation*, Public Management Service, 9 March 1995, Paris.

OECD (1996), *Regulatory Reform: Overview and Proposed OECD Work Plan*, Paris.

OECD (1996), *Regulatory Reform: A Country Study of Australia*, Public Management Service, Paris.

OECD (1997), *The OECD Report on Regulatory Reform: Synthesis*, Paris.

OECD (1998), *Regulatory Reform in the Global Economy: Asian and Latin American Perspectives*, Paris.

OECD (2000), 'Trade and Regulatory Reform: Insights from the OECD Country Reviews and Other Analyses', Working Party of the Trade Committee, December 2000, available at http://www.oecd.org/ech.

OECD (2000), The APEC-OECD Co-Operative Initiative on Regulatory Reform, November 2000, available at http://ww.oecd.org.

OECD (annual), *PUMA Series: Country Studies in Regulatory Reform*, Public Management Service, Paris.

Offe, Clause (1984), 'Alternative Strategies in Consumer Policy', *Contradictions of the Welfare State*, MIT Press, Cambridge, Mass.

Office of Regulation Review (1995), *Regulation and its Review: Second Annual Report*, Productivity Commission of the Commonwealth Government, Canberra.

Office of Regulation Review (n.d.), *Guidelines for Identifying Priorities for Portfolio Review Programs and Bodies to Undertake Reviews and Public Consultations*, Productivity Commission, Canberra.

Ogus, Anthony (1994), *Regulation: Legal Form and Economic Theory*, Oxford University Press, Oxford.

Ogus, Anthony (1998), 'Rethinking Self-Regulation', in Baldwin, R., Scott, C. and Hood C. (eds), *A Reader on Regulation*, Oxford University Press, Oxford.

Oliver, Dawn (1994), 'What is Happening to Relationships between the Individual and the State?' in Jowell, J. and Oliver, D. (eds), *The Changing Constitution*, Oxford University Press, New York.

Oliver, Dawn (1997), 'The Underlying Values of Public and Private Law', in Taggart, M. (ed), *The Province of Administrative Law*, Hart Publishing, Oxford.

Painter, Christopher (1994), 'Public Service Reform: Reinventing or Abandoning Government?', *Political Quarterly*, Vol. 65, pp.242-262.

Parker, Christine (2002), *The Open Corporation: Effective Self-Regulation and Democracy*. Cambridge University Press, Cambridge.

Pearce and Tombs (1990), 'Ideology, Hegemony and Empiricism: Compliance Theories of Regulation', *British Journal of Criminology*, pp.423-443.

Peltzman, Samuel (1989), 'The Economic Theory of Regulation after a Decade of Deregulation', *Brookings Papers on Microeconomics*, pp.1-59.

Pengilly, Warren (1994), 'The National Competition Policy Draft Legislation Package', Paper given at Conference *Trade Practices: A New Regime in the Making*, Hotel Inter-Continental, Sydney.

Phillip Morris v State of Victoria [1988] VR 825.

Phillips, Michael (2001), *The Lochner Court, Myth and Reality: Substantive Due Process from the 1890s to the 1930s*, Praeger Publishers, Westport.

Picciotto, Sol (1997), 'Fragmented States and International Rules of Law', *Social and Legal Studies*, Vol. 6, pp.259-280.

Pierson, Paul (1994), *Dismantling the Welfare State?*, Cambridge University Press, Cambridge, Massachusetts.

Pierson, P. and Castles, F. (2001), *Australian Antecedents of the Third Way*, Joint Sessions of the European Consortium for Political Research, Grenoble.

Pildes, R. and Sunstein, C. (1995), 'Reinventing the Regulatory State', *University of Chicago Law Review*, Vol. 62, pp.1-129.

Pinkney (1997) 'Probes Set to Anger Kennett', *The Herald Sun*, p.15.

Pollitt, Christopher (1990), *Managerialism and the Public Services: The Anglo-American Experience,* Basil Blackwell, Cambridge, Massachusetts.

Porter, Michael (1998), *The Competitive Advantage of Nations*, Macmillan Press, Basingstoke.

Posner, Richard (1974), 'Theories of Economic Regulation', *Bell Journal of Economics and Management Science*, Vol. 5, pp.335 ff.

Posner, Richard (1978), 'The Baby Shortage', *Journal of Legal Studies*, Vol. 7 pp.323 ff.

Posner, Richard (1987), 'Adoption and Market Theory: The Regulation of the Market of Adoption', *Boston University Law Review*, Vol. 67, pp.59-72.

Post, Robert (1995), *Democracy, Community, Management*, Harvard University Press, Cambridge.

Power, Michael (1997), The *Audit Society*, Oxford University Press, Oxford.

Productivity Commission (1991), *Statutory Marketing Arrangements for Primary Producers*, Australian Government Publishing Service, Canberra.

Prosser, Tony (1986), Nationalised Industries and Public Control: Legal, Constitutional and Political issues, Blackwell, Oxford.

Prosser, Tony (1994), 'Privatisation, Regulation and Public Services', *Juridical Review*, Vol. 3, pp.3-17.

Prosser, Tony (1997), *Law and Regulators*, Clarendon Press, Oxford.

Public Interest Advocacy Centre, Consumer Law Centre of Victoria, et al. (1995), *Voices in the Market: Consumer Consultation and Advocacy in an Era of Competition*, Consumers' Telecommunications Network, Surry Hills, Sydney.

Public Interest Advocacy Centre (1996), *Wear Away Rock with Water ... Utilities and Consumer Advocacy: A Feasibility Study into the Development of a Utility Consumer's Advocacy Network in New South Wales and Recommendations for Action*, Public Interest Advocacy Centre and E3 Group, Sydney.

Public Interest Advocacy Centre (1996), *Working the System: A Guide for Citizens, Consumers and Communities*, Pluto Press Australia Ltd, Sydney.

Public Interest Roundtable (1997), *National Competition Policy – Legislation Review: The Reality of Hilmer and Implications for the Public Interest*, Notes on speakers taken by the author who was present.

Pusey, Michael (1991), *Economic Rationalisation in Canberra: A Nation-Building State Changes its Mind*, Cambridge University Press, Melbourne.

Quiggin, John (1999), 'Rationalism and Rationality in Economics', *Queensland Economic Review*, Vol. 3.

Ranald, Pat (1995), 'National Competition Policy', *Journal of Australian Political Economy*, Vol. 36, pp.1-25.

Raz, Joseph (1977), 'The Rule of Law and its Virtue', *Law Quarterly Review*, Vol. 93, pp.195 ff.

Reich (1985), 'Public Administration and Public Deliberation: an Interpretive Essay' Yale Law Journal 94 1617.

Reich (1990), The Power of Public Ideas, Harvard University Press, Cambridge.

Reidenberg (2001), The Yahoo Case and the International Democratisation of the Internet, Fordham Law & Economics Research Paper No. 11.

Reiss (1984), 'Selecting Strategies of Social Control', in Hawkins, K. and Thomas, J. T., *Enforcing Regulation*, Kluwer-Nijhoff, Boston.

Richards (1996) 'An Outside Watchdog is the Best Security', *The Age*, 11 December, Melbourne.

Rix, Stephen (1993), 'The Political Context of Public Sector Reform Debate', in Johnson, R. (ed), *Water in Australia: Managing Economic, Environmental and Community Reform*, Pluto Press and Public Sector Research Centre, University of New South Wales, Sydney.

Rodriguez, Daniel (2000), 'Regulatory Incrementalism and Moral Choices: A Comment on Adlerian Welfarism', *Florida State University Law Review*, pp. 28 ff.

Roe, Jill (1976), *Social Policy in Australia: Some Perspectives 1901-1975*, Cassell Australia.

Ryan, Fergus (1992), *Report on the Performance Audit of the Auditor-General of Victoria*, Office of Auditor-General of Victoria, Melbourne.

Sabel, C., O'Rourke, D. and Fung, A. (2000), 'Ratcheting Labour Standards: Regulation for Continuous Improvement in the Global Workplace', Columbia Law and Economic Working Paper No. 185; SSRN Electronic Paper Collection, http://papers.ssrn.com/paper.taf?abstract_id=253833.

Salzman, James (2000), 'Labour Rights, Globalisation and Institutions: The Role and Influence of the Organisation for Economic Cooperation and Development' *Michigan Journal of International Law*, Vol. 21, pp.769 ff.

Samuels, Graeme (2001), Speech at *Conference on Regulatory Reform Management*, 9-13 July 2001, Sydney.

Sarat, A. and Kearns, T. (eds) (1993), *Law in Everyday Life*, Michigan University Press, Ann Arbor.

Sassen, Saskia (1996), *Losing Control? Sovereignty in an Age of Globalisation*, Columbia University Press, New York.

Sax (1992), 'The constitutional dimensions of property: a debate' Loyola of Los Angeles Law Review 26 23-37.

Schauer (2000), First Amendment Opportunism, KSG Working Paper No. 00-011.

Scheingold (1974), The Politics of Rights: Lawyers, Public Policy and Political Change, Yale University Press, New Haven.

Schlag, Pierre (1998), *The Enchantment of Reason*, Duke University Press, Durham.

Schmidt, Vivien (2000), 'Democracy and Discourse in an Integrating Europe and a Globalising World', *European Law Journal*, Vol. 6, No.3, pp.277-300.

Schmitter, Philippe (1985), *Private Interest Government: Beyond Market and State*, Sage, London.

Scholz, John (1984), 'Cooperation, Deterrence and the Ecology of Regulatory Enforcement', *Law and Society Review*, Vol. 18, No. 2, pp.179-224.

Schuck, Peter (2000), 'Law and Post-Privatisation Regulatory Reform: Perspectives from the US Experience', *Regulatory Policy in Latin America: Post-Privatisation Realities*, North-South Centre, University of Miami Press, Manzetti.

Schwarcz, Stephen (2002), 'Private Ordering of Public Markets: The Rating Agency Paradox', *University of Illinois Law Review* 2002 Vol., No.2, pp.1-28.

Schwartz and Rhodes, R. (n.d.), 'Internationalisation and the Liberal Welfare States: The UK, Australia and New Zealand', unpublished paper on file with author.

Scott, Colin (2000), 'Accountability in the Regulatory State', *Journal of Law and Society*, Vol. 27, No. 1, pp.38-60.

Scott, Graham (1996), 'The Use of Contracting in the Public Service', *Australian Journal of Public Administration*, Vol. 55, No. 3, pp.97-105.

Scott, James (1998), *Seeing Like a State*, Yale University Press, New Haven.

Seidman, Seidman and Payne (eds) (1997), *Legislative Drafting for Market Reform*, St Martin's Press, New York.

Senate Legal and Constitutional References Committee (1996), *National Well-being: A System of National Citizenship Indicators and Benchmarks*, Commonwealth Parliament of Australia, Canberra.

Shames, Michael (1995), 'Competition Among Equals', Conference on *Consumer Protection and Utilities Reform*, Canberra, Australia.

Shapiro, Martin (1981), *Courts: A Comparative and Political Analysis*, University of Chicago Press, Chicago.

Shapiro, Martin (1988), *Who Guards the Guardians? Judicial Control of Administration*, Georgia University Press, Athens.

Shapiro, Martin (1990), 'Judicial Review in France', *Journal of Law and Politics*, Vol. 6, pp.531-548.

Shapiro, M. and Sweet, A. (eds) (1994), 'Special Issue: The New Constitutional Politics of Europe', *Comparative Political Studies*.

Shapiro, Sidney (2000), 'Administrative Law After The Counter-Reformation: Restoring Faith in Pragmatic Government', *University of Kansas Law Review*, pp.48 ff.

Shepherd, George (1996), 'Fierce Compromise: The APA Emerges from New Deal Politics', *Northwestern University Law Review*, pp.1557 ff.

Shiva, Vandana, et al. (1997), *Ecological Costs of Economic Globalisation: The Indian Experience*, Research Foundation for Science, Technology and Ecology, New Delhi.

Shklar, Judith (1987), 'Political Theory and the Rule of Law', in Hutchison and Monahan (eds), *The Rule of Law: Ideal or Ideology?*, Toronto University Press, Toronto.

Silverstein, Helena (1996), *Unleashing Rights: Law, Meaning and the Animal Rights Movement*, Michigan University Press, Ann Arbor.

Sinclair, Darren (1997), 'Self-regulation and Command and Control: Beyond False Dichotomies', *Law and Policy*, Vol. 19, No. 4, pp.529-560.

Slaughter, Anne-Marie (2000), *The Network Inside Out*, Michigan University Press, Ann Arbor.

Slaughter, Anne-Marie (2000), 'Agencies on the Loose? Holding Government Networks Accountable', in Bermann, G. and Lindseth, P. (eds), *Transatlantic Regulatory Cooperation*, Columbia University Press, New York.

Spence, David (2002), 'A Public Choice Progressivism, Continued', *Cornell Law Review*, Vol. 87, pp.397-448.

Spiller, Pablo, (1994), 'The Institutional Foundations of Regulatory Commitment', *Journal of Law, Economics and Organisation*, Vol. 10, pp. 201 ff.

Steinwall, Ray (1994-1995), 'Notes on Recent Developments and Events' *Competition and Consumer Law Journal*, pp.2-3.

Stewart, J. and Kimber, M. (1996), 'The Transformation of Bureaucracy? Structural Change in the Commonwealth Public Service 1983-93', *Australian Journal of Public Administration*, Vol. 55, No. 3, pp.37-48.

Stigler, George (1971), 'The Theory of Economic Regulation', *Bell Journal of Economics and Management Science*, Vol. 2, pp.1-21.

Subordinate Legislation Act (1989), New South Wales.
Subordinate Legislation Act (1994), Victoria.
Summit of the Americas (2001), Declaration of Quebec City, Summit of the Americas.
Sunstein, Cass (1990), After the rights revolution: reconceiving the regulatory state, Harvard University Press, Cambridge, Massachusetts.
Sunstein, Cass (1994), 'Incommensurability and Valuation in Law' Michigan Law Review 92 779-861.
Sunstein, Cass (1996), 'Constitutional Moments and the Cost-Benefit State' Stanford Law Review 48 247-309.
Susskind, Richard (2000), Transforming the Law: Essays on Technology, Justice and the Legal Market, Oxford University Press, New York.
Taggart, Michael (1999), 'Reinvented Government, Traffic Lights and the Convergence of Public and Private Law', *Public Law* pp.124 ff.
Talbot, Alan (1995), *Auditing in the Public Interest: Performance Audit of the Auditor-General's Office*, Office of the Auditor-General of Victoria, Melbourne.
Tarrow, Sidney (1994), *Power in Movement: Social Movements, Collective Action, and Politics*, Cambridge University Press, Cambridge.
Taylor, Serge (1984), *Making Bureaucracies Think: The Environmental Impact Statement Strategy of Administrative Reform*, Stanford University Press, Stanford.
Teubner, Gunther (1984), 'Autopoeisis in Law and Society: A Rejoinder to Blankenburg', *Law and Society Review*, Vol. 18, No. 2, pp.291-301.
Teubner, Gunther (1988), *State, Law, Economy as Autopoietic Systems*, de Gruyter, Berlin.
Teubner, Gunther (1992), 'Regulatory Law: Chronicle of a Death Foretold', *Social and Legal Studies* Vol. 1, pp.451-475.
Teubner, Gunther (1993), *Law as an Autopoietic System*, Blackwell, Oxford.
Thompson, E.P. (1977), *Whigs and Hunters: the Origin of the Black Act*, Penguin, London.
Tshuma, Lawrence (2000), 'Hierarchies and Governments versus Networks and Governance: Competing Regulatory Paradigms in Global Economic Regulation', *Social and Legal Studies*, Vol. 9, pp.115 ff.
Veljanovski (ed) (1991), *Regulators and the Market*, Institute of Economic Affairs, London.
Victoria Legal and Constitutional Committee (1984), *Report on the Subordinate Legislation (Deregulation) Bill*, Parliament of Victoria, Melbourne.
Victorian Government (1995), *Guidelines for the Application of the Competition Test to New Legislative Proposals*, Melbourne.
Victorian Government (1995), *National Competition Policy: Steps to Assist Agencies in Complying with the Guidelines for the Application of the Competition Test to New Legislative Proposals*, Melbourne.

Victorian Government (1996), *Legislation Review Schedule*, Melbourne.

Victorian Government (1996), *Water Industry Regulatory Statement*, Office of State-Owned Enterprises, Melbourne.

Victorian Government (1997), *Audit Act 1994: Review Report*, Melbourne.

Victorian Parliament (1984), *Report on the Subordinate Legislation (Deregulation) Bill: Parliament of Victoria*, Legal and Constitutional Committee, Melbourne.

Victorian Parliament (1993), *Report upon an Inquiry into the Operation of the Subordinate Legislation Act 1962*, Scrutiny of Acts and Regulations Committee, Melbourne.

Victorian Parliament (1993), *Annual Reports on Statutory Rules Series*, Scrutiny of Acts and Regulations Committee, Melbourne.

Victorian Parliament (1994), *Annual Reports on Statutory Rules Series*, Scrutiny of Acts and Regulations Committee, Melbourne.

Victorian Parliament (1995), *Annual Reports on Statutory Rules Series*, Scrutiny of Acts and Regulations Committee, Melbourne.

Vincent-Jones, Peter (1999), 'The Regulation of Contractualisation in Quasi-Markets for Public Services', *Public Law*, pp.304-327.

Vogel, David (1986), *National Styles of Regulation*, Cornell University Press, Ithaca.

Vogel, Steven (1998), *Freer Markets, More Rules: Regulatory Reform in Advanced Industrial Countries*, Cornell University Press, Ithaca.

Walker, Dinneke (1995), 'Regulating for Consumer Protection: The Victorian Experience', Conference on *Consumer Protection and Utilities Reform Group*, Canberra.

Walker, Dinneke (1995), *Regulation of Victoria's Energy and Water Utilities: An Analysis of the Protection of Consumers and the Public Interest*, The Consumer Law Centre of Victoria Ltd., Melbourne.

Wallace, Laura (ed) (1997), *Deepening Structural Reform in Africa: Lessons from East Asia*, International Monetary Fund, Washington, D.C.

Walter (1999), 'Europe Gets Back in Gear', *New York Times*, p.19.

Watts, Michael (1993), 'Development: Power, Knowledge, Discursive Practice', *Progress in Human Geography*, Vol. 17, pp.257 ff.

Weatherill, Stephen (2000), 'New Strategies for Managing the EC's Internal Market', *Current Legal Problems* Vol. 53, pp.595-619.

Weinberg, Jonathan (2000), 'ICANN and the Problem of Legitimacy', *Duke Law Journal* Vol. 50, No. 1, pp.187-260.

White, G.E. (2000), *The Constitution and the New Deal*, Harvard University Press, Cambridge.

Wilensky, H. (1974), *The Welfare State and Equality: Structural and Ideological Roots of Public Expenditures*, University of California Press, Berkeley.

Wilhelmsson, T. and Hurri, S. (eds) (1999), *From Dissonance to Sense: Welfare State Expectations, Privatisation and Private Law*, Ashgate Publishing, Aldershot, England.

Williams, B. and Matheney, A. (1995), *Democracy, Dialogue and Environmental Disputes: The Contested Languages of Social Regulation*, Yale University Press, New Haven.

Williams, Walter (1988), *Washington, Westminster and Whitehall*, Cambridge University Press, New York.

Winn, J.K. and Yeh, T.C. (1995), 'Advocating Democracy – the Role of Lawyers in Taiwan's Political Transformation', *Law and Social Inquiry* Vol. 20, pp.561 ff.

Woolsey and Sohn (eds) (1981), *Regulatory Impact Analysis: Achieving Client Objectives under Cost/Benefit Assessments and Other Regulatory Reform Initiatives*, Law and Business, New York.

Yarmirr v Australian Telecommunications Corporation [1990] 96 ALR 739.

Yeatman, Anna (1990), *Bureaucrats, Technocrats, Femocrats: Essays on the Contemporary Australian State*, Allen and Unwin, Sydney.

Yngvesson, Barbara (1993), *Virtuous Citizens, Disruptive Subjects*, Routledge, New York.

Zedner, Lucia (1995), 'In Pursuit of the Vernacular: Comparing Law and Order Discourse in Britain and Germany', *Social and Legal Studies* Vol. 4, pp.517 ff.

Zifcak, Spencer (1994), 'New Managerialism: Administrative Reform in Whitehall and Canberra', in Rhodes, R.A.W. (ed), *Public Policy and Management*, Open University Press, Buckingham.

Interviews

Bardsley, Michael, Manager (Acting), Regulation Development Branch, Workcover NSW (1997), *Interview*, Morgan. February 5 1997.

Booth, Ian, Policy Analyst and Research Associate, Australian Chamber of Commerce and Industry, (1997), *Interview*, February 25 1997.

Boun, Policy Manager, Australian Consumers' Association (1997), *Interview*, February 28 1997.

Braithwaite, John, Professor of Law, Research School of Social Sciences and Member of Business Council of Australia (1997), *Interview*, Morgan. February 16 1997.

Cochrane, Legal Office, Office of Legislative Drafting, Commonwealth Attorney-General's Department (1997), *Interview*, Morgan. February 22 1997.

Coghlan, Paul, Assistant Commissioner, Office of Regulation Review, Productivity Commission, Canberra (1997), *Interview*, Morgan. February 15 1997.

Craven, Greg, Associate Professor in Law, University of Melbourne and former consultant to Legal and Constitutional Committee of Victorian Parliament (1996), *Interview*, Morgan. September 26 1996.

Cruickshank, Adrian, Member of Parliament of New South Wales (1997), *Interview*, Morgan. January 31 1997.

Downing, Terry, Senior Policy Officer, NSW Cabinet Office (1997), *Interview*, Morgan. February 7 1997.

El-Gamal, Barbara, Policy Officer, NSW Department of Community Services (1997), *Interview*, Morgan. February 14 1997.

Godard, Lisa, Secretary, Sydney Day Nursery Association (1997), *Interview*, Morgan. March 5 1997.

Goddard, Tania, Legal Officer, Immigration Legal Rights Advice Centre (1997), *Interview*, Morgan. February 3 1997.

Hilmer, Fred, Chairman of Fairfax and Former Chairman of the National Competition Policy Review (2001), *Interview*, Morgan. 9 April 2001.

Hogan, Michael, Director, NSW Public Interest Advocacy Centre (1996), *Interview*, Morgan, October 4 1996.

Ireland, Pauline, Policy Officer, Victorian Environment Protection Agency (1996), *Interview*, Morgan. September 30 1996.

Lim, Bob, Policy Analyst, Business Council of Australia (1997), *Interview*, Morgan. February 23 1997.

Moore, Gary, Director of New South Wales Council on Social Services (NCOSS) (1997), *Interview*, Morgan, February 20 1997.

Muir, Keith, Director, The Colong Foundation for Wilderness (1997), *Interview*, Morgan. February 21 1997.

Perton, Victor, Member of Parliament of Victoria, Chairman of Scrutiny of Acts and Regulation Committee (1997), *Interview*, Morgan. January 29 1997.

Senior Official A, Office of Regulation Review, Productivity Commission, Canberra (1997), *Interview*, Morgan. February 15 1997.

Senior Official A, Office of Regulation Review, Productivity Commission, Canberra (2001), *Interview*, Morgan.

Senior Official B and Senior Official C, Department of Treasury and Finance, Victorian Government (2001), *Interview*, Morgan. 2 April 2001.

Senior Official D, New South Wales Department of the Premier and Cabinet (2001), *Interview*, Morgan, 9 March 2001.

Senior Official E, New South Wales Department of the Premier and Cabinet (1997), *Interview*, Morgan. February 12 1997.

Senior Official F, National Competition Council (2001), Morgan. 3 April 2001.

Swan, Antony, Regulatory Policy Officer, Sydney Water Corporation (1997), *Interview*, Morgan. February 10 1997.

Index

trades unions, NCP, parliamentary
    inquiry, response 97-98
transparency, NCP 86, 87

UCAN (Utility Consumer Advocacy
    Network)
  aim 164
  utilities 164-166
utilities
  accountability 158-168
  consumer protection 158
  CPOs 161-163
  CSOs 158-161
  and GDP 150
  effects 150
  institutions created 151-153
  legislation review 149-168
    context 150-153
  and market values 151
  New South Wales/Victoria
    accountability 158-168
    comparison 153-157, 166-
    168
    objectives 149-150
    privatisation 150-151

and social citizenship 151
UCAN 164-166

variability, meta-regulation 39
Victoria
  Auditor General, review 190-199
  Competition Policy Task Force 120
  market values 126-127
  meta-regulation, agenda-setting
    136-138
    assumptions 137
    exclusions 137
    inclusions 136, 138
  NCC influence 125
  utilities
    accountability 157-168
    New South Wales, comparison
    153-157

Weber, Max, on law 19-20
welfare state policies 48, 49
  threats to 5-6
WTO (World Trade Organisation) 7
  demonstrations against 1
  function 20-21

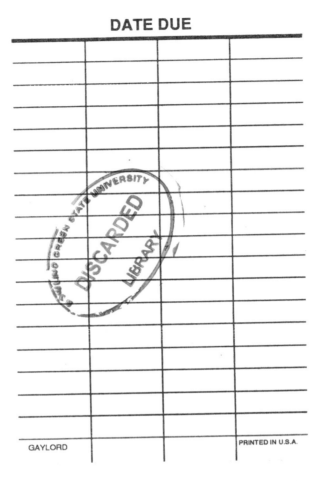